Spoken Word

The publisher gratefully acknowledges the generous support of the Eric Papenfuse and Catherine Lawrence Endowment Fund in Film and Media Studies of the University of California Press Foundation.

Spoken Word

Postwar American Phonograph Cultures

Jacob Smith

UNIVERSITY OF CALIFORNIA PRESS
Berkeley · Los Angeles · London

University of California Press, one of the most
distinguished university presses in the United States,
enriches lives around the world by advancing
scholarship in the humanities, social sciences, and
natural sciences. Its activities are supported by the UC
Press Foundation and by philanthropic contributions
from individuals and institutions. For more
information, visit www.ucpress.edu.

University of California Press
Berkeley and Los Angeles, California

University of California Press, Ltd.
London, England

Library of Congress Cataloging-in-Publication Data

Smith, Jacob, 1970–.
  Spoken word : postwar American phonograph
cultures / Jacob Smith.—1st ed.
    p. cm.
  Includes bibliographical references and index.
  ISBN 978–0-520-26703-9 (cloth : alk. paper)—
ISBN 978–0-520-26704-6 (pbk. : alk. paper)
  1. Sound recordings—United States—History—20th
century. 2. Sound recording industry—United
States—History—20th century. 3. Popular culture—
United States—History—20th century. I. Title.
  ML3790.S59 2010
  384—dc22

                                    2010017408

Manufactured in the United States of America

20 19 18 17 16 15 14 13 12 11
10 9 8 7 6 5 4 3 2 1

This book is printed on Cascades Enviro 100, a 100%
post consumer waste, recycled, de-inked fiber. FSC
recycled certified and processed chlorine free. It is acid
free, Ecologo certified, and manufactured by BioGas
energy.

Contents

Illustrations

Acknowledgments

Many people helped me to gather research materials for this book, including Jocelyn Koehler at the Camden County Historical Society; the staff at the Kinsey Institute and Wells Library at Indiana University; Peter Muldavin, "the Kiddie Rekord King"; Merle Sprinzen, who shared both her knowledge and fantastic collection of materials related to the Bubble Books; J.D. Doyle at Queer Music Heritage, who sent me Arthur Blake recordings; Denise Gose and Tammy Carter at the University of Arizona Center for Creative Photography; and Peter Liebert, Ian Buck, Kliph Nesteroff, and everyone at WFMU for making available so many audio treasures. The following people all generously gave their time and graciously consented to be interviewed: Barbara Holdridge, Phil Proctor, Rusty Warren, Will Jordan, Richard Fish, Bonnie Prudden, Don M. Sloan, and Tommy Smothers.

Several portions of *Spoken Word* have appeared elsewhere in an earlier form. Versions of chapter 1 appeared in the *Journal of Children and Media,* volume 4, number 1, February 2010, pp. 90–108, and will appear in *Childhood and Consumer Culture,* edited by David Buckingham and Vebjorg Tingstad, which is forthcoming from Palgrave in 2010. A version of chapter 3 will appear in *Sex Scene: The Media and the Sexual Revolution,* edited by Eric Schaefer, forthcoming from Duke University Press, 2011. Eric Schaefer and the readers at the *Journal of Children and Media* made useful comments that added much to the subsequent development of that material. Similarly, the two readers at the University of California Press helped me to streamline and better frame my argument. Many thanks go to Eric Schmidt at the University of California Press for all his patience and hard work, and to my editor, Mary Francis, without whose wise counsel and early encouragement this book might never have been written.

Various colleagues and friends have shaped my thinking and inspired this work. Colleagues at the University of Nottingham have provided friendship and fresh perspectives, in particular Roberta Pearson, Paul Grainge, Dave Murray, Mark Gallagher, Luke Robinson, Tony Hutchison, Ian Brookes, and Peter Messent. I have received continued guidance and encouragement from James Naremore, Chris Anderson, Richard Bauman, Greg Waller, Matthew Solomon, Robert B. Ray, and Patrick Feaster. I owe much to Glenn Gass for deepening my appreciation of both records and teaching. Many of the ideas found in this book were the result of discussions with Dale Lawrence, who kindly read an early draft. David Pace listened to Firesign Theatre with me, in addition to being a great friend, an inspiring teacher, and the world's greatest guide to Paris.

My sons, Jonah and Henry, patiently put up with the sounds of many strange records and accompanying long, boring lectures. Freda has long been my partner in making records and, more recently, in listening to and writing about records. I owe everything to her strength and insight. But most of all, I would like to thank my parents. Part of the joy of this project was the chance to eavesdrop on the sounds of their generation and, along the way, find the origins of some of their catchphrases, perhaps getting to know them a little better. I hope my work can stand as a small gesture of thanks for their love and support.

Introduction

NASA launched two Voyager spacecraft in August and September of 1977. These craft were to explore the outer planets from Jupiter to Uranus and then leave the solar system to become what Carl Sagan called "emissaries of Earth to the realm of the stars." As part of that mission, they carried a message for any extraterrestrial civilizations they might encounter, which included musical selections from around the world, greetings in sixty languages, and statements from President Jimmy Carter and Secretary General of the United Nations Kurt Waldheim. As artifacts of the cold war space race, the Voyager spacecraft were emblematic of postwar American society and technology. Equally emblematic of postwar American culture was the form in which NASA conveyed the Earth's message to the stars: affixed to each Voyager was a gold-coated copper phonograph record.

As the Voyagers' "golden records" were sent spinning into outer space, long-playing records (LPs) had been spinning in American homes for thirty years, becoming an integral part of many aspects of popular culture. From the 1940s to the 1970s, the phonograph industry experienced phenomenal growth in sales and cultural influence, producing recordings that were meant to serve a multitude of functions in the American home above and beyond the reproduction of popular music. Recordings of a diverse range of spoken word genres enjoyed robust sales in the postwar era and stimulated extensive critical discussion in the popular press. A generation of children grew up with their own record players and libraries of elaborately packaged and produced kids' records; recordings of poetry readings and dramatizations of stage plays served a variety of functions in the home; bawdy "stag party" records simulated the spaces of burlesque clubs and military barracks for male hi-fi aficionados; records of African American comics were a platform for a comic perspective on the sexual revolution; and young people in the 1960s and 1970s wove catchphrases that they had heard on comedy records into their everyday interactions. This book brings these and other overlooked aspects of phonography into the history of the postwar entertainment industry and media consumption in the American home.

It may come as a surprise to some readers that radio and television broadcasting will orient my discussion of the postwar record industry more than celebrated genres of popular music, such as jazz, folk, and rock and roll. In fact, spoken word records were frequently understood to be the home media alternative to network broadcasting in an era before the proliferation of cable television and videocassettes. Media scholars have approached the topic of American broadcasting from many perspectives, describing the social forces that shaped the institutions of broadcasting, its relationship to cultural discourses of home and family, its importance in the everyday lives of the audience, and the forms of entertainment that came to dominate the airwaves. That work can be supplemented through a comparative analysis of the record industry since, though network radio and television became the dominant forms of home media entertainment for most Americans in the decades after World War II, they shared the postwar American home with the phonograph.

I am interested in exploring the ways in which these adjacent media forms developed in relation to each other. As such, my analysis of the phonograph can contribute to several ongoing areas of discussion within the field of television studies. Lynn Spigel has argued that scholars need to understand television history "within the broader context of the history of postwar visual culture."[1] The case studies in the chapters that follow will illustrate that the same needs to be said of postwar audio culture. The home phonograph player, like radio and television, was integrated into the rhythms and spaces of postwar domestic life. Like television, the home phonograph served to connect public and private spaces, but the "window on the world" found on postwar LPs frequently represented spaces, language, and experiences that were not broadcast on network television. Phonograph records also facilitated social configurations of media consumption other than the "family circle" often associated with television. In fact, the record industry was, for a variety of reasons, able to market its products to relatively specialized, or niche, audiences. Media historians have argued that increasingly sophisticated regimes of market research and the growth of cable television helped to spur a tendency in the cultural industries to target small, specialized audiences during the last decades of the twentieth century. Niche marketing has typically been discussed in relation to television in the 1970s and 1980s, with the 1950s and early 1960s held up as bastions of mass audience radio and television broadcasting. The LPs discussed in the following chapters shed light on media "narrowcasting" during the "broadcasting era," and so add to our understanding of how the cultural industries have marketed their products.

In addition to broadening the discussion of the construction of media audiences, the postwar LP supplements our understanding of television "flow." Television scholars have begun to describe the process by which audiences could gain a degree of control over the ephemeral flow of the broadcasting schedule through the repetition provided by television reruns starting in the late 1950s, and the home videocassette recorder in the 1980s. LP records allowed listeners a level of control over home media entertainment decades before TV reruns or home video, and the reception of the LP in the postwar era can tell us about precursors to more recent patterns of home media consumption. Consider a 1967 article in which *New York Times* television critic Jack Gould announced the "long-awaited confirmation" that CBS Laboratories had developed a device that enabled viewers to playback prerecorded programs on their home TV sets: an early videocassette recorder. "There is no question," Gould wrote enthusiastically, "that the concept alone holds formidable implications for both show business and education." In an attempt to describe what he considered to be potentially the "the root of the next revolutionary change in the visual medium," Gould offered a comparison to a sonic medium: "Stripped of fancy language, the CBS playback device is a visual equivalent of the long-playing phonograph in sound." Indeed, Gould not only titled his article "Soon You'll Collect TV Reels, Like LP's," but also rhapsodized about the phonograph, calling it "by far the most democratic" of the mass media because of the way in which it allowed "individual selectivity" in home media consumption: "While using the same technical facility in the home, the individual has the widest possible range of artistic choice, from the symphony to pop, from serious dramatic plays to night club sketches. A huge medium appealing to millions has thrived on limitless diversity exercised not alone by a few smug impresarios but rather by the separate parts of the multitude."[2]

We should note how the emerging technology of the videocassette is understood here in terms of the LP. An examination of the culture of postwar phonograph records offers a new vantage point on prerecorded and repeatable home media entertainment before the videocassette.

Note how Gould made reference to the phonograph not just as a medium for music ("from the symphony to pop") but also as the source of "dramatic plays" and "night club sketches." Such spoken word drama and comedy records were a crucial part of the postwar phonograph industry but have been largely ignored in critical study. The 1950s and 1960s are often remembered as a golden era of both rock and classic pop music, the sales of which certainly made up the majority of record industry profits. But this was a complex period of transition in the phonograph industry, when popular musicians shared the charts with a remarkable variety of other acts. Part of my goal, then, is to trace the historical process by which rock became the dominant force in the American phonograph industry by the 1970s to the exclusion of these other genres. That dominance, according to Kier Keightley, was achieved by finding ways to sell the more profitable LP format to both an adult and a youth market.[3] Keightley argues that a "boomer historiography" has consistently disavowed rock music's commercial status, making much scholarship on the record industry "selectively blind to the industrial elements that contributed to the birth of rock music."[4] I would add that such a romanticized view of rock records has also made cultural historians deaf to postwar genres of recorded sound other than music. In a recent study of the postwar popular music industry, Tim Anderson encourages pop music scholars to redirect their attention from particular musical genres to the specific materiality of records themselves, a move he argues would make a "profitable shift toward communication studies."[5] But the records that Anderson examines are all recordings of music, and so the implications of his comments are not taken as far as they might have gone. I take Anderson's recommendation a step further, using an analysis of records to engage with scholarly work on radio, film, and television and so illustrate a means by which the investigation of the recording industry might be more fully integrated into the larger field of media studies. That said, my research on genres of spoken word recordings sheds light on popular music, and I will have occasion to discuss such topics as the music appreciation movement and overlooked precursors to rock culture.

The tendency to privilege popular music in historical work on the phonograph has obscured other types of sound recording that have existed since the birth of the record industry. Between the 1890s and 1920s, record companies released a wide range of material in a surprising array of genres, including historical reenactments, descriptive sketches, and comedy routines from the vaudeville and minstrel stage: a stunning diversity of cultural artifacts whose utility for historians is only beginning to be appreciated. Music became the dominant recorded genre only in the 1910s and 1920s, in part as a means to secure middle-class consumers, for whom highbrow music was an important form of social distinction. Patrick Feaster has described this shift in terms of the phonograph industry's growing emphasis on "fidelity" to a source, which overtook other definitions of audio entertainment as artful fiction. There was thus a tension between the identification of the phonograph as either a music box or artful mimic, the latter having roots in ventriloquism, oral mimicry, and dialect caricature.[6] As the industry sought to reach middle-class consumers, the definition of the phonograph as music box held sway, and other uses of recorded sound were relegated to the periphery of phonograph culture. After World War II, a resurgence of record sales and the development of long-playing formats set the stage for the reappearance of some of the diversity of the earliest days of recorded sound, making the postwar era a particularly dynamic period in which to study the phonograph industry.

The new technology of long-playing records, first introduced by Columbia Records in 1948 and the dominant source of industry revenue by the mid-1950s, was initially marketed primarily for its capacity to represent a larger repertoire of Western classical music. That technology was also used to disseminate a range of spoken word genres as industry and consumers explored the possible entertainment functions of the LP. In this regard, an important framework for my analysis is Rick Altman's "crisis historiography" of new media technologies. Altman's method takes into account the multiple and conflicting definitions of a new technology and considers "unsuccessful experiments and short-lived practices" as well as those that become established.[7] Altman describes how new media technologies tend to be recognized initially as several "different phenomena, each overlapping with an already existing medium." Such ambiguity leads to "conflicting definitions" of the media artifact, as various social forces struggle to gain control over it. Eventually, new technologies take on stable features as the result of culturally overdetermined factors.[8] Altman's framework can be applied to my previous gloss of the early phonograph industry: the phonograph was multiply defined as, among other things, a stenographer, a mimic, and a music box, with the success of the later being overdetermined by economic and cultural factors. Crisis historiography can also provide a way to understand the multiple definitions of the long-playing record in the fifties and sixties. For a time, that new media format was mobilized for children's entertainment, home education, cutting-edge comedy, risqué material, and poetic recitation. It was only when the economic ascendancy of rock music—spurred by the baby-boom demographic and a shift from singles to albums as rock's central medium—coincided with the emergence of new home media outlets that usurped some of the LP's social functions that a range of spoken word genres faded from the cultural stage. Spoken word LPs may have been a relatively short-lived media technology, but they still have much to tell us about the culture in which they were conceived, implemented, and consumed.

Altman applied his crisis historiography to a survey of early cinema sound practices, and his work is thus representative of writing on the social construction of recording technology by scholars such as Lisa Gitelman, Jonathan Sterne, and James Lastra, all of whom tend to focus on the early years of recorded sound, the emergence of the recording apparatus, and the development of film sound practices. The work of these authors has been invaluable, but their focus on the early period of modern media can obscure the fact that the cultural life of sound technologies has been an ongoing process, marked by continuing dynamics of continuity and change. The postwar era represents a particularly rich period for historical research since it was a time when the industry served a remarkably broad range of cultural functions, introduced significant technological innovations (long-playing formats, affordable home stereo sets, high fidelity, and multitracking on magnetic tape recorders), and experienced remarkable growth in record sales across diverse genres. Postwar spoken word records thus allow for a cultural history of sound technology and popular recording that moves beyond a focus on popular music and the recording apparatus and applies the theoretical insights of sound studies to a neglected period of sound media history.

As a result, the case studies that follow will move into largely uncharted territory in American media history and so will bring to light understudied contributions to media performance and the art of recorded sound. I showcase underappreciated contributions to sound performance found in unexpected genres: the makers of children's records experimented with the possibilities of multitrack recording well before the Beach Boys or the Beatles; recitations of modern poetry in the 1950s prefigure influential recordings by the likes of Bob Dylan; the performance styles of African American comics pushed the boundaries of ethnic caricature and developed influential uses of the microphone; and comedy LPs provide perhaps the best means by which we can understand some of the most influential modes of comedic performance of the postwar era. The recordings described in the following chapters allow us to hear with fresh ears the development of postwar performance styles and sound recording techniques.

One of the overriding aims of this book is to illustrate the diversity of genres and styles found on postwar records. That aim, however, poses a certain challenge in terms of method, since each chapter has required that I contextualize a different constellation of performers, traditions, and cultural discourses. Therefore, while the entire book is grounded in scholarly work on media history and performance, individual chapters will draw upon work on children's culture, debates about the "middlebrow," the aesthetics of poetry recitation and improvisation, the sexual revolution, theories of mimicry, and the construction of media publics. What becomes clear is that no single theory can account for all of the spoken word records of the postwar era, although several key themes run through the book and are summarized in the conclusion. I should also emphasize that my choice of case studies is not meant to suggest a pantheon or offer a comprehensive or definitive history of spoken word records. Another book could be written on the same subject focusing on the likes of Shelley Berman, Richard Pryor, Rae Bourbon, Jonathan Winters, Ruth Draper, Mitch Miller, Lord Buckley, Moms Mabley, the Children's Record Guild, Jim Copp, Redd Foxx, Cheech and Chong, Hecky Krasno, Dick Gregory, Bill Cosby, Bob Newhart, and Kermit Schaefer. That said, the records that I have chosen to examine are not merely my personal favorites but are meant to illuminate the most prominent genres of spoken word records released during the postwar decades, as indicated by my analysis of the popular and trade press. With the plural "phonograph cultures" in my title, I have also sought to take into account a variety of taste cultures, from under-the-counter "smut" to high culture poetry; a range of niche demographics, including children, housewives, and African Americans; and a cross-section of reception practices.

Each chapter moves rather freely across the years between 1940 to 1980, but they are arranged in chronological order as indicated by the peak of each given genre's cultural prominence. I register that peak by a representative recording: chapter 1's discussion of children's records hinges on Capitol's Bozo records of the mid- to late 1940s; chapter 2 has to do with high culture spoken word records, specifically Dylan

Thomas's 1952 and 1953 recordings for Caedmon Records; chapter 3 covers sexually explicit "party albums" during the era of the sexual revolution, including Rusty Warren's blockbusters of the early 1960s; the recorded performances of celebrity mimics are the subject of chapter 4, including Vaughn Meader's *The First Family* album, which was, on its release in 1962, the biggest-selling LP of all time; and in chapter 5, I examine postwar comedy albums, concluding with Steve Martin's chart-topping records of the mid-1970s. Such a structure provides a rough chronology of the spoken word LP during the era of its most significant cultural resonance while also allowing me to develop several key themes: the nature of the intermedial relationship between the phonograph and network broadcasting; the role of the phonograph industry in the emergence of niche marketing; and the development of performance styles and production techniques during an incipient era of prerecorded home entertainment. With some of these larger goals in mind, what follows is a short description of the structure of the book.

In chapter 1, I examine the rapid expansion of the children's record market in the 1940s, which was fueled by the baby boom, a general recovery in the record industry, and the influence of the music appreciation movement. Children's records from this era have much to tell us about the increasing importance of children to American consumer culture as well as postwar cultural discourses about children's use of media. After a discussion of phonograph records made for children in the earliest decades of the phonograph industry, I set the stage for the postwar era through an examination of the marketing of "Bubble Books" released by Columbia and Victor Records in the 1910s and 1920s. The Bubble Books were the first hybrid of book and record marketed to children and, as such, represented a pioneering instance of cross-media synergy between book publishing and the record industry. The market for children's records experienced a remarkable surge in the 1940s and 1950s, when records were often discussed as a welcome antidote to television. Some of the best-selling children's records of the 1940s and 1950s present a fascinating tension: marketed as home lessons in the appreciation of Western classical music, they trained children in modes of listening more in tune with genres of recorded popular music. In fact, experimentation with multitrack studio techniques for the children of the baby boom created an audience who could recognize and appreciate the studio-based progressive rock of the 1960s.

"Kidisks" were heard by children but in many cases were marketed to and bought by mothers: one of the ways in which women played an active role in postwar phonograph culture. Chapter 2 examines the role of women in the postwar record industry through the case study of Caedmon Records, founded by Marianne Mantell and Barbara Holdridge in 1952. Not only was Caedmon the only female-owned record company of the era, but it pioneered the market for "highbrow" spoken word records, beginning with Mantell and Holdridge's recordings of Dylan Thomas's poetry recitations. Such records are an example of American "middlebrow" culture, since they represented an attempt to popularize high culture. Though cultural critics of the time vilified such "midcult" products, recent scholarship has begun to reexamine that form of cultural production. My analysis of Caedmon adds to that reevaluation of American cultural history. The press discourse that surrounded Mantell and Holdridge illustrates some of the tensions surrounding nondomestic women during the postwar years. Besides describing Mantell and Holdridge's success story, women's magazines recommended highbrow records by companies like Caedmon as a means of self-improvement for housewives. Just as radio and television production and consumption were profoundly influenced by their introduction into the domestic sphere, so LPs were shaped by the rhythms of female domestic labor and suburban social life, and women were encouraged to make "educational" records part of their domestic routine: as one article put it, to "intrigue their mind while their hands worked." Key aspects of the postwar middlebrow LP market were thus closely linked to social discourses having to do with gender, education, and cultural taste.

Inspired by the success of Caedmon, the major record companies offered their own highbrow alternatives to radio and television broadcasting. Some smaller record companies took the opposite tack, and chapter 3 examines adults-only records and their connection to the sexual revolution. Adult-themed records made between the 1950s and mid-1970s provide an overlooked case study of mass media erotica meant for consumption in the home before cable television or the explosion of porn on videocassette. Under-the-counter recordings of erotic material, which have been referred to as either "blue discs" or "party records," have circulated since at least the 1930s but attained a new degree of cultural visibility in the 1950s and 1960s. Party records were often intended for a culture of male hi-fi aficionados, but the home stereo was not solely the domain of men. During the same era, records made by female comics such as Rusty Warren presented bawdy material from a female perspective and reached legions of female fans. Warren's records were intended for mixed-gender social gatherings, but some long-playing phonograph albums were intended to function as home lessons in sex therapy for couples. At the same time, black-owned independent record companies were releasing records of the performances of risqué African American comedians such as Redd Foxx to predominantly African American audiences. Some of these African American comics used the home phonograph as a medium for their perspective on the sexual revolution. Rudy Ray Moore is best known for his starring role in the Dolemite blaxploitation films of the mid-1970s, but he first achieved media notoriety as the creator of a series of adult party records in the early 1970s. Moore and his collaborator, Lady Reed, presented an African American perspective both on blue discs of a previous era and on the best-selling sex manual *The Sensuous Woman* (1969). By placing Moore and Reed's LPs in a larger genre of erotic records, we can better appreciate the ways in which their work functioned to critique performance styles and attitudes heard on white erotica and provided an African American voice in the media discourse of the sexual revolution. Rapper Chuck D. famously asserted that rap records were the "black CNN" for his generation. In the same way, records made by African American comics such as Moore were the "black Comedy Central" in the era before cable television. As all of the case studies in chapter 3 show, the LP was well suited to the frank discussion and performance of sexuality, a point that phonographic performers often made by contrasting party records with network radio and television.

A notable subgenre of comedy LPs in the postwar era was that of celebrity impressions: the subject of chapter 4. In fact, modern media such as the cinema, phonograph, and radio made it possible for far-flung audiences to recognize unique celebrities by their characteristic voices and gestures. Pre-1920s phonograph recordings captured the broad ethnic caricature of the nineteenth-century minstrel and vaudeville stage, but by the postwar era, comedy records by impressionists such as Arthur Blake, Will Jordan, Vaughn Meader, George Kirby, David Frye, and Rich Little offered what Susan Glenn calls the "comedy of personality": "the imitation, sometimes in a satiric vein, of the particular style and repertoire of *specific individuals*."[9] LP records provide perhaps the best means of exploring this tradition of comedic imitation in the American media. The LP played an important part in this history because it provided an outlet for political impressionists, whose routines were often regulated on network radio. The phenomenal success of Vaughn Meader's *First Family* LP spurred what was considered to be a renaissance of postwar mimics. My investigation considers imitative performance in broad terms and takes into account a variety of mimics, actors, and impressionists. Such an approach reveals the cultural rules of gender and racial mimicry that held sway at the time as well as the hierarchies of what I call imitative performance. Imitation was an important category for evaluating performance during the postwar era, and besides figuring in cultural hierarchies about acting, it became a central trope in the acts of comedians in the 1970s who sought to critique the previous generation of show business. Nonetheless, postwar imitative performances took part in the social construction of media celebrity, since professional mimics functioned both as unofficial Hollywood studio publicity and as a factor in the expansion of the legal rights that celebrities held over representations of their personae.

Celebrity mimics were only one facet of a robust market for comedy records in the 1950s and 1960s: a market that represented a return to the early decades of the record industry, when company catalogs offered comedy routines from the minstrel and vaudeville stage. Postwar comedy LPs documented changes in the spaces of American comedy performance at the same time that they showcased techniques used by performers to go beyond those particular spaces to create and sustain a wider public of record listeners. LPs by nightclub and cabaret comics of the late 1950s and early 1960s featured a jazz aesthetic associated with a sense of spontaneous improvisation and closely connected to specific urban nightspots. Records preserved the innovative approaches of nightclub comics such as Lenny Bruce and Mort Sahl as well as a cabaret style descended from the Compass Theater in Chicago. In both cases, comedy records can help us to understand approaches to improvisational performance. By the end of the 1960s, the LP became the medium for a revival of audio theater, a recorded version of radio drama in the era of television. The records made by groups such as the Firesign Theatre commented on emerging forms of television programming and reception and featured a rock aesthetic that utilized the possibilities of the multitrack recording studio to create dense, fantastic sonic spaces and encourage repeated listening. In the late 1970s, Steve Martin's comedy LPs hit the top of the charts, capturing Martin's stadium rock aesthetic, which included his signature catchphrases. Martin's success came at the end of the comedy album's largest cultural impact, and by the early 1980s, the comedy album was displaced as the home medium for edgy satire by cable television.

As I hope these brief chapter descriptions indicate, spoken word LPs illuminate understudied aspects of American media history at the same time that they add to scholarly dialogues within media studies. The products of the record industry and the cultural meanings they acquired offer an important supplement to our understanding of American postwar media culture. Duke Ellington once explained that his composition "Harlem Air Shaft" was meant to capture all the sounds of that city: "So much goes on in a Harlem airshaft," he said. "You hear fights, you smell dinner. You hear people making love. You hear intimate gossip floating down. You hear the radio. An airshaft is one great big loudspeaker."[10] Postwar spoken word recordings provide an airshaft into the diverse and compelling sounds of postwar American culture; they are emissaries to us across expanses of time, just as the Voyager golden discs were meant to be emissaries across expanses of space.

CHAPTER I

Turntable Jr.

In August 2001, the last episode of the *Bozo's Circus* television show was aired on WGN in Chicago. Though the show had been a staple of local Chicago television for forty years and over seven thousand episodes, the final WGN broadcast received national press coverage that hailed Bozo as the longest-running children's television character in America, seen at one time on stations from coast to coast. Bozo's television debut had been in Los Angeles in 1949, and in his heyday there were Bozos on the air in most major American cities, as well as in Brazil, Mexico, Thailand, and Greece. Among the many performers who played Bozo on local TV stations were Muppets creator Jim Henson and NBC weatherman Willard Scott, who went on to be the first television Ronald McDonald—a figure who borrowed much of his visual style from Bozo.[1] Sadly, Bozo's reign as juggernaut of postwar children's television was coming to an end by the 1990s, the victim of competition from cable stations such as Nickelodeon and Cartoon Network. The last Bozo broadcast in Chicago marked the end of an era and drew a variety of local celebrities, including Smashing Pumpkins lead singer Billy Corgan, who performed a version of Bob Dylan's "Forever Young."

There was another music industry personality in the WGN studio that day, one who was probably not recognized by many in the audience: Alan Livingston, a former Capitol Records executive. Best known as the man who signed both Frank Sinatra and the Beatles to his label, Livingston had another legacy, one that inspired the *Saturday Evening*

Post to write in 1955 that he had "pioneered a branch of show business" that was earning twenty million dollars a year and had even influenced American educational theories. Livingston had managed this feat by conceptualizing and producing a children's phonograph record called *Bozo at the Circus* in 1946: a disc that not only introduced Bozo the Clown to the world, but was at one time the best-selling album in phonograph history and the fountainhead of a postwar boom in children's records. It was from Livingston's record that the Bozo entertainment franchise sprang: the proliferation of regional television Bozos actually began at Capitol Records, where Bozo clown suits were kept in all of its regional offices for actors to play the famous clown at personal appearances.[2] That the longest-running children's television character of the postwar era originated in the record industry is a telling indication of the largely unrecognized importance of the phonograph in children's media culture.

Juliet B. Schor has described a contemporary American consumer culture in which children form the link between advertisers and the family purse and children's tastes and opinions shape corporate strategies. Schor states that the centrality of children to the consumer marketplace is a relatively recent phenomenon and that not long ago children were merely "bit players" who were approached by marketers primarily through their mothers. Schor, like many other scholars, refers to the widespread introduction of television as an important turning point in the use of the media as a platform for marketing to children because of the way in which it allowed advertisers a more direct link to young audiences.[3] But the work of scholars such as Daniel Cook, Ellen Gruber Garvey, Lisa Jacobson, and William Leach has indicated that children were seen as more than bit players in home consumption decades before television and even radio. Jacobson argues that middle-class children became targets of advertising more than half a century before television and warns that identifying the 1950s as "the pivotal historical moment" in marketing to kids risks falling into a "technological and economic determinism" that can obscure "a host of earlier efforts to inculcate brand consciousness."[4] The phonograph was one such earlier effort at marketing to children, despite being overlooked in examinations of early twentieth–century children's media culture. Consider that in 1924, the Victor Phonograph Company could eagerly refer to the novel opportunities provided by reaching the "boundless and almost untouched children's market." Victor was embarking on a marketing campaign for one of the earliest lines of mass media products targeted specifically at young children: Bubble Books, the first book and record hybrid for kids.[5]

The phonograph industry provides an important missing chapter in the history of the design and marketing of media products for children. Phonograph records have been largely absent from the scholarly history of children's media entertainment. Overviews of children's media typically move from discussions of dime novels to the nickelodeon film theater and from there to radio and television, without any mention of the phonograph industry.[6] In Norma Odom Pecora's overview of media industry output for children, she has this to say about the recording industry: "Teens have been central to the music industry since the 1950s and the advent of Rock and Roll, but the younger market has been ignored both in terms of product and technology."[7] As I will demonstrate, records for children were actively marketed to parents and children by the phonograph industry decades before Disney and television. Of particular interest in the pre–World War II era are the Bubble Books, which were released by Columbia Records (and later Victor) in the 1910s and 1920s. Advertising materials for Bubble Books reveal a lost phase in the development of influential approaches to marketing media products to children and index the anxieties that surrounded the arrival of such products into the home. Notably, children's records such as the Bubble Books did not provoke the kind of public controversy inspired by dime novels, early cinema, radio, and television, despite aggressive marketing by the record industry in popular magazines, department stores, and even in schools. The fact that children's phonograph records sparked such little public debate is certainly one of the reasons that children's records have been off the scholarly radar but also poses some significant questions concerning the study of children and the media: Why did children's records not inspire the same controversy as other forms of children's media? Why do some forms of new media for children provoke more cultural concern than others? The following analysis, then, is concerned not only with adding the phonograph industry to historical accounts of children's media and with documenting early strategies for marketing children's media products, but also with identifying aspects of that marketing that allowed these pioneering instances of home media products for children to be woven into the fabric of everyday American family life.

The Bubble Books provide a new perspective on the emergence of a children's market in American consumer culture and helped to set the stage for children's records of the 1940s and 1950s: the time of a remarkable surge in what the trade press called the "Brat-wax," "pee-wee platter," or "kidisk" market. Postwar recordings such as *Rusty in Orchestraville, Sparky and the Magic Piano,* and *Genie the Magic Record* index debates about child-rearing and the role that media entertainment should play in children's lives. Some of the best-selling children's records of the 1940s and 1950s present a fascinating tension: marketed as home lessons in the appreciation of Western classical music, they trained children in modes of listening more in tune with genres of recorded popular music. In fact, experimentation with multi-track studio techniques on records made for baby boom children blazed a trail for the studio-based rock and roll of the 1950s and 1960s. From Bubble Books to Bozo, children's records have much to tell us about the development of modern media texts that were thought to be good for children. When Alan Livingston discussed the development of his blockbuster Bozo records, he often noted the influence of records made for children in the early decades of the twentieth century. In order to understand developments in the postwar children's record industry, it is necessary to first examine children's records in the early years of the phonograph industry.

JUVENILE RECORDS

It can be argued that the history of the children's phonograph record begins with the history of recorded sound itself, since the oft-repeated "creation story" of the phonograph has Thomas Edison reciting the nursery rhyme "Mary Had a Little Lamb" into his tinfoil recording device. Phonograph historian Patrick Feaster has pointed out that this heart-warming anecdote is quite probably a rewrite of history: given Edison's penchant for salty humor, the first test was likely to have been quite different. Nonetheless, from the very beginning, the phonograph was cast as a device with a certain affinity for children's entertainment. In fact, one of Edison's earliest intended uses for recorded sound was to make children's dolls that could speak.[8] In 1890, Edison outfitted his West Orange, New Jersey, laboratory as a production line for dolls containing tiny phonograph players. The dolls did not sell well, and the company folded in 1891, by which time the market for entertainment phonograph cylinders had begun to take off.[9] Though the phonograph would not speak to American children through dolls, the major phonograph companies actively sought to develop a child market for phonograph players and records as early as the 1890s and 1900s.

Consider that the first Victor Talking Machine product to be nationally advertised was the Toy Gram-o-phone, which is shown in a December 1900 ad in *Munsey's Magazine,* with copy that reads, "The most wonderful Christmas gift ever offered for children."[10] In a November 1907 advertisement in *McClure's Magazine,* we see the image of two little girls amazed by the phonograph horn, while the copy proclaims, "The Edison Phonograph as a Christmas Present": "No single thing furnishes so much entertainment, amusement and enjoyment to a family, especially where there are children and young folks, as an Edison Phonograph."[11] Compelling evidence exists that the phonograph was indeed being given to children as a Christmas gift. On a rare amateur home recording circa 1899–1901, we hear a father or grandfather describing the gift of a graphophone (the Columbia Company cylinder player) to his children: "My children, when I heard you play the flute and the piano . . . it occurred to me that you would enjoy a graphophone immensely, and that perhaps it would be the most appropriate . . . [Christmas gift] I could possibly give you." The patriarch goes on to describe the gift as both a "source of enjoyment" and as an aid to more serious study.[12]

The phonograph industry continued to actively pursue the child market both indirectly through parents and through direct appeals to children, as is illustrated by the use of a Victor promotional brochure entitled *The Victor: For Every Day in the Week* (1907), which promoted the phonograph as a multipurpose form of children's entertainment. In the Victor trade journal *The Voice of Victor,* the company advised retailers on how to use the brochure: "This booklet can be used in conjunction with your window display . . . in some localities it may be better to distribute them upon dismissal of school."[13] In the brochure, we see the image of a phonograph player being delivered to a home, as copy proclaims, "There certainly is pleasure for us every day in the week with the Victor." A series of illustrations follow, depicting the various ways in which the phonograph could entertain children: on Monday, a group of youngsters wear military uniforms and march around the nursery to the sounds of John Philip Sousa; and on Tuesday, the children listen to Mother Goose stories on the phonograph player and put on a Punch and Judy show.

Such Mother Goose stories, or juvenile records, were made by performers such as William F. Hooley, who identified himself as Uncle Will and began recitations of material such as *The Death of Cock Robin* by telling listeners: "Now, children, draw your little chairs nearer so that you can see the pretty pictures." Also consider pioneer recording artist

Len Spencer's Columbia 1899 recording of Cinderella, on which we hear Spencer say, "Now children, draw your little chairs around the Graphophone Grand, and Uncle John will tell you the story of Cinderella and the glass slipper." At the end of the tale, Spencer says, "There now, wasn't that a nice story? Run off to bed now little ones, kiss Uncle John 'good night.'" Gilbert Girard was the premiere vocal mimic of the early phonograph industry and frequently applied his talents to making records for children. On titles such as *A Trip to the Circus* (Victor 1901) and *Auction Sale of a Bird and Animal Store* (Edison 1902), Girard and Len Spencer presented animal mimicry, an auctioneer performance, and broad jokes: a range of offerings that could appeal to both children and adults. *A Trip to the Circus* is introduced as a "descriptive selection for the little folks," and then we hear Spencer announce, "Now children, hold tight to my hand, and don't get too near to the animals." "Oh, see the elephants," Spencer declares, and Girard provides a loud trumpeting sound. On Girard's later recording *Santa Claus Visits the Children* (Victor 1921), we hear Santa arrive on his sleigh and announce: "Come children, gather near. A few nice stories you shall hear." Girard goes on to recite Mother Goose verses interspersed with his impressive repertoire of sound effects. We find here an early model for children's records, wherein a rudimentary narrative framework structures a series of spectacular sound effects meant to capture the attention of young listeners. As we shall see, the calibration of these different types of sonic appeal became a recurring structural dynamic of children's records.

"Juvenile records" from the early decades of the twentieth century demonstrate that the phonograph industry was quick to recognize the importance of the child audience for home media entertainment. In fact, a major campaign to market children's records began in 1917, when Columbia Records formed a partnership with Harper and Brothers Books to manufacture 5½-inch diameter records and market them to children.[14] The Bubble Books were the brainchild of Ralph Mayhew, who in 1914 was working for Harper and Brothers on a children's book of verse in which he planned to have "a child sitting blowing bubbles which ascended and burst into the little pictures and nursery rhymes."[15] In a 1921 interview with *Printer's Ink* magazine, Mayhew described how he first conceived of combining children's books with phonograph records: "I had a habit," Mayhew stated, "of crawling out of bed occasionally of a Sunday morning, putting a record on the phonograph, slipping back into bed with pencil and paper and working on little verses for my Bubble Book. One Sunday morning, while thus engaged, the idea suddenly occurred to me of incorporating small phonograph records in my Bubble Book, with appropriate music to accompany the nursery rhymes. I had never heard of putting a book and records together, and the idea rather struck my fancy."[16] Mayhew was eventually able to convince Harper and Brothers and Columbia Records to back his idea, and the first edition of the Bubble Books was pressed in 1917. The first Bubble Book—which contained three single-sided 5½-inch records featuring musical versions of traditional children's verses sung by Henry Burr and an accompanying package with illustrations by Rhoda Chase—met with immediate success: "Hardly had the salesmen gone out when the orders began to pour in," *Printer's Ink* noted, adding that nine thousand copies were sold in the month after it was released.[17] These initial strong sales figures continued over the next several years: according to one 1920 advertisement, more than one and a half million Bubble Books were sold between January and May of that year.[18] Indeed, the Bubble Books sold well enough to inspire subsequent editions through the early 1930s, with the copyright and patents controlled by the Victor Company after 1924.[19] The Bubble Books were the first book and record hybrids marketed to children and so represent a pioneering instance of cross-media synergy between book publishing and the record industry. An examination of the ad campaign designed to sell Bubble Books reveals early strategies for developing a child audience for home media products and the kinds of media texts that were considered to be beneficial to children.

THE BOOKS THAT SING

At a time when American toy manufacturers were entering the mass market, Columbia and Harper and Brothers began advertising Bubble Books in both the popular and trade press.[20] In regards to the latter, Daniel Cook warns that the use of trade journals as evidence "demands circumspection," since the "bald, forthright approach to markets" found in such discourse was intended for a very particular audience. Cook suggests that trade material should be considered as "providing an entrée into a historically situated semantic domain" and can provide insights into the process by which commercial portrayals of children and childhood are constructed.[21] Trade advertisements for Bubble Books in *Talking Machine World* were targeted to record store owners and reveal some of the motivations and assumptions behind influential strategies for marketing children's media entertainment.

For example, retailers were encouraged to use children to reach adult consumers indirectly. *Printer's Ink* magazine claimed that phonograph dealers across the country were reporting that "they sell phonographs to many people who explain that they 'don't care for talking machines' themselves but that they must have one to play the Bubble Book records for their children. Naturally, having taken the machines into their homes, they overcome their first prejudice and buy other records as well, so that the Bubble Books have been a means of stimulating phonograph and phonograph record sales."[22] "The easiest way to win the good-will of customers is through their children," stated a 1923 *Talking Machine World* ad targeted to phonograph dealers: "You know how freely the most reticent mother will talk, if you get her started on the subject of her little boy or girl."[23] A 1924 Victor company publication noted that nothing ingratiated a merchant with the public as much as "being of service to children. Parents will feel more than ever well disposed toward you . . . for bringing a desirable thing to their children's hands."[24] Children were also thought to be able to influence their parents through what marketers have described as the "nag factor," or "pester power," in which children are encouraged to make purchase requests of their parents.[25] A 1921 *Talking Machine World* ad asked, "How many children are working for you? No, we don't mean in the store but outside, in your customers' homes. The dealer that sells Bubble Books has one or more persistent salesmen in every home in his town."[26]

Not only were children a means of reaching parents, but trade press ads also asserted that they were potentially "serial purchasers." That is, the importance of the child market lay in the fact that children were eager to purchase multiple items in a particular line, or as the Bubble Book ads bluntly stated, "When you sell one—you sell a habit!" Ralph Mayhew was not the first person to recognize the "serial" potential of the children's market. Ellen Gruber Garvey has described how children in the 1880s and 1890s collected advertising trade cards, which they arranged in scrapbooks: "No single trade card," Garvey writes, "was enough."[27] Nonetheless, the idea of exploiting children's seemingly limitless appetites struck *Printer's Ink* as a novel aspect of Bubble Book marketing: it was Mayhew's "keen marketing imagination" that had perceived that a second Bubble Book could be sold to the same people "who had bought the first one. And they were right."[28] "With most kinds of merchandise the sale is the end of the transaction," stated the copy in a 1922 *Talking Machine World* ad, "but with Bubble Books it is another story. When you sell your first Bubble Book you have only just begun.

For there is one sure thing about Bubble Book buyers—they always come back for more."[29] A Victor company trade journal described how one of the most "satisfying features" of selling records to children was the fact that "every sale sows the seeds" for an "endless chain" of future sales.[30] A 1919 ad visualizes the child as both a serial purchaser and as a link between the marketplace and the home: an illustration depicts a pied piper holding a portable gramophone, leading a line of dancing children from the city to "Ye Talking Machine Shoppe," while the copy beneath reads, "Lure the children to your store with these enchanting little volumes, and they will take you right into the heart of the family. When the youngster has bought one he always comes for more."[31] Bubble Books could thus create a serial market for records in a manner similar to film serials in the 1910s, which Terry Staples argues were designed to stimulate regular cinema-going in children.[32]

Trade press advertisements for Bubble Books demonstrate strategies for marketing children's media products that have since become commonplace. The trade press ads I've been describing were, however, only one aspect of what was considered to be an unprecedented advertising campaign for children's products. In fact, the use of a large-scale print advertising campaign was itself a notable aspect of the marketing of Bubble Books. A 1920 ad in *Talking Machine World* announced a "great national Bubble Book campaign" at a cost of $75,000.[33] The trade journal the *Bookseller, Newsdealer and Stationer* stated that this would be "the largest advertising campaign ever devoted to books . . . the sum to be expended in the advertising campaign for them exceeds anything ever before spent on a single juvenile line."[34] Advertisements in that campaign appeared in mass-circulation magazines such as *Ladies' Home Journal* and *Woman's Home Companion* and provide a commercial discourse that ran parallel to the trade journals described above.

It will not come as a surprise that popular press ads for Bubble Books targeted women, since it was thought that they did the bulk of both the family's consumer spending and child rearing. The growth of a market for both mass-produced toys and children's records was tied to the emergence of new family roles that were in turn shaped by campaigns against child labor, the decreasing size of the middle-class family, and the introduction of scientific discourses of child rearing.[35] Ellen Seiter stresses that children's consumption be placed in the context of the increasing demands placed on women's time, demands that made "children's goods appealing, even necessary for mothers."[36] Seiter argues that it was the "increasing labor and time intensity" of middle-class mothers' work

FIGURE 1. Bubble Book advertisement: Bubble Books take the phonograph industry right into the heart of the family. Courtesy of Merle Sprinzen, private collection.

that "set the stage for the proliferation of children's consumer goods": "In order for the volume of toy sales to have increased, families had to move to houses with space to keep the toys and children had to have mothers who were so busy that they needed new ways to keep children entertained."[37] Daniel Cook also points to the importance of mothers for the marketing of children's goods and describes the emerging belief among marketers in the 1920s and 1930s that "mothers are like no other class of trade because they will forego their own happiness to provide for their children, a circumstance favorable to selling better grades of merchandise."[38] During this same period, advertisers were fashioning contemporary theories of child guidance into a "cogent merchandising strategy," and advertisements often encouraged middle-class women both to "invest more emotional energy in their role as mothers" and to "recognize that they would be judged more heavily than ever by their successes or failures in this role."[39] Bubble Book ads targeted to retailers sometimes made explicit reference to new regimes of parenting. A 1924 *Talking Machine World* ad noted that parents were making a "study of their children these days": "They have learned from child psychologists that the first six years of life are the most important. Impressions gathered during these—the formative years—are lasting. That's why they want the best of everything for their children."[40] The rhetoric found in this ad corroborates Nicholas Sammond's claim that an increasingly important part of a mother's parental responsibilities at this time came to be the regulation of her child's consumption of brand goods.[41]

In their appeal to mothers, marketers downplayed the Bubble Books' status as a sound recording and described them instead as a unique hybrid of toy and book. Popular press advertisements suggested that children would be captivated by Bubble Books as though by a toy: "When they're tired of balls and tops and blocks and marbles and dolls, here's something new."[42] Bubble Books' quasi-toy status was also encouraged by innovative packaging, with one edition featuring cutout toys to accompany listening: "Make the little people in the Bubble Books dance to the music of their own songs," an ad urged. Children could place cutout figures in the center of their Bubble Book records as they played, so that the "little Bubble Book friends go round and round—just as though they were dancing," the ad copy suggested. "Then you can work out little plays and have the Bubble Book people do the things that the records sing about."[43] We might see these cutouts as an early example of what Schor calls "trans-toying," whereby everyday objects such as toothbrushes are turned into playthings.[44] Here the

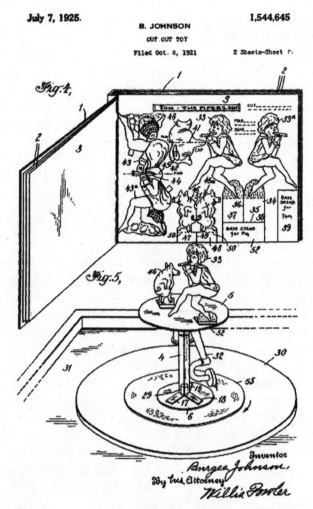

July 7, 1925.

B. JOHNSON

CUT OUT TOY

Filed Oct. 3, 1921

1,544,645

2 Sheets—Sheet 1.

FIGURE 2. The spinning phonograph becomes a toy: Bubble Book cutout figures. Accessed at http://www.google.com/patents.

spinning phonograph record itself becomes a toy, further blurring the line between plaything, record, and book.

Though ads suggested that children would enjoy Bubble Books as they would a toy, parents were also urged to see their booklike qualities. As their name and slogan ("the books that sing") indicated, they were to be regarded as a type of book. Parents were urged, for example, to start a Bubble Book "library." A 1919 ad in *Ladies' Home Journal* stated that "the Bubble Books are not play things for the moment only. They are books of permanent value that will train your children's taste for poetry and rhythm and beauty of color."[45] The Bubble Books' hybrid status was offered to mothers as the vehicle for guilt-free relaxation, since children would be educated by their booklike qualities at the same time that they would be captivated as though by a toy. In a section entitled "Long Hours of Peace and Quiet," ad copy stated that "mother can sit quietly by sewing or reading, for she knows the children will be entertained for hours together, and at the same time they are learning."[46] In an ad entitled "It Keeps Them Happy on Rainy Days," a mother explained that "rainy days used to be the bane of my life. . . . The children used to drive me to distraction asking me for something to do. . . . But now, since I got them some Bubble Books, they just wish for the rainy days because it means real joy for them. They are busy and happy the livelong day . . . and the best part of it is that while they are playing with these magic wonder books they are learning something worth while."[47]

It is safe to assume that the success of the Bubble Books owed much to the powerful appeal of ads such as these, wherein a female voice addressed mothers busy with new kinds of housework and parental expectations. Phonograph records, it was suggested, could benefit mothers and children as a hybrid of book and toy that offered mothers time for relaxation and educated children at the same time. We find here an approach to selling children's records that is similar to Ellen Seiter's discussion of the "Toys That Teach" articles that appeared in *Parents* magazine in the 1920s and 1930s.[48] Seiter argues that this rhetorical strategy was meant in part to balance "conflicting feelings toward consumption and its hedonistic and emulative aspects" and adds that such educational claims were "usually limited to desks, toy typewriters, or chalkboards and to specialized educational toy manufacturers such as Playskool."[49] Bubble Book ads reveal a similar approach being used for media products beginning in the 1910s.

The use of a "toys that teach" strategy for the Bubble Books can be placed in the context of larger record industry initiatives to market their products in American schools. In a 1924 discussion of "the school field," the trade journal the *Voice of Victor* asked, "Do you know that there are over 24,000,000 children in the schools of America? Imagine the effect on Victor prestige if *all* of them were hearing the Victrola daily in their classrooms, learning of its quality and the joy it brings. . . .The importance of reaching [children] in school, while their tastes are being formed, cannot be over-emphasized."[50] Later that year, the *Voice of Victor* cheered the "steady, constant, upwards climb of the line of Victors placed in schools in every state in the Union" and noted that the number of cities whose schools had adopted the Victrola as part of their curriculum was up from 4 in 1911 to 13,000 in 1924.[51] Phonographs were included in school curricula in a variety of ways, the most common of which was as part of music appreciation programs: a topic to which I will return later in the chapter. For now, note that one way in which record companies incorporated their products into school music appreciation activities was by sponsoring music memory contests. These served to "concentrate the attention of children, parents and teachers on a certain number of selections of good music for a given period each year, culminating in a final contest between competitive teams": "These teams hear a given number of the selections from the total number heard during the period of preparation, the team recognizing the greatest number being adjudged the winner." Memory contests were a boon to the industry since they required an ongoing regime of repetitive study, in which records furnished "the repeated hearings necessary for memorizing."[52] Music memory competitions resemble the contests found in children's magazines that sought to promote child readers' engagement with advertisements.[53] Record industry initiatives in the school field were also symptomatic of an era in which marketers were supplying schools with "enrichment materials" such as "commercially sponsored toothbrush drills and Lifebuoy wash-up charts."[54] Though I have found little direct evidence of Bubble Books being used in these kind of school initiatives, the toys that teach marketing rhetoric of the Bubble Book campaign was one component in a larger record company strategy for marketing to children via discourses of education, both at home and in schools.

The "education" that Bubble Books provided consisted of a repackaged oral tradition of children's nursery rhymes and songs. *Printer's Ink* described how the Bubble Book staff engaged in "an elaborate study of nursery songs and stories": "Mr. Mayhew haunts second-hand book shops and sends all over the world for the different versions of famous old nursery rhymes and tunes. Sometimes as many as twenty-five different versions of one song are collected, and as many different versions of the words. From these [the Bubble Book] editorial board painstakingly works out what it believes to be the best authenticated version of both words and music. As it sees its task, it is not the mere manufacturing of ingenious little books; it is training child minds, teaching music, rhythm and English, and nothing is too much trouble to get things right."[55] Short forms of children's entertainment like nursery rhymes were well-suited to the time limitations of early records: with only approximately four minutes of recording time per side, it was difficult to develop longer narrative forms. But nursery rhymes also helped to associate these mass-produced records with oral traditions of parenting. Consider the following ad from a 1920 issue of *St. Nicholas Magazine:*

> When your grandmother was a child, she loved those songs, and she, in turn, rocked your mother's wooden cradle gently to the same quaint, old nursery rhymes. And your mother loved them and sang them, just as you love them. Only you don't have to sing them to your children. They can listen to them to their hearts' content as they are sung by the BUBBLE BOOKS. For the pictures in the BUBBLE BOOKS are new and charming—lovelier than any you could get when you were a little girl . . . the songs themselves . . . are not only the songs your grandmother sang—not only the ones your mother knew and you loved—but *all* the dear, familiar rhymes and melodies that all children have loved from time immemorial and will go on loving to the end of time.[56]

The rhetoric of this ad connects Bubble Books to a timeless matrilineal oral tradition and at the same time attempts to upstage that tradition by arguing for the supremacy of the modern media: records could stockpile and reproduce *all* the dear, familiar rhymes, and with accompanying pictures lovelier than anything available in the past. Further, while the ad portrays the mother as the vehicle of a beloved tradition, it imagines a future in which her role was replaced by the phonograph. Note how a 1918 ad in *Ladies' Home Journal* presents "Tom the piper's son," who asked mothers, "Let me sing to your child . . . I've always wanted to tell those children of yours my story, and to sing them a song—and now at last I can do it."[57]

Also consider a fictional sales scenario found in the *Voice of Victor* trade journal, in which "a little mother drops into the store on her way home from the sewing club to buy a few records for her three small daughters." The mother explains that she is looking for records of songs that would help her little girls in learning to sing, since her own voice "is not good any more, and not at all the sort I should want them to imitate." The salesman replies, "Yes, indeed, we have many beautiful little songs recorded especially for children; and they have been made, too, with just such a situation as yours in mind. Very careful attention has been given to enunciation, voice quality, thought-content, rhythm, melody, and instrumentation." At one point, the salesman asks whether the girls were familiar with "old Mother Goose." "Surely," replies the mother, "she is a much-loved member of our household!" "Then, let me play for you these 'Mother Goose Songs'" returns the salesman. The mother is impressed: "These are wonderful! I know I shall enjoy them quite as much as the children. And what a delight for them to meet their dear little story friends in these songs."[58]

We might identify this sales pitch as what Cook calls the "storybook strategy" in 1920s discourse on marketing to children: the attempt to "associate products with children's characters and imagery" that made commercial appeals "invisible or at least innocuous to parents."[59] But we also find here a vivid dramatization of some of the same themes found in the *St. Nicholas* ad cited above: the substitution of the phonograph for the mother's voice and a tradition of oral nursery rhymes. In his examination of trade press for children's clothing in the first decades of the twentieth century, Cook found that the mother came to stand as "a gatekeeper at the interface between home and market, between the sacred and profane, who must arbitrate between these spheres": "As the middle term between market and child, the mother as consumer in a sense purifies economic exchange by imbuing commodities with sentiment."[60] Bubble Book ads like the one described above were aimed at mothers as the "middle term" in the chain of family consumption but implied that the phonograph could "cut out the middleman" between oral tradition and the child; the middleman being the mother, who was reminded of her parental responsibilities even as her role was threatened. Bubble Book ads took part in a larger tendency of advertising copy of this era to address feelings of regret at the loss of earlier traditions and to offer consumer goods to assuage anxieties about the passage to a culture of mass consumption. Such ads suggested that the modern consumer could simultaneously enjoy both the modern and the traditional via the product, and so, in Roland Marchand's words, civilization could be "redeemed."[61]

Bubble Book ads claiming that traditional characters like Tom the piper's son wanted to speak directly to children may have made their media products more innocuous to parents, but that rhetoric also reveals some of the underlying anxieties that parents were feeling concerning their children's consumption of mass-produced media. It was, of course, the record companies and Harper and Brothers, not Tom the piper's son, that were looking for new ways to speak directly to children. Bubble Book marketers explored several avenues for such a direct link to the child audience, one of which was through the use of radio.

BUBBLE BOOK BROADCASTING

Phonograph retailers were urged to start a Bubble Book Hour both on local radio stations and in their stores. A 1923 *Talking Machine World* ad declared, "Children love to hear their favorite nursery rhymes and games. And the radio 'powers that be' know that the best way to interest parents in their radio is to please children. That's why the songs and stories of the Bubble Books are broadcast from every radio station."[62] In another ad, Harper and Brothers wrote, "More than 1,000 letters are being received every week by us as a result of the broadcasting by radio of the Bubble Books."[63] Retailers were also urged to play the records in their stores at a regularly scheduled time: "Announce the fact that one afternoon a week . . . you will give a recital of the 'books that sing.' Such a weekly event will draw to your store the parents as well as the children. You can see how a Bubble Book Hour will stimulate sales in all other departments of your store."[64] It is hard to know how many retailers engaged in either form of "broadcasting," but the *New York Times* radio programming schedule indicates that station WJZ in Newark, New Jersey, regularly featured "The Bubble Book That Sings" at 6:30 P.M. in 1922. The *Christian Science Monitor* listed "Bubble Book Stories" at 6 P.M. on New York station WJY in 1923.[65]

Another form of Bubble Book broadcasting involved promotional parties held in department stores across the United States. *Printer's Ink* noted that "so remarkably have the Bubble Books fitted into the life of the children of America that Bubble Book parties have now become quite the rage in the tiny tots' social world."[66] I have found evidence of such events taking place in 1921 and 1922 in Wisconsin, Iowa, Indiana, California, and Connecticut. The *Appleton [WI] Post-Crescent* reported in 1921 on a "Tippy Toe Bubble Book" party at the Appleton Theatre that featured games, pantomime, elaborate scenery and costumes, and appearances onstage by Mother Goose, characters from the Bubble Books, and "many little girls from Appleton."[67] Bubble Book parties were well-suited to a contemporary marketing scene in which department stores in major American cities were establishing year-round toy departments that were "not simply selling spaces but fantasy places, juvenile dream worlds."[68] William Leach notes that strategies for enticing children to such spaces included parades and "little fairy-tale playlets for children in makeshift theaters in toy departments or in store auditoriums."[69] Similarly, Miriam Formanek-Brunell describes how doll retailers and manufacturers sponsored doll's tea parties, doll carriage contests, and parades in department stores during the 1910s and 1920s.[70] Bubble Book parties should be added to historical accounts of toy departments as spaces of both marketing and spectacle, but they also stand as precursors to marketing techniques made famous by Walt

Disney. Disney connected his animated creations to the spaces and experiences of shopping: note that Mickey Mouse became a "fixture in department stores across the country" after Disney sold the licensing rights for Mickey merchandise in 1929.[71] Also consider that the Mickey Mouse Club, whose members numbered one million by 1932, took part in "collective rituals" with child peer-groups in addition to cinema-going: children saluted the American flag, joined in community singing, and took part in activities such as "picnics, competitions, prizes and fund-raising."[72] Bubble Book marketing explored similar kinds of collective rituals in department stores across the country.

The comparison with Disney can allow us to return to the question posed at the beginning of this chapter: why is it that some children's media become more controversial than others? Sammond has argued that Disney succeeded where other producers of children's films failed because he was most able to profit from concern about children's cinema-going, exemplified by the Payne Fund Studies of the mid-1930s, that fostered a desire for products thought to be beneficial to the development of the child audience. The Disney company managed to offer itself as the solution to anxieties about "movie-made children" by providing parents with a trusted brand "that did not require assessment of individual products."[73] The record industry followed some of the same marketing strategies as Disney and also succeeded in marketing its media products in ways that did not provoke controversy.

If we consider the various aspects of the Bubble Book marketing campaign described previously, we find that common sources of adult anxiety about children's media were avoided or defused. Children's media consumption has often caused adult concern because of the ways in which it threatened established notions of childhood and child rearing. Children's media products often served as an introduction into a world of commodities, a problematic prospect, since "the sacralization of childhood fostered expectations that children should be shielded from commercial exploitation of any kind."[74] Class hierarchies have frequently been a subtext for struggles over children's entertainments: debates about children's reading of dime novels, for example, became "intertwined with larger class tensions, as Protestant reformers sought to fortify their waning cultural authority."[75] The spaces of media exhibition were often felt to erode distinctions between public and private recreation, either by drawing child audiences to public amusements or by bringing urban, working-class entertainments into middle-class homes.[76] Media entertainment could also cause a troubling blurring of the boundaries between childhood and adulthood. In his study of the child cinema audience in the 1920s, Richard deCordova observes that "many children seemed to prefer the films aimed at their parents to the films made for them": an upsetting development for adult reformers since it "called into question the difference between adult and child desire."[77] The nickelodeon movie theater could also disrupt systems of family control, since children went to the cinema without parents and were outside the purview of adult supervision.[78] Many debates about children and television have hinged on the question of parental authority: Spigel states, "The bulk of discussions about children and television were offered in the context of mastery."[79] Finally, adult concern about children and media has frequently manifested in discourses of child passivity and metaphors of addiction.[80]

By laying out these recurring areas of adult concern about children's media consumption, we can see how ably the Bubble Books managed to circumvent them. The Bubble Books' "authentic" nursery rhymes were clearly age appropriate and represented a traditional form of middle-class children's culture; phonograph records were safely consumed in the home, under the aegis of parental supervision; the small-scale 5½-inch format of the Bubble Books and children's toy phonograph players were distinct from larger adult records and Victrolas; with the phonograph, unlike with radio, parents had control over content brought into the home; and finally, children arguably took an active role in the playing of records on their own phonograph players, as well as in activities associated with the Bubble Books such as play with cutout dolls, records made to accompany dances and games, and local Bubble Book parties. The fact that Bubble Books managed to sidestep many criticisms of children's media allowed them to be marketed across various platforms and without significant controversy. Jacobson claims that early-twentieth-century children's advertisers were able to avoid organized opposition by aligning themselves with the "very institutions of early-twentieth-century childhood that sought to sequester childhood as a wholesome, play-centered stage of life": they secured the cooperation of the public schools; romanced the "companionate family"; and associated their products with "children's developmental needs and mothers' quests for more leisure."[81] The marketing strategies used by the record industry followed a similar pattern with similar results, enabling records such as the Bubble Books to proliferate in middle-class homes and schools, on the radio, and in department stores without major opposition.

Though they certainly did not match Mickey Mouse in terms of cultural impact, the Bubble Books were a significant part of pre–World War

II children's media culture. The phonograph has a unique position in the history of the cultural industries as the first form of prerecorded media entertainment consumed in the home. The market in children's records trailblazed by the Bubble Books exploded in the 1940s and helped to fuel a postwar resurgence in the phonograph industry. An important catalyst in that postwar explosion was Alan Livingston's *Bozo at the Circus* (Capitol 1946). Livingston's Bozo record was a hybrid of book and record on the model of the Bubble Books, albeit with one major innovation: Livingston devised a system to closely synchronize book and record such that, when Bozo blew his whistle on the record, the listener was to turn the page of the book. This simple device was one factor in the surprising success of the first Bozo record, which had made five million dollars by 1955, with eight more Bozo albums following, all bestsellers. Like the Bubble Books, the Bozo series involved a major promotional campaign, including newspaper and magazine advertising as well as window displays and radio performances. If the Bubble Books represented an early example of media industry synergy, Bozo became a full-fledged multimedia franchise along the lines of Mickey Mouse: two million dollars worth of Bozo tie-in merchandise had been sold by 1952, including coloring books, balloons, decals, puppets, blocks, comic books, tablecloths and napkins, paper plates and cups, picture puzzle books, lamps, and dolls.[82] In 1956 a critic in the *New York Times* could look back on the Bozo book-record format and declare that it had given "the whole field a tremendous spurt."[83] Though certainly innovative, the Bozo records were only one factor in a surge of interest in children's records after World War II, when kidisks spoke to a new set of cultural concerns about children's media entertainment.

BRAT-WAX

The Bubble Books' success story just described occurred during a particularly robust period for the phonograph industry. By the end of the 1920s, however, the market had taken a nosedive. The record industry was particularly hard hit by the stock market crash: the Edison Company ceased record production altogether, and RCA Victor issued no catalog in 1931.[84] In the wake of the economic crisis, many American families opted for the free entertainment of the radio networks as opposed to phonograph records. As one 1955 article put it: "Most phonographs went to the attic when radio came in. The depression finished off many record companies, and the survivors quit trying to sell children's records."[85] By the early 1940s, the record industry had managed a recovery via several strategies: increasing degrees of conglomeration with the radio and film industry; promoting cheap records (techniques associated with Jack Kapp at Decca Records); and capitalizing on the rise of the jukebox market and the success of swing records.[86] The record market had substantially returned to form by the early 1940s: in January 1942 a *New York Times* article stated that the industry was "bigger and better than ever," noting that 1941 had seen the most sales yet, with about 110 million records sold, 10 million more than the previous high–water mark of 1921. The article went on to describe a general increase in phonograph culture: "Where collectors of records were numbered in the thousands a few years ago, they are now in the hundreds of thousands. Where records had a special vogue as Christmas gifts, they are now purchased steadily throughout the year. Record clubs have taken root, and books and magazines devoted to the field appear in increasing numbers." The *Times* noted that it was not just music records that were spurring sales, but also records devoted to poetry, drama, and dance and language lessons and, notably, children's records.[87]

The year 1946 was an annus mirabilis of the children's record industry. That year *Variety* declared in a front-page headline that the production of "kiddie disks" had become "big business."[88] "Outside of a few pioneers," the article stated, "few diskeries had ever capitalized on the moppet market until last year, when some 9 million kiddie platters were sold during December alone. Close to 20 million were sold during all of 1945." In light of this, the major record companies were planning to allocate between 17 and 25 percent of their total output to the children's market, and an estimated 30 percent of all records sold during the Christmas rush would be "for the moppets."[89] That same year, the *Los Angeles Times* described the "rapidly growing children's department" at Victor Records: "Five years ago, [the department] couldn't find space in a closet for such platters. All other major companies have had an equal expansion of their kids' corner, and independent outfits are popping up every day." The article went on to state that although less than 2 million children's records were sold in 1941, more than 27 million were to be pressed in 1946, and even that number wouldn't be enough to meet the demand.[90] Sales of children's records continued to skyrocket during the mid-1940s, up to 50 million in 1947, at which point children's records accounted for approximately 15 percent of the entire record business. By 1948 there were "more than 600 different titles on the market, six times as many as in 1944."[91] The "kidisk Klondike" continued over the next fifteen years. In 1951 *Variety* wrote that the children's market had hit a new high, racking up an estimated 15 million dollars in sales, enough to put kidisks "neck and neck" with the sale of classical music recordings.[92] *Harper's Magazine* stated in 1951 that kidisks, previously considered to be "a stepchild of the record industry," now accounted for "50 per cent of the total sales of records at Gimbel's at Christmas time and around 25 per cent during the rest of the year."[93] Sales remained strong through the 1950s, and by 1960, *Variety* estimated the kidisk market was worth $50 million.[94] As a point of comparison with the film industry, United Artists had total revenues of $19.6 million in 1951 (kidisks: $15 million), and Universal Studios had total revenues of $58.4 million in 1960 (kidisks: $50 million).[95]

There are many ways to explain the massive growth in the children's record market in the late 1940s. Besides the general revival of record sales, children were increasingly able to get hold of records in venues besides record stores and listen to them in places other than the home. *Variety* claimed that an important factor fueling the kidisk Klondike was the fact that chain stores were beginning to stock a wider range of kids' records.[96] *Billboard* wrote that "peewee platters" had given the record industry an entrance into the larger department stores, noting that "department stores, as a whole, have welcomed kidisks, with some of them going into big merchandizing campaigns."[97] Children were also getting the record habit from public libraries. The Washington Public Library added a music collection of symphonic recordings to its collection in January 1940, and the following year the New York public libraries extended their services to lending phonograph records.[98] Libraries such as these would eventually carry a range of children's records. By 1960 the *Library Journal* would have a special edition on the use of phonograph records in libraries.

Children were also listening to records in schools. As we have seen, record companies had been developing strategies for reaching the school market since the 1910s. Popular press coverage indicates that the industry continued to pursue that project in the postwar era. Consider that, in 1945, the *Los Angeles Times* reported that the children's divisions of record companies were being bombarded with requests from educators for records on music history and dramatizations of American history.[99] *Variety* noted in 1946 that educators were becoming "more interested in the moppet field because they feel that entertainment is the ideal medium for teaching, since pupils' minds are relaxed and open."[100] By

1954 the New York Board of Education had even started a program to bring the sound equipment in the New York City public schools up to "high-fidelity standards," arguing that the phonograph had become as much of a "basic teaching tool" as the blackboard and textbook. The article went on to state that most instruction in "history, literature, foreign languages, social studies, health and physical education, typing and shorthand" was supplemented by "specially devised disk and tape recordings. Even 'behavior' problems are sometimes handled by means of carefully selected records."[101]

The market for educational records was part of a larger postwar obsession with education. Parents increasingly saw children's leisure time as a crucial aspect of preparation for the job market: Sammond writes that, as children were removed from labor markets, their leisure time increasingly became taken up with "productive activity": "In an increasingly rationalized and competitive labor market, the productivity of one's childhood consumption is imagined as providing the potential edge necessary to marginally differentiate one's self over one's competitors."[102] Or, in the words of a record label executive quoted by the *Wall Street Journal* in 1962: "Parents realize how tough it is going to be for their kids to get into college . . . they want to give their children a head start. This gives them an impetus to buy educational records as they never have before."[103]

Libraries and schools helped make phonograph records a ubiquitous part of many postwar American children's lives. Children's records were primarily consumed in the home, however, where they appealed to many postwar parents because they seemed to provide an alternative to television. Aniko Bodroghkozy has argued that television was discursively linked to children from its inception: "Television, a postwar technological phenomenon, and the baby boom, a postwar demographic phenomenon, both led to profound political, social, and cultural changes in the landscape of American life. Arriving in U.S. homes at about the same time in the late 1940s and 1950s, these electronic and anthropoid new members of the family circle seemed allied in fomenting social revolution."[104] Indeed, many critics feared that the new medium had usurped parental control and authority, becoming a "threatening force" that circulated "forbidden secrets to children" in ways that parents could not fully control.[105] Critics writing about children's records during the 1950s and 1960s often expressed concern about television's influence on children. Consider, for example, how records were often praised for their lack of advertising. A *New York Times* critic wrote in 1956 that there was growing demand from parents for "educational records without the sponsor's jingles."[106] What is more, records were thought to provide children and parents with more agency in their media consumption than television. Whereas watching television was often thought to make children into passive, media-addicted "telebugeyes," the phonograph was seen by some critics as a more interactive form of children's media entertainment. Consider a *New York Times* article from 1955 that told parents who were concerned about their children's excessive television viewing to counterbalance such entertainment by "providing a new stock of well-selected records." Foremost among the "pleasurable stimulation of good recordings" mentioned by the article was the way in which the child enjoyed "personally choosing a record from his own collection; he holds it in his hand; he sets it in motion, playing his favorites over and over at will. The freedom of choice and action affords pleasure and satisfaction."[107]

As the previous quote suggests, critics prized record consumption for the ways in which it allowed the child to physically engage with the low-priced record players that the industry had recently made available to children. *Variety* reported that virtually every manufacturer had phonograph players that retailed for under $20.[108] In 1958 the *New York Times* suggested that "the child is able to manipulate a simple record player (one speed) at about two years of age, and a three speed at about age 3 . . . a child can have his own good machine at 4 or 5."[109] One writer argued that such basic phonograph players allowed children to "master the simple technique of starting the player and putting a record on" even before they had acquired the ability to read.[110] The presumed benefits of such hands-on record consumption were detailed in a *New York Times* article from 1957:

> From an early enough age when a child has the manipulation skill to put on his own records, it is wise to have him enjoy and experiment with his own record player. It does not need tweeters and woofers; every last glockenspiel note is unimportant. It should be a good machine so that he can manhandle it without breaking the family budget on repairs but not so good that it is going to cause constant cautioning remarks about taking care . . . the musical accomplishments belong to him because he has gone through the satisfying physical act of putting on his player and hearing music come out with the same cocked headful of surprise as Victor's dog listening to His Master's Voice. The records will be scratched and the tone arm will have the wires out half the time, but this is child's work. Any adult can place the arm gently or put on a record without gouging it, but it takes a child to disconnect the arm

and run the needle over the ridges with skill. And still the child listens and gains affection for his battered records and record player.[111]

The child's operation of the record player is again characterized as a "satisfying physical act" in and of itself, a form of "child's work" that is implicitly opposed to passive television viewing.

We should note the slippage in this article from a generic child to an explicitly male one, which is not surprising given how closely the vision of the child record consumer presented here resembles the predominantly male hi-fi hobbyist, with his hand-made stereo console, cherished for the functionality of its design (see chapter 3). For example, a 1954 article in *High Fidelity* entitled "Raise Your Own Audiophiles," features a photo of "Tom Jr." and "Tom Sr." having a tinkering session on a 45-rpm record player.[112] Like the toy trains, chemistry sets, and cameras described by historian of children's culture Gary Cross, the phonograph was a child's consumer product that was used to teach boys to "admire the technologies of the future" and "imagine themselves in control of modern power."[113] The author of the 1957 *Times* piece cited previously even concluded by arguing that a child's record listening would encourage individual expression and nonconformity: "Milk, not children, can be homogenized."[114] The child's record player was thus thought to provide valuable lessons in an active male practice that was a beneficial alternative to television, an inoculation against postwar conformity, and a safe entry point into children's consumer culture.

What becomes clear is that the success of children's records in the late 1940s and 1950s was overdetermined: fueled by the general resurgence of the record industry; the baby boom; new avenues of record reception; and the rhetorical importance of records in debates about mass culture. The content of the records themselves was shaped by postwar discourses of child rearing, and an examination of some best-selling and critically acclaimed kidisks can tell us about the role that recorded entertainment was meant to play in the lives of postwar children. A 1951 *House Beautiful* article entitled "Robby's First Records" was one of many advice columns for parents that recommended those children's records that combined narrative with lessons in the appreciation of orchestral music. As an outstanding example of such a record, the article suggested *Rusty in Orchestraville* (Capitol 1946), written by Bozo-creator Alan Livingston. That record, along with another Livingston creation entitled *Sparky's Magic Piano* (Capitol 1948), reveal the influence of one more factor in the postwar rise of children's records: the music appreciation movement.

INSTRUMENTS THAT TALK

The *New York Times* estimated that in 1954, pupils in New York schools spent at least two hours a week listening to recordings in music appreciation classes.[115] In fact, the music appreciation movement was an important factor in the rise of the children's record market and shaped the form of some of the best-selling children's records of the immediate postwar era. The origins of music appreciation can be found in the early decades of the 1900s, the time of what Mark Katz describes as a "revolution in American music education": "In the nineteenth century the primary goal was to teach students how to *make* music, particularly through singing. In the twentieth century, however, the focus began shifting from the practical to the aesthetic. The ideal became known as appreciation—generally understood as the intelligent enjoyment of music, typically classical music, as a *listener.*" "The goal of appreciation," Katz continues, was to develop in students an understanding of music "beyond their own ability to perform," and the phonograph was valued for its ability to demonstrate the "good music" that even music teachers could not perform. Record companies such as Victor and Columbia even printed the first American music appreciation textbooks in the 1910s and 1920s.[116]

The Victor Company trade journal, the *Voice of the Victor,* featured numerous articles on the importance of the school audience throughout the 1920s and described the company's national program of music appreciation, spearheaded by Mrs. Frances E. Clark, who gave the address "Music Appreciation of the Future" at the National Supervisors' Conference in Cincinnati in 1924, which was attended by over twelve hundred supervisors of public school music from across the United States. Mrs. Clark stated, "We devote no end of time and money, public and private, to training people to be unintelligent performers, when what we *ought* to do is train them to be intelligent listeners."[117]

The music appreciation movement continued to play an important role in American cultural life through the 1930s, influencing a range of media practices.[118] Between the years 1928 and 1942, the NBC radio network broadcast the *NBC Music Appreciation Hour,* which featured Walter Damrosch, the conductor of the New York Symphony Orchestra and a "musical counsel" to NBC. Frank Biocca describes Damrosch's program as part of an "ambitious national project involving the coordination of numerous school systems in every part of the country, every major phonograph company in the nation, and the production of a music text."[119] For Biocca, Damrosch's broadcasts demonstrated the larger hopes held by "music elites" that radio would transform the tastes of the American public. This initial excitement about the educational potential of radio was inspired in part by the conviction that, given adequate airtime, the inherent superiority of classical music would stem the growing popularity of vernacular forms of music such as jazz.[120] William J. Bogan, the superintendent of Chicago schools, expressed this sentiment at a 1930 music educators conference on the pros and cons of radio, at which he stated his belief that "if people could be educated to enjoy music they would turn from jazz immediately."[121]

It eventually became clear, however, that American network radio would not function to educate the masses in the way in which the music elites had hoped.[122] As radio broadcasting turned increasingly to sponsored entertainment and later to recordings of popular music, children's records provided an alternative medium for the lessons of music appreciation: *Harper's Magazine* wrote that many postwar parents who were buying children's records were "thinking in terms of musical education."[123] Some of the best-selling postwar children's records reflect the influence of the music appreciation movement. The liner notes to Capitol Records' *Rusty in Orchestraville* proclaim the record to be "the most refreshing and painless course in music appreciation ever offered to youngsters who are studying, or will someday study music," adding that it "fills the need for a sugar-coated musical appreciation course for juveniles." These notes were addressed to parents, who are called "the legion of perplexed and fretting moms and dads who entertain high hopes for their children's mastery of music." The narrative heard on the record develops the theme of "fretting parents" concerned about their child's "mastery" of music.

The record begins with the following narration: "Once there was a little fellow named Rusty, just about your age. His mother wanted him to be a musician, and once a week she would take him to Miss Spear the piano teacher to study. Everyday at home Rusty would have to sit at the piano and practice the scales." "Scales," we hear Rusty complain, "they're no fun! If I could play a real piece maybe, but just plain old scales. I don't think I like this old piano anyway. Mom isn't home so I'll just sit in this big old chair, she'll think I've been practicing all the time." Rusty falls asleep and wakes up in Orchestraville, where he meets the Conductor, who claims to rule over all the instruments. The Conductor introduces Rusty to various talking instruments in the orchestra, and Rusty gets to play each one. The Conductor explains that in

Orchestraville, "any little boy can play any instrument he wants" without any practice. "Gee, that was fun!" Rusty exclaims after playing Vera the Violin. These encounters with the instruments motivate exposing the listener to some of the classical repertoire.

Next the Conductor tells Rusty that the composer Joseph Haydn had "practiced his music lessons very diligently" when he was a little boy and so grew up to become a "great musician." The Conductor explains that Haydn's *Surprise Symphony* was written with a sudden crescendo to rouse those in the audience who might have fallen asleep. The orchestra plays the piece, and when the surprise occurs, Rusty laughs. "Shhh! Quiet Rusty!" the Conductor quickly scolds. After the performance, Rusty finally gets a chance to play Peter the Piano, who had been avoiding him because of the "unpleasant things" Rusty had said about practicing his piano. As Rusty becomes lost in pleasure playing Chopin's *Minute Waltz,* he awakes from his dream. His mother tells him to "get right back to practicing," to which Rusty eagerly responds: "Oh yes, Mother. I'll practice hard. I'm going to be a great musician." The record ends with Rusty dutifully practicing his scales. It is hard to miss the lessons of music appreciation beneath the sugar coating of the narrative and sound effects: the sampling of the classical repertoire; demonstrations of the instruments in the orchestra; information about the lives of the "great composers"; and even concert-going etiquette when the Conductor harshly silences Rusty for giggling during the *Surprise Symphony.*

Similar lessons can be found on another record made by Capitol entitled *Sparky's Magic Piano.* A narrator tells us that Sparky was "a little boy just about your age" who had been taking piano lessons for a year. One day, his piano teacher (again named Miss Spear) arrives at his house for his lesson. She starts a metronome as Sparky plays his piece, which serves to underscore his hesitant and uncertain performance. When he makes a mistake, Miss Spear cries out, "No, no, Sparky!" He finishes and asks, "Was that all right Miss Spear?" "Well, not too bad for the first week, but you need more practice, much more practice." "More practice," Sparky complains, "I've been practicing every day for a whole year. I can't even learn a piece in a week. When will I be able to play real good? How long does it take? Sometimes I don't know if it's worth it. I don't get to play outside as much as other kids." Before leaving, Miss Spear wonders aloud, "I wish there was some way I could show you how wonderful it is to play well. If only I could some way let you see what it's like." Miss Spear demonstrates the importance of records to the music appreciation movement when she decides to play a recording of the Chopin Waltz in E Minor for Sparky: "Someday you'll be able to play like that, if you keep at it. Listen to the whole thing Sparky. Maybe you'll appreciate the piano more."

As he drifts off to sleep, Sparky wonders what it would be like to play as well as the recording. Like Rusty, Sparky finds himself in a dream world in which musical instruments talk and he can play the Western classical repertoire without practicing. He is startled when his piano says to him, "I'm going to show you what it's like to play the piano well. Sit down on my stool, put your fingers on my keys, run your hand over my keys." "Why, I'm playing just like my teacher," Sparky exclaims. As was the case with Rusty, the record tries to convey the visceral pleasure of this experience: Sparky laughs and says, "This is fun!" Unlike on the Rusty record, Sparky's mother appears in the dream, rushing into the room when she hears him playing the piano so well. "Sparky, I can't believe it!" she gushes, and quickly calls Miss Spear to come over. To demonstrate his newfound piano prowess, Sparky plays *Flight of the Bumblebee* at top speed—a studio effect achieved by speeding up the tape. "Sparky," Miss Spear announces matter-of-factly, "you're the greatest pianist in the world."

After this impressive debut, Sparky's mother immediately puts him on a nationwide concert tour. At his first concert, Sparky confesses that he is scared by all the people but goes on with a successful performance. What follows is a kind of audio montage where we hear a selection of classical pieces performed at different prestigious concert halls across the country: at Symphony Hall in Boston, Sparky plays Liszt's Hungarian Rhapsody no. 2; at the National Mall in Washington, he plays Chopin's Waltz in C-sharp Minor; at the Civic Opera House in Chicago, he plays Beethoven's *Moonlight Sonata*; and finally at New York's Carnegie Hall, Sparky plays the Prelude in C-sharp Minor by Rachmaninoff. After his New York appearance, Sparky finishes to great applause and walks off stage. His mother hisses: "Sparky, why did you walk off the stage? Go back and play an encore. They want to hear another piece." "All right," he says in a resigned tone of voice, "one more piece." Sparky tells the crowd that he will play "the *Spinning Song* by Mendelssohn" but is shocked when the piano announces, "Oh, no, you won't!" "What do you mean, I won't?" Sparky asks in a whisper. "Your time is up," the piano mockingly replies, "I will no longer play for you!" Sparky begins to panic in front of the packed house: "Oh please, don't stop now. Just one more piece." From the wings, his mother calls out: "Sparky, play!

Everyone is watching!" Next we hear the murmuring of the audience: "Why doesn't he play? What's the matter with him? He seems to be talking to himself." "Piano, you must play for me, you must," Sparky begs as he pounds on the keys, "Play piano, play for me; it won't play!" Sparky awakes from the dream to find himself with his mother. "I dreamed I could play the piano better than my teacher, better than anybody," he tells his mother. "Don't worry Sparky," she replies, "you'll be able to play the piano well someday, if you keep up your practicing." "I will," he says, "I'll practice my piece right now, and I won't give up until I can play as good as I did in my dream. Well, anyway, as good as my teacher." The record ends as we hear Sparky practicing his piece.

Both the Rusty and Sparky records use the motif of a dream world of talking instruments to show children the pleasures of music making within a tradition of Western classical music. The fact that the description of such pleasures is transposed into the realm of fantasy reveals the need to mystify the necessary drudgery that is required to produce performers in that tradition. In Christopher Small's bleak assessment, such musical training works to "take children away from day-to-day contact with the infinite variability of the human race and place them in an educational monoculture where their only contact is with contemporaries of similar background and interests" and so deprives them of "an essential dimension of the experience of growing up."[124] Both the Rusty and Sparky records hint at the price of success on these terms: the boys cannot play outside; they move though a world populated only by adults; and they must endure hours of dreary practice only to someday face a nonstop succession of stressful concert performances. The ideal of concert performance takes on an absurd and vaguely sinister light on the Sparky record: note the ease with which Sparky's mother pushes him into a life of public performance and her insensitivity to the stresses of that life; the incongruous image of a small boy mastering the dense, sensual Romantic musical repertoire; the rather forced moments when Sparky testifies to the pleasures of musical performance; and Sparky's painful public humiliation in front of a callous audience. In fact, the record provides a vivid picture of concert hall performance as—to quote pianist Glenn Gould, himself a child prodigy who would have known more about Sparky's plight than most—the "last blood sport."[125]

The element of absurdity in these successful records did not go entirely unnoticed. In fact, their narrative structure, tone, and message were satirized by a man whom Henry Jenkins has called the poet laureate of postwar permissive child rearing: Dr. Seuss (Theodor Geisel).

Seuss's only live-action Hollywood film project, *The 5000 Fingers of Dr. T* (1953), is the story of Bartholomew Collins (Tommy Rettig), a young boy who, like Rusty and Sparky, finds himself forced to practice the piano by his mother, a fate that he escapes by entering a dream. Though he uses the same narrative tropes as the Capitol music appreciation records, Seuss systematically subverts their message: where Rusty meets a kindly Conductor, Bart encounters Dr. Terwilliker (Hans Conried), a cruel megalomaniac; instead of meeting a happy community of orchestra instruments, Bart finds them locked in Dr. T's dungeon; instead of a dream world where musical performance is effortless and pleasurable, Bart is trapped in a nightmarish musical internment camp; and crucially, instead of waking from the dream with a renewed determination to practice until he is a "great musician," Bart wakes up and runs out of the house to play baseball with his dog.

It is not surprising that Seuss would reject the message of Capitol's music appreciation records. Henry Jenkins argues that Seuss was an important figure in a postwar shift in attitude toward permissive child rearing that saw "the explicit display of parental authority as thwarting their offsprings' independence and free will."[126] Jenkins describes the differences between prewar and postwar models of child rearing as follows:

> The prewar paradigm saw the relations between parents and children primarily in terms of discipline and authority; the postwar model saw parent-child relations increasingly in terms of pleasure and play. The prewar paradigm, grounded in behaviorism, stressed the importance of forming habits of behaviour necessary for productive life; the postwar paradigm, grounded in Freudianism and most often labelled "permissiveness," sought to limit inhibitions upon basic impulses and desires . . . the prewar model prepared children for the workplace within a society of scarcity, the postwar model prepared them to become pleasure-seeking consumers within a prosperous new economy.[127]

Capitol's music appreciation records and Seuss's film emerge as sites in which such changes in parenting were contested. We might see this struggle in terms of Raymond Williams's idea of residual and emergent forms of culture.[128] That is, Rusty and Sparky represent a residual prewar paradigm, with their stress on the formation of productive behavior, that is, piano practice. That rhetoric made the Capitol discs an easy target for Seuss's satire, with Seuss representing an emergent, "permissive" paradigm.

The Capitol records, however, offered somewhat contradictory messages about the child's ideal role in consumer culture. Note that the

Rusty and Sparky records trained children to be consumers of records as much as performers of music. In fact, one of the ironies of these records is that the great majority of Rustys and Sparkys would never experience the pleasure of concert performance, no matter how much they practiced. Small reminds us that few children would ever become performers of classical music: the majority of students were instead to be "told *about* music rather than being involved in its creation."[129] This majority, who were "considered not to have the ability to take an active part in a musical performance," would be trained instead as musical consumers: "They are fated to be no more than consumers of the music that is produced for them by professionals. They pay for the commodity, music, but they have no more say in what is produced than do consumers of any other commodity; they have only the choice of either buying or not buying."[130] As one example of this approach to education, consider Robert L. Garretson's 1966 music education manual, *Music in Childhood Education,* which stated that the great majority of students would "ultimately join the vast army of consumers of music," who were of great importance, since "it is upon this segment of the American people that the future growth of music in America depends." The book even contains instructions for teaching children to listen to records: "The teacher should assume a position generally somewhere near the record player," Garretson advises, "and assume an attitude of thoughtful attention."[131] The children who listened to Rusty's and Sparky's adventures were learning to appreciate the products of the modern record industry, an important aspect of which was to enjoy the novel sounds made possible by new techniques of studio production.

That is, though the stated purpose of these records was to instill the desire to play the piano, the attention and imagination of child listeners was captured through the use of studio effects. Before examining the use of sound technology on the Capitol kidisks, note how the piano is opposed to studio effects in the climactic scenes of *The 5000 Fingers of Dr. T.* Dr. T's army of reluctant piano students arrive to play his musical composition on a giant, surreal piano, but Bart sabotages the event through the use of a strange concoction called the MusicFix, which takes music out of the air. Bart removes the sound of the piano during the concert, and in its place we hear sound effects created through the manipulation of magnetic tape: Dr. T's words are looped and sped up. On the soundtrack, then, the generational battle is played out between technologies of music making: the piano versus the tape recorder. The exploitation of new magnetic tape sound technology can also be heard on many postwar children's records.[132]

GENIE THE MAGIC RECORD

The Capitol children's records sought to teach children about orchestral music, but they did so through the use of cutting-edge studio techniques. Alan Livingston may have been selling music appreciation, but his interest in records had to do with the creation of novel sounds. Livingston recounted how his own childhood record consumption had been focused around the enjoyment of "peculiar noises": "When [Livingston] grew old enough to monkey with the phonograph, he spun records slow or fast with his finger, to hear how strange they sounded. A little later he ruined many of the family's records by boring off-center spindle holes in them. Played this way, they produced unearthly noises."[133] Indeed, it was the recognition that "a kid record should have queer, humorous sounds" that shaped the creation of the first Bozo record, which used studio technology to alter the voices of circus animals: a lion's voice is drenched in reverberation to suggest his vast size; the hippo's is lowered by slowing the playback of magnetic tape; and the hyena's is similarly sped up. After successfully making animals talk on the Bozo records, Livingston decided to make musical instruments talk on the Rusty and Sparky records, an effect he achieved by acquiring the license to use a device called the Sonovox. The Sonovox worked by playing a recording through two specially designed hand-held speakers that were placed on each side of the throat. Whatever sounds were on the recording were transmitted to the larynx, so that the sound came out of the throat as if it was produced there and could then be shaped into speech by silently mouthing the desired words. Sounds could thus be made to speak, or as a 1939 *Time* magazine article put it: "A grunting pig, relayed through the human voice-box, can be made to observe: 'It's a wise pig who knows his own fodder.'"[134] Sparky's talking piano and the instruments Rusty meets in Orchestraville were created using this device, which provided an arresting means of personifying orchestral instruments in a manner similar to other popular postwar children's records such as *Peter and the Wolf* or *Tubby the Tuba*.

Of course, Livingston's work at Capitol was only one part of the kidisk industry, and another striking example of studio effects can be heard on a record made by the actor who played the plumber Zabladowski in

The 5000 Fingers of Dr. T: Peter Lind Hayes. Though Zabladowski was Hayes's only significant film role, he enjoyed a career as a television and nightclub performer in the 1950s, frequently with his wife Mary Healy, who plays Bart's mother, Heloise, in Dr. Seuss's film. Hayes also created one of the most popular postwar children's records, one that made the phonograph disc, not musical instruments, talk. *Genie the Magic Record* (Decca 1949) begins with a laugh by Hayes, who identifies himself as the eponymous Genie. Hayes speaks as the phonograph record and announces that he can do anything: "Alaka-zoot I'm a whistle; alaka-zing I'm a telephone," after which we hear those respective sound effects. Genie goes on to become barnyard animals, a glass of milk, and a circus, at which point we meet the "smallest man in the world," whose voice is sped up, and the "tallest man in the world," whose voice is drenched in reverb. "I bet I can sing 'Farmer in the Dell' faster than you can," Genie announces, and we hear a loop of Hayes's voice that gradually speeds up. There are even moments of overt reflexivity, as when the record says on the start of side two, "Ouch! Whoops, be careful with that needle, it scratches. I'm sure glad you turned me over; that fuzz on the phonograph tickles." Though the record ends with Genie turning into a violin, oboe, and piccolo, musical instruments are not given priority over the myriad other sounds that came before, and so the listener's attention is directed less toward learning the components of the orchestra than toward the phonograph's infinite capacity to represent sound. On another children's record Haynes made with Decca, *The Little Tune That Ran Away* (1949), not only do the instruments share the sonic stage with other sounds, the orchestra even becomes the vaguely sinister antagonist of the narrative: the eponymous "little tune" runs away from the orchestra because it plays him so badly. What follows is a desperate chase, in which the tune is played by a car horn, a police whistle, cats, dogs, farm animals, and a train whistle. The record thus feels like a parable wherein sound is liberated by the phonograph from the confines of orchestra instruments into a broader sonic world. Through the use of such studio techniques, Hayes's records, like Livingston's Bozo discs, directs the listener's attention to "peculiar sounds" and to the record as a medium.

Part of the appeal of such spectacular sound effects was their efficacy in encouraging children to listen to phonograph records multiple times. In 1951, *House Beautiful* described records as "a unique form of entertainment" in that they were "based on repetition": "A television show generally is seen once—the same with radio and movies. But a child will listen to a phonograph record he likes a hundred times, and still not be satisfied. What a tremendous impression such records must make on a child's young mind! He hasn't just seen or heard a story or piece of music—he has memorized it." The author continued by stating that the child's "demand for repetition" made "suspense and dramatic story plot . . . the least of our considerations." "Bozo at the Circus," the author noted, had "practically no plot at all": "Yet I know of children who have worn out as many as nine albums, and still wanted the same album instead of another. The reason for this is that certain ideas properly depicted on a phonograph record will create in a child's mind imaginative situations which are so pleasing to him that he wants to relive these situations many times over. Certain sounds, both vocal and musical, will be so appealing or humorous to a child that he will almost never tire of hearing them."[135]

The connection between studio effects and repetition has been closely associated with genres of recorded popular music, particularly rock and roll. Theodore Gracyk argues that rock production exploited the limited human perception and memory of timbre, creating complex, studio-based sounds that encouraged audiences to listen to structurally simple works again and again: "As with memories of pitch and color, memories of timbres 'fade' after a moment, becoming more imprecise with the passage of time," Gracyk writes, and "when timbre is the basis for expressive qualities of a work—and it seems to be very important for recorded rock—it will have an expressive impact in direct experience that will be absent in our memories of it. Hence listening to it will be important in a way that remembering it is not."[136] Gracyk, like other rock critics, sees the 1950s as a watershed in studio technique: recordings being made by independent companies such as Sun Studios in Memphis or Chess Studios in Chicago signaled the birth of a form of studio-based musical creation that would reach its cultural apotheosis in the mid-1960s multitrack recordings of the Beatles and the Beach Boys: both of whom were on the roster at Capitol Records. As we have seen, this kind of sonic experimentation for a postwar audience had begun a decade before Elvis with the children's records of the 1940s.[137]

Livingston's Rusty and Sparky records thus can be seen as a complex compromise: they are an introduction to the repertoire and performance practice of classical music, but children's attention was held through the use of studio-produced novelty sounds more akin to recorded popular music. Postwar child record listeners, you might say, were being trained to appreciate *Dark Side of the Moon* as much as the *Surprise Symphony* and to associate the phonograph more with the creation of fantastic sonic worlds than the faithful reproduction of concert hall performance.[138] What is certain is that the market for children's records that was established by the Bubble Books became a central part of children's media consumption in the decades after World War II. Postwar children's records emerge as an important site of contestation concerning shifting ideas about child rearing and the place of children's media consumption. Like the Bubble Books of the 1920s, postwar kidisks were taken into American homes under a banner of education and with the help of marketing techniques that avoided significant opposition from parents. The postwar kidisk boom also forged ties between a generation of Americans and the record industry. Indeed, the press often framed the discussion of "brat wax" in terms of the industry's attempts to secure a future market: "Aside from big royalties," *Variety* wrote, record companies felt that through kidisks, they could "build future fans and build a record conscious group of youngsters."[139] Similarly, *Harper's Magazine* wrote, "The record manufacturers are at least as interested in making future customers for their wares as they are in just selling to children."[140] The baby boom children who wore out their Bozo records would continue to have a particularly close relationship with the phonograph over the next three decades.

CHAPTER 2

Hi-Fi Midcult

In 1952 two young women, recent graduates of Hunter College, went to the Kaufmann Auditorium in New York to hear the poet Dylan Thomas give a reading of his work. After the performance, Barbara Holdridge and Marianne Mantell tried to see Thomas but could not get past a crowd of admirers. Determined not to give up, they sent an usher backstage with a note for the poet, in which they stated that they had a business proposition for him, being careful to sign only their first initials to conceal their gender.[1] After a time, the usher made his way back through the crowd with instructions for the women to call Thomas at his hotel. Holdridge and Mantell phoned the poet for several days with no reply; in the words of one account, "Thomas led a classically Bohemian life, in which waiting at the phone for business calls did not play a large part."[2] Eventually, Holdridge and Mantell managed to get in touch with the poet, schedule a meeting, and make their business proposition: they would record sixty minutes of Thomas reciting poetry to be released by their fledgling company, Caedmon Records, in exchange for a five hundred dollar advance against the first thousand records and a 10 percent royalty thereafter. Thomas agreed, and the first recording session took place on February 22, 1952, where Thomas read several of his poems and the story "A Child's Christmas in Wales," which had been published in *Harper's Bazaar* in 1950.[3] Four years later, *Billboard* wrote that those "esoteric disks" had sold 35,000 copies and so achieved "hit" status.[4] The *Atlantic Monthly* reported in 1954 that a clerk in one of New York's largest record stores had exclaimed, "Dylan Thomas? We can't get enough of him. Why, he moves damn near as fast as Toscanini."[5] By 1960 the records Thomas made for Caedmon had sold 400,000 copies in the U.S. and abroad.[6] Indeed, the copyrights of the Caedmon records came to be the most lucrative of all Thomas's estate and began Holdridge and Mantell on an influential and lucrative career in the record business.[7]

The origin story of Caedmon Records that I've sketched here has been told and retold in press coverage of Holdridge and Mantell's company, biographies of Thomas, and record industry trade journals. The story clearly provides a certain fascination, with a cast of characters and narrative twists worthy of a film screenplay: the stunning voice of a self-destructive Byronic poet is captured in his twilight years, saved from obscurity in the nick of time by a fortuitous meeting with two young female entrepreneurs who, in a male-dominated industry, were forging an innovative company by mass-producing high culture. In fact, the narrative of Thomas's meeting with the Caedmon founders can serve as a nexus for the central concerns of this chapter: the role of women in the postwar phonograph industry; debates about high culture media products made for a popular audience; and the upsurge of interest in spoken word entertainment during the 1950s. Carefully unpacking the key elements in Caedmon's success story will illuminate some important ways in which the record industry took part in postwar American cultural life.

For example, Caedmon provides a rich case study of the role of women in the postwar cultural industries. Popular press coverage of Holdridge and Mantell illustrates prominent tendencies in the postwar discourse surrounding women who worked outside of the home. Joanne Meyerowitz is among feminist historians who have questioned the common perception of the postwar era as a time only of domestic drudgery for women. In her analysis of the coverage of women in popular magazines, she found articles that offered a certain validation of nondomestic activity for women and even "subverted the notion that women belonged at home."[8] A similarly complex and ambiguous message about nondomestic female labor can be found in press articles about Holdridge and Mantell, who represented a rare instance of women in executive positions in the postwar record industry.

Women's magazines described the careers of Caedmon's female founders but also recommended spoken word recordings of poetry and literature as a means of self-improvement for housewives. The content of spoken word LPs, like that of radio and television broadcasting, was shaped by the rhythms of female domestic labor and suburban social life. Women were encouraged to make "educational" records part of their domestic routine and even the focus of social gatherings. Indeed, the educational value of such records was thought to help remedy the fact that men had far greater access to a college education than did their wives in the years after World War II. The education provided by Holdridge and Mantell's records involved the popularization and commodification of high culture poetry and drama, and so Caedmon should be placed in the context of debates about American "middle-brow" culture. Caedmon's success came at a time when debates about the middlebrow helped to encourage the emergence of niche, or narrow-cast, media products, with the company's records marketed to the same upscale, middle-class audience that was watching European art films in the 1950s and 1960s. Dylan Thomas's LPs were the fountainhead of Caedmon's success but were also emblematic of the complex cultural hybrids associated with the middlebrow. The story of Caedmon's association with Thomas can serve as an entry point to such key aspects of the high culture spoken word LP market. To begin, let us focus our attention on the two young Hunter College graduates in that narrative, for whom Thomas's poetry reading was a launching pad for careers as record industry executives.

SUCCESS STORIES

Journalists were fascinated by the fact that Caedmon was owned and operated by women, but from one perspective, the prominence of women in the record industry should not have been a surprise at all. Musical performance had long been understood as an important part of the traditional female task of making the American middle-class home a space of moral uplift. As the piano's central place in the parlor was usurped by the phonograph, the job of the selection, purchase, and playing of records was frequently assumed by women. The early phonograph industry worked under the assumption that women were overseeing music culture in the home and playing the dominant role in the consumption of records. As we saw in chapter 1, women were key figures in the educational departments of the major record companies. Other middle-class American women became involved in the retail side of the phonograph business, working as salespeople in the record sections of department stores.[9]

Women continued to be associated with record retailing in the early 1940s, as can be seen in the 1941 film *Penny Serenade*. In the opening of that film, we see Julie Gardiner (Irene Dunne) packing her bags to leave her husband Roger (Cary Grant) after the recent death of their daughter and a subsequent chill in their marriage. Julie comes across an album of 78 rpm phonograph records entitled "The Story of a Happy Marriage," which includes discs purchased at various moments in her life with Roger as well as keepsakes such as a pair of baby shoes. Julie plays one of the records, which triggers her memory and motivates a flashback to her and Roger's courtship: a transition achieved visually by an iris out of the spinning record. The flashback takes us to a record store where Julie is working. We see Roger walk past the shop window and turn his head as he hears that the record on the shop's phonograph player is skipping. As he glances into the store, he notices Julie. Roger goes into the store and, hoping to strike up a conversation, makes a few half-hearted enquiries to another young female salesperson in the shop. At one point he asks to see a record that is kept on a high shelf. The saleswoman makes a long-suffering expression, suggesting that this is not the first time a man has made such a request, presumably to get a look at her legs, and she casually produces another copy from behind the desk. Roger finally approaches Julie and asks if he can hear the flip side of the record currently playing in the shop. She takes the disc into a listening room, and he follows with an armful of records to prolong their time together.

When we next see the two walking home, Roger has a large box of records under his arm. "Mind if I ask you a personal question?" Roger asks when they reach the steps to Julie's apartment, "Have you got a Victrola inside?" "Why yes, of course," she replies. "Would you let me hear this one?" he asks, "Otherwise I'll have to take it home and imagine how it sounds." "Don't you have a machine at home?" Julie responds, confused. He confesses that he doesn't, and she declares, "Why on earth did you buy twenty-seven . . ." What follows is a wonderful wordless exchange of close-ups as Julie catches on to his real intentions. The scene ends as she nonchalantly removes the record from its sleeve and walks into her apartment, with Roger following behind her. This sequence provides us with an intriguing illustration of how phonograph records could function as a site of family memory along the lines of a photo album but also reveals the extent to which young women were associated with the sale of phonograph records. Indeed, the record shop is presented as an environment in which jaded saleswomen had to develop strategies to repel the unwanted come-ons of male customers.

Despite this long-standing tradition of female labor in record shops, women had little hope of attaining executive or decision-making positions in the record industry. In a 1988 study, Patrick Parsons concluded that female employees had long been a small minority in terms of over-all employment at record companies, and to the extent that they did find work, they were systematically excluded from positions associated with "deciding what gets created."[10] Parsons found that only 5 percent of record industry employees in 1966 were female, and those 5 per-cent were almost all in publicity and promotion office positions. Several features of the record business militated against the rise of women to senior-level positions. Note, for example, that there has often been a "stag party" culture surrounding the radio promotion of records, which involved the exchange of prostitutes and strippers for airplay. Female employees often found their career in record promotion limited by their exclusion from, or uneasiness with, this misogynist business culture.[11] Similarly, in a study of women in the record industry, Sue Steward and Sheryl Garratt cited a spokesman for EMI Records who argued that women were precluded from artist and repertoire positions ("a & r") because they required "very odd hours, and going out alone at three in the morning to listen to weird music in weird clubs."[12] Given such barri-ers to female advancement, Barbara Holdridge and Marianne Mantell's rise to executive positions in the record industry stands as a notable exception. As we shall see, their success in part relied on the develop-ment of a business model that found avenues for promotion besides the bribing of radio executives and that took them in search of talent to places like the Kaufmann Auditorium rather than seedy nightclubs.

Holdridge's account of her start in the record industry provides further evidence of the limits placed on female career development. In an email interview, Holdridge stated that "there were no women in managerial positions in record companies in 1952" and that the Caedmon found-ers were seen as "mavericks in what was still a male business world."[13] Holdridge admitted that their gender made it tough to get started in the industry: "We went to several rental agents before we found one who would rent an office to us. The bank also was skeptical."[14] Before starting her own company, Mantell had worked for a small record label, Period Records, but had become bitter about the industry. "There was a dearth of anybody in the record business who knew anything about the record business," she told the *Washington Post* in 1961. "They could pronounce LP and money and cash and dollars and cents but they didn't know anything about music . . . I tried to sell one guy the idea of doing a program of medieval records. One day I said, why don't we record poetry. Another day I said, let's do American poetry. He smashed his fist down and said, 'Let's do medieval American poetry.'"[15] In the face of such industry philistinism, Mantell was said to have discovered that "she was not cut out to be an Organization Woman."[16] Meanwhile, Holdridge was working as the assistant editor at Liveright Publishing. The two decided to pool their skills and start their own company and soon had their fateful meeting with Dylan Thomas.

Holdridge and Mantell's focus on "high culture," or "educational," content was an important factor in their ability to carve out a niche for themselves as female record executives. Such an orientation could be read as a continuation of the music appreciation initiatives of the 1920s, initiatives, as we have seen, in which women such as Mrs. Frances E. Clark at Victor played a key role. Holdridge and Mantell were, however, not the first people to explore the potential of the phonograph as a medium for high culture recitation. Indeed, such a function was a prominent part of Thomas Edison's early speculations about sound recording.[17] Jason Camlot describes a "well-developed Victorian yearning" for a technology that would "make the reading experience more immediate" and "capture the character and subjectivity of an author without the mediation of the printed page."[18] As early as 1890, Edison's agents in England had recorded famous poets such as Robert Browning and Alfred Tennyson.[19] Early catalogs of the American phonograph industry included poems read by James Whitcomb Riley, excerpts from Charles Dickens's *A Christmas Carol* read by Bransby Williams, and other assorted poetic recitations. Closer to Caedmon's time, Columbia Records released Orson Welles's full-length audio versions of Shakespeare plays in the late 1930s and early 1940s. Michael Anderegg characterizes Welles's Mercury Text Records as "pioneer efforts" in the record industry and describes a Columbia promotional document concerning the project that featured the heading "Cashing in on the Classics."[20] None of these efforts, however, cashed in on the classics to the same degree as Caedmon, which grossed $10,000 in its first year. By 1966 Holdridge and Mantell were said to be enjoying a "cultural bonanza," worth $14 million.[21] Fueled initially by the Thomas LPs, Caedmon grew to a full-time staff of eight, including a shipping clerk who would soon be shipping crates of his own LPs: Mike Nichols of Nichols and May fame (see chapter 5). Caedmon also made use of the services of independent recording engineer Peter Bartok, the son of the famous composer. This small, independent operation is representative of an era when independent labels held a prominent place in the record business. I will return to the importance of independent labels in my discussion of African American comics in chapter 3, but for now we should note that just as independent companies such as Chess, Atlantic, and Sun were dominating the pop music charts in the mid- to late 1950s, independent companies such as Caedmon were making important contributions to spoken word genres.

As we have seen, the remarkable success of the female-owned Caedmon was unique in the male-dominated record industry. One factor in Caedmon's success was the company's ability to garner national press attention. It is not surprising that such press coverage focused on Holdridge and Mantell as nontraditional working women. As such, press accounts of Caedmon provide evidence to support recent scholarship that has questioned the assumption that a single, uncomplicated domestic ideal held for women during the postwar era. Susan Hartmann notes that although the Cold War helped to sustain traditional gender roles, political leaders also looked to women's employment to aid in the political crisis.[22] Joanne Meyerowitz argues that postwar women in increasing numbers were joining the labor force and participating in public life despite the baby boom and a culture of discrimination.[23] Meyerowitz bases her claims for a more complex view of postwar gender culture on an examination of popular periodicals, in which she found ideals of domesticity coexisting with an ethos of female individual achievement that "celebrated nondomestic activity, individual striving, public service, and public success."[24] Indeed, popular magazines often featured female success stories that spotlighted women with unusual talents and careers.

Press coverage of Caedmon resembled the magazine stories described by Meyerowitz, in that it featured a "bifocal vision" of women as both traditionally feminine and as public figures. That bifocal vision functioned to resolve tensions between domesticity and public achievement by "ignoring the difficulties that women usually faced in pursuing both" and by serving as a reminder that even publicly successful women had to maintain "traditional gender distinctions."[25] "There is nothing flamboyant, Madison Avenue-ish, or even business-like about these two soft-speaking young women," the *Pasadena Independent Star-News* wrote of Holdridge and Mantell. "They could easily pass for suburban housewives and mothers—which they are." "Twice a week," we are told, "these young mothers leave their respective suburban homes and head for New York. Here, Caedmon Records now occupies an entire floor—8,000 square feet—of a mid-Manhattan office building."[26] This account

FIGURE 3. The founders of Caedmon Records: Barbara Holdridge and Marianne Mantell in the Caedmon office with the office cat. Photograph by Rollie McKenna. © Rosalie Thorne McKenna Foundation. Courtesy of Center for Creative Photography, University of Arizona Foundation.

is typical of the way in which the spaces of the home and the Caedmon office were often described in terms of the other. Consider another article in which we are told that Holdridge and Mantell "run their huge operation from two cluttered desks, in one large cluttered room. Books, manuscripts, records, taping and other recording equipment litter the room, 'Believe it or not we're good housekeepers at home,' said Marianne."[27] A similar press account noted that, despite their success, the Caedmon founders "still share the same cluttered desk" and give pet names to the philodendron pots in the office.[28] It is difficult to imagine descriptions of sloppy desks or evaluations of the treatment of office plants in press coverage of male record executives such as Atlantic Records' Ahmet Ertegun, Moe Asch at Folkways, or the Chess brothers. Holdridge and Mantell's nontraditional, nondomestic work made them newsworthy, but was consistently framed in terms of the domestic.

Meyerowitz found that postwar press stories tended to downplay the obstacles that nondomestic women faced in the public arena.[29] Despite accounts of dim-witted male executives who wanted to release medieval American poetry records, press coverage of Caedmon tended to paint a rosy picture of the helpful men who surrounded Holdridge and Mantell. In one article, Holdridge stated that their gender had "been a help in getting their business started": "It's as simple as this," she said. "You have boy friends to take you out to dinner when you're broke . . . other male friends helped with legal and accounting services."[30] "Chivalry isn't dead after all!" summed up one article. "Two young women have built a thriving business—with the help of obliging males." Accounts of Caedmon's early years often described how the women had to use a wheelbarrow to move newly pressed LPs to their office: "They weighed 300 to 500 pounds," Mantell stated. "We couldn't lift the wheelbarrow up curbs, so we would wait for a man to come along and help us. One always did. We had our dates help in the office, and friends designed the record covers. I think 40,000 men helped us in those days."[31] Press accounts thus emphasized Holdridge and Mantell's need for male assistance, describing those men who had helped them instead of those who had hindered them, or indeed the larger institutionalized sexism that they faced.

One also finds a pervasive tendency in the press to describe the physical appearance of the Caedmon founders, illustrating Meyerowitz's assertion that articles about nondomestic women made frequent reference to a "narrowly defined" femininity. The *Haywood [CA] Daily Review* referred to the "two dewy-eyed brunettes of 24," while *Good Housekeeping* wrote that Holdridge and Mantell were "both still in their middle twenties and both attractive."[32] The male author of that article went on to describe how all of Mantell's "appalling erudition" was "wrapped up in a blond bit who gives you the feeling that you could lift her up with one hand and that this might be a rather pleasant thing to do."[33] Thus, despite acknowledging their achievements in the cultural industries, articles such as these asserted restrictive definitions of female attractiveness and behavior.

The press discourse surrounding Caedmon thus provided the same kind of ambiguous message about female achievement that Meyerowitz found in her study. On the one hand, the press presented nondomestic options to women and praised those—like Holdridge and Mantell— who had asserted themselves as public figures. On the other hand, these articles "reinforced rigid definitions of appropriate behavior and sexual expression" for women and did not "overtly challenge traditional gender roles."[34] The case of Caedmon shows us how the record industry continued to be an important area of nondomestic female labor in the postwar years, although that labor was constrained by restrictive notions of gender.

It would be a mistake, however, to suggest that Holdridge and Mantell were merely passive onlookers in Caedmon's representation in the press. In fact, Holdridge asserted their active participation in exactly the kinds of press discourses I've been describing. "Neither of us ever sensed any hostility or condescension in any of the many articles that appeared in magazines or newspapers," Holdridge stated. "As individualists and women entrepreneurs, we knew that there was male skepticism and resentment out there, but we were not women's libbers, in any antagonistic way. Our independence and entrepreneurship did not cause us to be alien to our wholeness as women, and our non-Caedmon interests embraced home arts as well as business and recording endeavors. We ourselves routinely commented to the press on all of the men who helped us (and remember, there were few women, even later, in a position to do so). We welcomed their gallantry and assistance, thought it amusing that so many men rushed to help us lift our cart filled with heavy boxes of records on and off sidewalk curbs, and were grateful to them all, while aware that there were men in the industry who resented our success and reportedly had fits of pique. The newspaper and magazine writers wrote just what we fed them, and the media publicity helped us enormously in our marketing efforts."[35] Holdridge's statements suggest that we should be careful of ascribing too much agency to the press in their presentation of Caedmon and thereby erase the pragmatic perspective of the company's female founders as well as their active role in shaping the press discourse that surrounded them.

Nonetheless, the founding narrative of Holdridge and Mantell's initial meeting with Dylan Thomas so often retold in the press should be seen in light of the foregoing discussion. Though the protagonists were female entrepreneurs who were establishing an important independent record company, the repetition of that narrative encourages us to see them as star-struck, "dewey-eyed" fans as much as canny business innovators. Dylan Thomas becomes one of the 40,000 chivalrous men who kindly helped Holdridge and Mantell to forge their company. The prominence of this story in press discourse can thus be seen as a subtle way to enforce gender norms for two exceptional nondomestic women. At the same time, Caedmon's founders were certainly aware of the appeals of this narrative and its utility in crafting a discourse that helped the company to achieve its remarkable success.

More can be learned, however, if we consider the story of the Kaufmann Auditorium, not from the perspective of Holdridge and Mantell as entrepreneurs, but with an eye to the setting of the event: a crowded poetry reading full of young fans eager to see a traveling performer with a reputation for lyrical virtuosity and a mesmerizing voice. That scene might strike contemporary readers as a strange hybrid of rock concert and university lecture. Indeed, to understand the success of Caedmon's spoken word LPs, we need to situate them in the context of a rise in reading aloud in the American cultural scene of the 1950s.

READ IT ALOUD

Dylan Thomas's legendary reading tours of the United States in the early 1950s were part of a growing market for public recitations of various kinds at this time. The New York Museum of Modern Art launched a series entitled "Evenings with Modern Poets" in 1950 that drew capacity audiences to hear Dylan Thomas as well as Marianne Moore, W.H. Auden, E.E. Cummings, William Carlos Williams, and Robert Frost.[36] The *New York Times* saw the series as symptomatic of a change in the public's attitude toward the reading of contemporary poetry: "As little as fifteen, or even ten years ago, the prevailing attitude might have been summed up in the word 'queasy.' Poetry was apt to be regarded, if at all, as something dutiful, like churchgoing."[37] Besides poets such as Thomas and Frost, a figure who helped to establish reading aloud as public entertainment in the 1950s was the Hollywood film actor Charles Laughton. According to the *New York Times* in 1955, Laughton had provided "most of the impetus" for the revival of public reading.[38] The careers of Laughton and Thomas can serve as barometers for the cultural dynamics of reading aloud at this time and so help us to contextualize the rise of Caedmon Records.

Laughton began reading Bible passages and classic literature to American soldiers in Los Angeles hospitals after World War II. Encouraged by friends to make his readings accessible to a larger audience, he took his act to Ed Sullivan's television show. In the wake of a successful appearance there, Laughton met with MCA booking agent Paul Gregory, who organized a national reading tour for the actor, including appearances at colleges and community events. Writing in 1953, *New York Times* critic Jack Gould noted that Gregory and Laughton were responsible for a "minor miracle" in show business: "The unpredictable nature of the entertainment world seldom has been more vividly illustrated than in the revival of the art of reading aloud. While Hollywood and Broadway have had their usual troubles with productions boasting lavish settings and big casts, individuals and small groups are trouping the country with little more than a handful of books and registering spectacular box-office successes."[39] In the wake of his performances as a solo reader, Laughton teamed up with Charles Boyer, Cedric Hardwicke, and Agnes Moorehead, and under the name the First Drama Quartet, they gave spoken word performances of George Bernard Shaw's *Don Juan in Hell* across the country. The First Drama Quartet's production was released as a phonograph record by Columbia in 1952 and, by one account, "outsold all other Columbia two- and three-disk albums" of the time.[40] Laughton was even featured on a *Time* magazine cover story that year. The *Time* article described how the actor had "turned the old pastime of reading aloud into a booming big business" and so had tossed a "sizable bone to the culture-starved": "One might have thought the movies, radio and television had never been invented."[41]

As that quote indicates, the rise of reading aloud was consistently framed in relation to the media and, in particular, to television. In 1952 the *Christian Science Monitor* expressed hope that the recent interest in reading aloud would enrich "a generation brought up on movies in technicolor and television in the living room."[42] When the *New York Times* noted in 1952 that reading aloud was "developing into a craze," the author asked sarcastically, "What has got into us? Is there something wrong with the television set?"[43] Laughton himself urged parents to make reading a "pleasure as television is a pleasure" for their children.[44] In fact, family togetherness was another frequently mentioned benefit of reading aloud. *Coronet* magazine explained Laughton's belief that reading aloud would "strengthen family bonds."[45] Elsewhere, Laughton stressed that reading was "a shared experience which draws people closer together. Husbands and wives, families or groups of friends can enjoy the comfortable satisfaction that comes from laughing together, learning together."[46]

In rhetoric such as this, the proponents of reading aloud continued a Victorian tradition of family reading as a "private drama of enculturation" that was opposed to the "shadowy and disreputable" world of the stage.[47] Mark Morrisson describes how the "verse-recitation movement" in Victorian England privileged "oral cultural production over visual spectacle," the latter being associated with "artifice, theatricality, and—especially—the working-class music hall."[48] For Alison Byerly, Victorian uneasiness about the theater found "a perfect outlet in reading performances, which represented a domestication of theater, a compromise for people who wished to be entertained but were suspicious of overt theatricality."[49] Even public readings by celebrity authors such as Charles Dickens were given an "unpretentious staging" consisting of a reading desk and lamp to frame the performance as an extension of "familiar domestic activity."[50] The "craze" for reading aloud in the 1950s, of which Charles Laughton was a central part, can be seen as an update of these Victorian discourses on entertainment, with a residual distrust of spectacle transferred from the stage to television.

Though reading aloud was seen as antithetical to television, Laughton brought it to the nation's airwaves. Echoing the verse-recitation movement's suspicion of visual spectacle, Laughton voiced his belief that the modern world had been "brought up to look rather than to listen," and he intended his television program entitled *This Is Charles Laughton,* to "redress the balance."[51] The critical skepticism that greeted *This Is Charles Laughton* reveals an assumed gulf that existed between his brand of spoken word performance and the television audience: "Some pessimists contend that the TV audience will be scared to death at the sight of a book, never having seen one," quipped the *Christian Science Monitor.*[52] Such elitist predictions were somewhat confirmed by the program's poor showing and short run, though a more important factor than the television audience's presumed illiteracy was certainly the show's lack of visual appeal. *New York Times* television critic Jack Gould found the program to be a "distinct disappointment" and described its lack of close-ups and a camera technique that was "more akin to a photographed stage appearance than indigenous television."[53] *Time* bemoaned the fact that all viewers had to look at was "Laughton himself, a fat man in a rumpled suit, leaning on a stool placed on a table."[54] Along similar lines, *Coronet* magazine suggested in 1952 that Laughton had "a physique like a bundle of wet wash."[55] Laughton's "untelegenic" appearance and his show's "unpretentious staging" were in line with a tradition of reading aloud going back to Charles Dickens, but they certainly hampered his appeal on network television. Despite limited success on television, Laughton remained an influential missionary for the cause of reading aloud in the home and continued to make appearances on the stage, in the popular press, and on phonograph records.

Charles Laughton's multimedia campaign for reading aloud and *This Is Charles Laughton* resemble attempts at this time to bring educational content to American television. Educators had been standing on the sidelines of broadcasting since the defeat of the Wagner-Hatfield amendment in 1934, but calls for educational broadcasting were renewed in the early 1950s.[56] At that time, Freida Hennock, the first female commissioner of the Federal Communications Commission, spearheaded a campaign for educational television.[57] FCC hearings on educational television began in November 1950, and in April of that year, the FCC outlined its decisions regarding channel allocation.[58] Hennock had argued that 25 percent of television frequencies be set aside for noncommercial stations, but the FCC only agreed to approximately 10 percent, or about 242 channels.[59] The first noncommercial educational television stations (ETV) went on the air in 1953, and there were 18 in 1955 and 40 in 1959.[60] Laughton's brand of reading aloud may have gone against the grain of "indigenous" network television, but it resembled popular ETV programming such as the lectures on Shakespeare given by the University of Southern California's Dr. Frank Baxter.

The television networks responded to the ETV movement in several ways. The Ford Foundation–funded *Omnibus* was broadcast by CBS on Sunday afternoons between 1952 and 1956 and on other networks until 1961. According to Anna McCarthy, *Omnibus* was meant in part "to show policymakers that there was no need for state funded television," since commercially sponsored programming could ably contribute to American's cultural education.[61] Besides *Omnibus,* educational imperatives on network programming of the early 1950s included Sylvester "Pat" Weaver's cultural mandate at NBC known as Operation Frontal Lobes. With programs such as *Matinee Theater* and Arlene Francis's *Home,* Operation Frontal Lobes promised to bring "culture and education to the masses in a palatable form."[62] Despite such lofty ambitions, none of those programs survived for very long: by the end of the decade, Marsha Cassidy describes how demographic shifts in the television audience had required the networks to concentrate on programs with "mass appeal and higher profit margins."[63] McCarthy notes that even *Omnibus* achieved only limited success and had consistently low ratings.[64] Charles Laughton's short-lived television program was another high-profile network educational initiative of the era, and reading aloud was an efficient, though debatably palatable, approach to the production of educational broadcasting. Though reading aloud lacked the mass appeal needed for mainstream television success, Caedmon's record sales during these years were steadily climbing: the LP provided the niche, educational content that the television networks struggled to deliver.

Charles Laughton's reading aloud campaigns, legislation on educational television, and CBS's *Omnibus* can all be placed in the context of debates about American hierarchies of taste. As many social historians have noted, the postwar era was the time of what Daniel Belgrad refers to as a "reconfiguration of social tensions on a cultural level": "The social distinctions that had once been associated with economic status were translated in the 1940s and '50s into cultural positions, as an elite defended its 'higher' tastes, whether modern or genteel, against the onslaught of abundance."[65] Barbara Wilinsky argues that cultural taste and leisure activities became increasingly important as arbiters of suburban middle-class distinction at this time, as members of that group sought "to distinguish themselves from one another and from other classes."[66] One result was an ongoing struggle over what were considered to be "highbrow" and "middlebrow" canons of taste. Such distinctions often had to do with attitudes toward the cultural industries. Marianne Conroy writes that the term *middlebrow* designated "a new stratum of taste that arose with the spread of commercial culture, a stratum distinguished from 'highbrow' forms of elite culture by its implication in commerce and popular formulae and from 'lowbrow' forms of mass culture as well, by reason of its claims to social or aesthetic importance."[67] As Janice Radway puts it, the space of the middlebrow was occupied by products that sought to hide their "machine-tooled uniformity behind the self-consciously worked mask of culture."[68]

One of the key voices in the critique of the middlebrow was Dwight MacDonald, who, in his well-known 1960 essay "Masscult and Midcult," bemoaned the growing presence of "Midcult," a "peculiar hybrid" created from mass culture's "unnatural intercourse" with high culture. Midcult was said to share "essential qualities" with mass culture, such as "the formula, the built-in reaction, the lack of any standard except popularity," but it hid these behind a "cultural figleaf": "In Masscult the trick is plain—to please the crowd by any means. But Midcult has it both ways: it pretends to respect the standards of High Culture while in fact it waters them down and vulgarizes them."[69] As examples, MacDonald pointed to the Museum of Modern Art's film department, the Book-of-the-Month Club, and CBS's *Omnibus*.[70] Although not mentioned by MacDonald, Caedmon was operating in the same middlebrow realm as the examples listed above, since their records were making "high brow" poetry and literature accessible to a popular audience through mass production and marketing.

Caedmon's "hi-fi midcult" reached a fairly specialized niche audience, one sometimes explicitly opposed to the television audience. A *New York Times* reviewer noted that Caedmon's recordings of T.S. Eliot and

Dylan Thomas offered encouraging signs for "those who are afraid that we are a nation of low-brows, mesmerized before a TV screen."[71] By one account, Caedmon appealed to the same "culturally sophisticated audience" who were "reading paperbacks, listening to FM radio, and patronizing European films."[72] In terms of the latter, Wilinsky has documented the rise of American art cinema and films whose concern with realistic, adult themes reflected a "shift from a focus on the mass audience to a concentration on the more selective (and select) adult audience."[73] In fact, the critique of middlebrow culture ran parallel to the emergence of marketing to such select niche audiences. Note that MacDonald saw one ray of hope in the midcult phenomenon: the discovery that "there is not One Big Audience but rather a number of smaller, more specialized audiences that may still be commercially profitable," which resulted in "the sale of 'quality' paperbacks and recordings and the growth of 'art' cinema houses, off-Broadway theatres, concert orchestras and art museums and galleries." MacDonald concludes, "The mass audience is divisible, we have discovered, and the more it is divided, the better."[74] As a company working at the nexus of just these kinds of cultural debates, Caedmon was particularly successful at balancing niche appeal and mass production.

As with other forms of the middlebrow, recordings of modern poets were held by some to democratize elitist high culture. Randall Jarrell, consultant in poetry at the Library of Congress, declared in 1956 that the hi-fi stereo was putting poetry back in American life: on records "you don't have to puzzle over what the words mean, you just listen to your high-fidelity phonograph."[75] Other commentators made similar points about the LP's ability to popularize forms of modern poetry that could be inscrutable and intimidating. "Does modern poetry give you a pain in the neck?" asked the *El Paso Herald-Post* in 1953. "Are you unable to make head or tail of it? Can you see neither honest rhyme nor reason in it? Me, too. But I have news for all of us who have been tussling with modern verse: Our trouble is that we have been trying to read it. That way lies madness. Modern poetry doesn't read so good, it seems, but it listens just dandy. The trick is to listen, rather than look." The author added that Caedmon's owners had assured her that modern poetry was "more easily understood on records than on paper."[76] As part of postwar middlebrow cultural production, Caedmon was making high culture palatable to a popular audience.[77]

Holdridge and Mantell espoused a populist view of their work, with Mantell stating that their success was due in part to a feeling among their audience that "critics and scholars had taken literature to such a remote point that it was getting dull and uninteresting": "In recording the author you are doing something tremendously important," Mantell stated, "you get an insight into the poem as the poet wrote it. . . . The records give stature to poets who have been relegated to critics and scholars."[78] Like the middlebrow debate more generally, Caedmon represented a cultural turf war, with media producers providing an end run around established scholars and critics, allowing poets to speak directly to a popular audience and consumers to gain access to valuable knowledge that could be translated into signs of social distinction.[79] As such, Caedmon was responding to larger trends of the 1950s, whereby, according to W.T. Lhamon Jr., "the clogged arteries of official modern culture finally popped open" as a result of a widespread realization that "the prestigious wing of every art had cut itself off from its potential public to follow its own heedless autonomy."[80] In areas such as painting, music, and architecture, both avant-garde and popular artists sought a more immediate and intimate connection with their audiences. Caedmon facilitated such a connection in the field of modern poetry.

Note, for example, how a striving for intimacy between reader and listener shaped Caedmon's approach to marketing and producing their records. A sense of intimate connection with the poet was a key to the company's promotional rhetoric. In a 1969 Caedmon ad placed in the *New York Times,* the copy explains that, "since a poet hears a poem in his mind's ear as he writes it, he knows how he wants it to sound. And you too will hear how the poem ought to sound—with a new understanding not only of the poem, but of the poet himself—when you listen to the great poets of our age reading from their own works on Caedmon Records."[81] In the studio, Holdridge and Mantell attempted to make literature "a newly intimate experience": "Our recordings made the poets seem human and vibrant, speaking directly to the listener rather than being encapsulated on the printed page. Instead of filtering the lines through only their own inner voices, listeners heard the poet himself convey his emotions and cadences with his own voice and intensity." Holdridge described how the studio audience at Caedmon recording sessions tended to consist solely of the two founders, who comprised "a highly responsive, caring, admiring and involved audience. Because [authors] were reading directly to us, that connectedness and spontaneity came through to all subsequent listeners." The sense of "connectedness" was amplified by their preference for "a more intimate 'room' sound" as opposed to "a 'hall' sound."[82] In Patrick Feaster's terms, Caedmon rejected a descriptive mode of phonography concerned with depicting "an event as it might be passively overheard" in favor of a substitutive mode that seeks to "replace an event as its functional equivalent, inviting an identical response from its listeners."[83] Instead of replicating an overheard concert hall event, Caedmon's recordings suggested the intimate experience of a copresent reading.

Dylan Thomas was one of the people who took fullest advantage of such a direct, intimate media channel between poet and popular audience. Indeed, Caedmon's uncertain status between highbrow literature and popular culture industry is embodied in Thomas, who mixed the world of letters with popular media, working as he did in radio and film in addition to becoming a rather unlikely star of the recording industry. Further, the earthy subject matter of much of Thomas's work suggests a point of comparison to the art cinema scene of that era. Eric Schaefer claims that a thin line often separated art cinema and sexually explicit exploitation films.[84] Indeed, hallowed Italian Neorealist classics were sometimes marketed to American audiences primarily for their frank portrayal of sexuality and were screened in the same theaters as "lowbrow" sex films. Similarly, Thomas's poetry was appreciated by many Americans for its titillating subject matter and the poet's bohemian reputation. John Malcolm Brinnin wrote that "the tumescence" of Thomas's poems fed rumors of his own lechery, and that the uncovering of sexual imagery in his poems rapidly became a "national undergraduate pastime."[85] For example, one can hear Thomas describe the "butter fat goosegirls, bounced in a gambo bed, their breasts full of honey, under their gander king" on Caedmon's recording of "In the White Giant's Thigh."

Thomas's unusual hybrid of poet and popular recording artist could seem jarring and incongruous to some. Consider a *New York Times* cartoon from 1956, in which we see three middle-aged men drinking coffee in a working-class diner. They all look up at a radio on the wall above them, from which they hear, "And now, as requested by J.G. of Hollis, Long Island, a Dylan Thomas recording." The humor of the cartoon comes from the incongruity of the Welsh poet on pop radio. In 1964 *Newsweek* even compared Thomas's continued appeal to the "James Dean cult," stating that "today's hunger for vicarious boisterousness and for virile, rhapsodic verse can be measured by the increasing sales of everything that Dylan Thomas wrote and recorded and by the variety of the people who now read and listen to his works."[86] We might also consider a track on the first Mike Nichols and Elaine May comedy album, *Improvisations to Music* (Mercury 1959). Recall that Nichols had briefly been employed at Caedmon as a shipping clerk, where he certainly spent time handling Dylan Thomas LPs. On a track entitled "Everybody's Doing It," we hear Nichols perform what Janet Coleman has described as one of his "favorite party gags": a wonderfully spot-on Dylan Thomas imitation.[87] The humor of the track is derived from the juxtaposition of Thomas's trademark recitation style with a brash saloon tack-piano and commercial slogans. "When I was a boy in Youngstown, the voices of the poets cried quick, they do not cry today," Nichols intones. "You did it! You son of a gun, in your grey flannel suit, you drowned the poets! The flannel in the mouth choking the voice of the silver bird that cries no more." Then follows in the same solemn tones, "Winston tastes good like a cigarette should. You get a lot to like in a Marlboro." At this point, Elaine May chimes in with "Smoke Kools! Smoke Kools!" As I will discuss in chapter 5, Nichols and May were important players in postwar comedy records and often took aim at network sponsorship, but for now, "Everybody's Doing It" provides another example of how Thomas invited comment as a liminal figure who straddled taste distinctions.

As a final illustration of Thomas's uncertain position in existing hierarchies of taste, consider an anecdote from Brinnin's account of life on tour with Thomas in 1953. When the two went to see pop singer Johnnie Ray at a nightclub in Boston, Brinnin described how, as the singer "tore, shredded, and annihilated one song after another, Dylan applauded and cheered with the devastated shop-girls and, with the most insatiable of them, called for half a dozen encores."[88] That anecdote seems intended to astound the reader with the image of the British bard enjoying a "shop-girl's" pop entertainment. In this and the previous examples, Dylan Thomas and his Caedmon LPs embodied the middlebrow's "unnatural" cultural intercourse that so troubled critics such as MacDonald: here was a Romantic poet whose mystic imagery was packaged and sold by the modern cultural industries, an intellectual man of letters who could be compared to a Hollywood teen idol. Thomas's affinity for Johnnie Ray illustrates how, in both his temperament and association with the record industry, Thomas prefigured the rock and roll performers who would make their entrance on the cultural stage just a few years after his death. Lhamon contrasts an early 1950s poetry scene that was "almost entirely academic" and relegated to the "two-dimensional space" of books, to the immediacy of rock and roll heard on records.[89] Dylan Thomas's records blurred the lines between highbrow book-based poetry and records by rock performers.[90]

The "peculiar hybrid" of poet and pop star heard on Thomas's records reemerged a decade after Thomas's death in the form of a young singer-songwriter from Hibbing, Minnesota. That singer, while in the process of constructing a new persona, first considered calling himself Robert Allen, then Robert Allyn, and finally, after encountering poems by Dylan Thomas, settled on Bob Dylan.[91] An early *New York Times* review noted that Bob Dylan had adopted his surname "out of his absorption with Dylan Thomas" and that it showed in his "language of colorful precision with images a-tumble, sometimes childlike, but hardly ever out of control."[92] Bob Dylan's work has often been described in relation to LP culture via the influence of Harry Smith's six-album set, *Anthology of American Folk Music,* released in 1952 by Folkways Records. Caedmon's Dylan Thomas recordings should be added to the list of Bob Dylan's phonographic precursors. Certainly the experience of listening to Bob Dylan tracks such as "Gates of Eden," "Desolation Row," or "A Hard Rain's a-Gonna Fall" is as close to the experience of listening to the "language of colorful precision with images a-tumble" of Thomas's Caedmon LPs as it is to records by Chuck Berry, Leadbelly, or Doc Watson. Indeed, part of Dylan's enduring influence on the record industry—along with mid-1960s albums by the Beatles—was to indicate that LPs, previously associated with an upscale adult market for classical music and jazz, could be sold to a youth market heretofore serviced by popular music on less profitable single records. As Keir Keightley argues, it was the shift from predominantly sales of singles to the more stable and profitable LP that enabled rock to become the "dominant force" within the record industry.[93] Caedmon's LPs need to be added to this history, as a blueprint for rock album acts of the 1960s and as an early genre of LPs sold to both an adult and, as we shall see, a youth market. As with the studio techniques heard on postwar children's records described in the previous chapter, a consideration of spoken word LPs illuminates celebrated developments in the 1960s, when rock acts entered both the LP and the hi-fi midcult market.

Returning to Caedmon's primal scene at Thomas's 1952 poetry reading, my initial comparison to a rock concert might now seem less incongruous. Phonograph records were an important medium for figures such as Charles Laughton and Dylan Thomas, whose spoken performances were eagerly consumed by American audiences looking for alternatives to network broadcasting and ways to display social distinctions. The meeting between Holdridge and Mantell and Thomas is emblematic of a period that saw the proliferation of hybrids of popular and high culture. We have thus far considered Thomas's New York reading from the perspective of Caedmon's founders and with regard to the cultural significance of reading aloud. The Kaufmann event can yield further insights if we shift our attention to the audience. Who was coming to these public recitations, and who was buying Caedmon's records? How were highbrow LPs meant to function in the postwar home?

INTRIGUE YOUR MIND WHILE YOUR HANDS WORK

The press was fascinated by the question of who was buying Caedmon's highbrow records. In 1961 the *Washington Post* asked, "Would a Texan spend some of his money on a phonograph record of poems recited by Dylan Thomas?" The surprising answer was "yes."[94] A year later, the *Blytheville [AR] Courier News* was shocked to discover that some of the people who ordered records from Caedmon lived in small towns, wrote "on wrapping paper," and "put 'i' and 'e' in the wrong order when they ask[ed] for a recording of a Shakespeare play."[95] Such accounts register the perceived novelty of Caedmon's elite cultural content being made available to a mass audience. Literate young adults were one cross-section of that audience that proved to be crucial to Caedmon's success, or, as the *El Paso Herald-Post* put it in 1953, Dylan Thomas records were "the rage of the long-hairs in the bobbysox brigade."[96] *Good Housekeeping* declared in 1956 that Caedmon had discovered a large group of poetry fans "a little older than the bobby-soxers, who love to put verse records on their phonographs late at night, when they are going to sleep, the way teenagers like to play jazz."[97] In a 1965 interview, Holdridge noted, "Young people put us in business . . . our first market was college students and today we still get a large share of our business from young people who are interested in fine literature, poetry and drama."[98] These references to the young adult audience provide further evidence that Caedmon represented a precursor to the teen album market of the 1960s.[99] It was another demographic, however, that received a disproportionate amount of attention in popular press coverage of highbrow spoken word records: female homemakers.

The home phonograph, like radio and television, had to fit into the spaces of the American home and the rhythms of female domestic labor. Kenney argues that the record industry had long considered its products to be an antidote to housework: "Recorded music could offer solace and 'transcendence' to the overworked and lonely housewife and a burgeoning, exciting, and swiftly evolving world of recorded sounds into which women were encouraged to retreat."[100] Despite the prominence of a male-dominated high-fidelity subculture in the postwar era—a subject to which I will return in the next chapter—recorded sound was also an important part of many American women's lives. Pamela Wojcik has argued that "a flexible and positive feminine discourse about phonography" coincided with a masculine discourse surrounding hi-fi technology.[101] An examination of Caedmon Records can add to our understanding of the feminine practices and discourses surrounding phonography.

The home hi-fi stereo held many potential appeals to postwar housewives, including the enjoyment of spoken word records under the cover of the children's records described in the previous chapter. The use of famous film stars to narrate kidisks was understood as a means to reach the parents who bought the records, not the children for whom they were supposedly made: children didn't care about the casting of noted personalities, a record buyer at Gimbel's department store told *Harper's Magazine* in 1951, "names of course, mean nothing to the children."[102] As with the use of recognizable Hollywood stars as voice talent in recent computer-animated films, celebrity voices on children's records represented an appeal to parents more than children. Note as well the inclusion of epic and melodramatic narratives in the repertoire of kidisks, such as Decca's 1946 *Lost Horizons* starring Ronald Colman and *The Snow Goose* featuring Herbert Marshall. Such titles suggest that mothers might well have enjoyed listening to records that were ostensibly marketed to children. Ann Gray has made a similar argument about the videocassette market. Gray writes that watching videos with children justified "different kinds of pleasures" for women who would otherwise have felt guilty about watching children's and fantasy genres of entertainment.[103] In an era before videocassettes, children's records may have served as an alibi for the female consumption of similar genres of recorded entertainment.

We should not overlook the erotic appeal of the voices of stars such as Herbert Marshall and Ronald Colman. In a *House Beautiful* article from 1963, reference was made to the pleasure that the voice on spoken word LPs could provide to women: "Your imagination is more active when the seductive voice of an actor lulls you into the enjoyment of simply listening," the author wrote, adding that "being read to by the world's most skillful voices would be judged a pleasure by anybody's scale of values. But when you can control these voices to read you the world's greatest literature while you are lolling at ease or doing some needed task with your hands, it is a deluxe delight of the first order."[104] These passages hint at pleasures of hi-fi listening beyond catching up on classic literature.[105] Dylan Thomas in particular was described in terms of the sensual quality of his voice. Note how Brinnin described his vocal presence at public recitations:

> The enormous range and organ-deep resonance of his voice . . . gave new music to familiar cadences and, at times, revealed values in the poems never disclosed on the page. When he concluded the evening with a selection of his own works—encompassing both tenderly lyrical and oratorical passages with absolute authority, it was difficult to know which gave the greater pleasure, the music or the meaning. Some of his listeners were moved by the almost sacred sense of his approach to language . . . some were entertained merely by the plangent virtuosity of an actor with a great voice.[106]

A typical review of Thomas's records described his "barrel-bodied voice" with its "organ-like resonance" and his "lilt and incantatory style."[107] *Holiday* magazine wrote in 1953 that Thomas was "more than excellent. He is exciting. Most of the time I don't know what he's talking about, but it doesn't matter much. His rapt tones—bardic, I suppose is the word—have an incantatory quality that sets the imagination a-shiver. He reads as we fancy Homer might have sung."[108] Critic Edward Canby wrote in *Harper's* of Thomas's "glorious bardic flow of such English as must have been spoken in the great Elizabethan days, so rich, so varied, so vigorous."[109]

The "incantatory" quality described in reviews such as these is what Jed Rasula calls an "oracular declamatory style" that has been a persistent feature of Western poetry reading: a droning mode of recitation suggestive of "the bardic posture of superior wisdom."[110] The incantatory style negotiates between speaking and singing, and so between two ways of perceiving the voice. Reuven Tsur describes a poetic mode of sound perception, one that is able to activate both speech and nonspeech modes of listening and so overcome the usual "channel separation" of speech and nonspeech perception.[111] Thomas's style of recitation facilitates such an audio balancing act. He pitched his deep, powerful voice near the top of his range, in a singsong musical cadence thick with expressive tremolo, recorded, as we have seen, in a manner meant to emphasize these nuances. Not only did this give his voice a musical quality, but it suggested a kind of delicate emotional intensity beneath the "barrel-bodied" voice. Thomas keyed the poetic mode of listening in part by making his vowels hover around a regular range of pitches, but never becoming so regularized as to fall into a clearly defined key or dominant pitch. In other words, his speech is always threatening to become song but never quite does. His consonants were spoken with relish, often with an emphasis on the last consonants of each word, which created a temporal undertow to the forward propulsion of verbal meaning. His words were thus given shape on both sides, becoming sonic objects d'art, allowing the listener to savor each word, retrospectively accentuated as if by backlighting. What results is a vocal performance that was both bardic and musical.[112] Thomas, a reviewer noted, could turn out to be "to poetry what Caruso was to music."[113] Thomas's visceral performance of high culture invited comparisons to the famous operatic tenor and phonograph star, although, given Caedmon's intimate approach to recording and Thomas's erotically charged material, it might have been more accurate to think of the poet in relation to a radio crooner.

One effect of the erotic appeal of Thomas's voice was that his records could function as a vocal stand-in for courtship: Library of Congress poetry consultant Randall Jarrell estimated in 1956 that "hundreds of young men were playing Dylan Thomas to hundreds of girls in Greenwich Village."[114] We might also note the young poet Sylvia Plath's habit of lending her Dylan Thomas records to young men in whom she was interested.[115] A *Newsweek* feature on Caedmon described a letter from a female listener who wrote to say that she played her Thomas LP "as the last thing she does every night before going to bed—whatever that signifies."[116] The sensual pleasure of the incantatory voice, then, was clearly part of the appeal of spoken word recordings for some female listeners.

Though the erotic quality of the reader's voice was certainly a selling point, articles in newspapers and women's magazines more typically stressed the spoken word LP's utility for housewives as a means of self-improvement. Postwar spoken word records were said to provide models of proper speaking. In one article, Charles Laughton and Dylan Thomas were offered as "a first-hand demonstration of just how potent an instrument the human voice can be": "Listen to . . . them and you'll be inspired to try reading aloud to yourself. What such practice can do to your conversational voice is exactly what should happen to any woman who aspires to be a charmer."[117] A book entitled *Spoken Records* published in 1963 noted that the best spoken word records communicated "more than entertainment" and contained "essential soundings in spoken language which have become increasingly missing from the American oral tradition, because of the long exclusiveness of writing in our educational pattern. The better records can and do carry implicit ear training and incentives to more distinguished use of spoken language than adults of the present age have generally received in their schooling."[118] In rhetoric such as this, spoken word LPs became practical tools for improving the voice, an area in which women were often judged.

LPs of the world's great literature read by skillful readers were also offered as a way to stimulate women's minds while their hands were busy with routine household tasks. In 1961 the *Saturday Review* claimed that LPs featuring Shakespeare read by Ronald Colman and Lincoln's speeches read by Raymond Massey appealed to "busy housewives who listen as they work," and thus were "operating on a higher level than the conventional busy housewife with her radio and television."[119] The author of a 1961 article in *House Beautiful* noted that LPs provided a way to make women's "precious time pay off double": "You can listen to these talking records while doing almost any routine and therefore mindless household task. I listened to the complete and unabridged 'Meditations of Marcus Aurelius' while cooking, washing dishes, darning socks, knitting, tidying bureau drawers, and doing my nails. And I refinished furniture while renewing my acquaintance with Washington Irving, Jonathan Swift, and H.G. Wells."[120] The author noted, "Once you get into the habit of listening while working, you're so oblivious to tedious chores that you are willing to take on more of them": "Now, with the availability of such spoken literature, you have been robbed of that old excuse about 'I haven't the time to read.' They've made the time for you."[121] Spoken word records could thus subtly add to the pressures on postwar homemakers, who were expected to be literate and well-read companions as well as full-time domestic laborers.

The LP's educational potential for busy housewives should be understood in a postwar context in which institutionalized gender imbalances existed in university admissions policies. Colleges and universities experienced tremendous growth after the war, due in large part to the 1944 G.I. Bill. Holdridge stated that, when she and Mantell started in 1952, "the G.I. Bill was producing a generation of college-educated young men who had studied English and American literature and were avid for our recordings."[122] Notably, feminist historians have argued that the G.I. Bill represented an educational subsidy that largely excluded women. By 1947 male veterans made up nearly half of college enrollments, and their entry onto college campuses came at the expense of women: "Many schools scaled back female admissions to permit male attendance to more than double."[123] Elaine Tyler May writes that the number of women in college was also rising at this time but represented a smaller percentage of the student population. Furthermore, women were less likely to complete their degrees: many women achieved upward mobility "not through their occupations but by attaching themselves to well-educated men who had good occupational prospects."[124] As May notes, many of the women who attended but did not necessarily complete university went on to discover that "professionalized homemaking was not enough to keep their minds alive."[125] For some critics, high culture records were thought to remedy these problems: *House Beautiful* wrote that such records helped to bridge the "intellectual gap between husbands and wives when one has gone to college and the other hasn't." Records were also said to help to ease the imbalance between parents and their "student offspring": "When children come home from college with minds fired by some philosopher or historian, a parent who hasn't cracked a book on the subject in 25 years will find the records a face-saving college refresher course."[126]

Spoken word LPs like Caedmon's were not heard only by isolated housewives, but could also become the focal point of other, more social forms of media consumption. *Time* wrote in 1963 that "theater, poetry, and other spoken-word recordings" were an important part of "the surprising girth and growth of the U.S. culture boom" and that Caedmon releases were being heard in "play-listening house parties."[127] Caedmon's advertising made reference to similar contexts of domestic listening. A 1961 ad in the *New York Times* pictured two young couples gathered around the stereo, while the copy described how "President Kennedy, his family and distinguished guests" had enjoyed "a command performance of *Macbeth* and other Shakespeare plays at the White House. Now you too can command performances of whatever Shakespeare play you desire in the comfort of your own home. . . . Enjoy your own Shakespeare festival with your living room as the stage." A recurring feature in *House Beautiful* magazine described spoken word LPs as a way to keep adult socializing in the home and thus avoid the hassles of "baby-sitter, weather, and traffic problems": "You can enjoy listening to these records alone, in a cozy twosome, or in a group. In a group where listeners discuss what they hear, you can almost see sparks fly when the flint of one mind strikes the tinder of another."[128] "Many hostesses," the author continued, "plan parties around the recordings, using them as conversation-starters or subjects for lively group discussions." As an example, the article made reference to the Academic Recording Institute's Time for Ideas records, which were compared to college seminars on topics such as anthropology, American history, and philosophy. The creator, Mack Reed, explained why he made the series: "My wife and I agreed, along with our friends, that we were falling into an intellectual rut. We were tied down with four kids and TV. We didn't read the same books—at least not at the same time—which precluded discussion along that line. When you have a bunch of kids, it's almost impossible to attend lectures, and neither of us encouraged the other to go out nights alone."[129] In another article, the same author recommended throwing "theater parties" in which groups of friends would gather to listen to a recording of "a full-scale stage hit with a star-studded cast": "If going to a live performance means battling for tickets, driving miles, and fighting traffic, your friends will prefer to take their drama in armchair comfort with congenial company, in the enticing atmosphere of your home. Besides, the spirited group discussion or debate that follows, say, Shaw's *Saint Joan* or Sartre's *No Exit,* is a bonus of participation that the live theater seldom offers."[130] Lynn Spigel notes that it has become a "truism among cultural historians and media scholars that television's growth after World War II was part of a general return to family values." "Less attention," she writes, has been devoted to media-related "neighborhood bonding and community participation."[131] The communal reception of educational records illustrated here provides a case study in that alternative history of postwar media reception.

The coverage of configurations of home reception such as these in women's magazines demonstrates the ways in which Caedmon marketed drama and modern poetry to a female audience and so provides another way to account for the rare success of this female-owned record company. We might draw a parallel here to the cosmetics industry, where promotional strategies such as "house-to-house canvassing" had allowed businesswomen with less access than men to credit and business education to rise to the highest levels of success and authority.[132] At the same time, we have seen how marketing and press discourse depicted these recordings taking on a variety of functions in the postwar American home. High culture spoken word LPs served as an antidote for household imbalances in education; as a form of sensual pleasure and intellectual engagement for individual homemakers; as a companion to housework; and as a prop for social interaction among couples. By multiplying the pragmatic functions of modern poetry and drama, Caedmon embodied the threat of middlebrow culture to undermine "the notion of aesthetic autonomy" through a bid to be "at once politically effective, morally responsible, commercially successful, and culturally respectable."[133] Not only was Caedmon commercially successful and culturally responsible, its releases even became a key part of national classroom education. Holdridge and Mantell's company was lifted into the economic stratosphere by postwar government spending on education. Title 1 of the Elementary and Secondary Education Act of 1965 led to a "phenomenal growth of spending for education": between 1954 and 1964, outlays for education rose 142 percent, including approximately $100 million for school libraries, textbooks, and audiovisual materials.[134] In a 1967 interview, the Caedmon founders asserted that 40 percent of the company's business came from the purchase of educational records by schools and community libraries.[135] Holdridge stated that Title 1 had given schools money to buy audiovisual equipment, which had then necessitated the purchase of educational recordings and so made "all the difference" between Caedmon's stature as a "small though highly regarded recording company and the multi-million dollar company" it became in the 1960s: "Previously, schools had purchased ones and twos. Now they bought hundreds at a time." The new importance of the school business made Caedmon "a hot property for acquisition by major American companies."[136] Indeed, Caedmon was incorporated into HarperCollins in 1986.

By the time of Caedmon's sale to HarperCollins, the spoken word record was no longer the only electronic medium for high culture in the home. Another alternative to network television materialized with the transformation of the scattered educational television stations into the Public Broadcasting Service (PBS) in the late 1960s. A decade after Freida Hennock's campaign for educational TV, FCC chair Newton Minow obtained increased funding for educational stations and Congress established the nonprofit Corporation for Public Broadcasting in 1967. In the face of pressure from conservative administrations, PBS reduced its public affairs and experimental formats, replacing them with "high-toned cultural programming and imports of British television dramas."[137] American television audiences could, by the 1970s, enjoy dramatizations of classic literature in the home on PBS's *Masterpiece Theater* (1971–) or *Great Performances* (1972–).

If PBS partially supplanted the LP as a medium for high culture media entertainment in the home, audiocassette technology proliferated such entertainment outside the home. In 1986 *Time* described a burgeoning "books on tape" market then worth $250 million and foresaw a "big future" for the trade, predicting a "50% to 100% growth in the next five years."[138] In some respects, the consumption of books on tape continued the practices of spoken word LPs. Writing in 1995, Sarah Kozloff estimated that 50 percent of audio book consumption was intended as a distraction from "tedious, arduous and or solitary activities" such as ironing and knitting.[139] Notably, Kozloff argued that the other 50 percent of listening occurred while driving in cars, where listening was primarily done alone.[140] Similarly, *Time* stated that a key factor in the booming audio book trade was the recent prevalence of tape decks in cars, adding that "Walkman-style cassette players" had become "as much a part of the urban landscape as Reeboks and Perrier."[141] One result of the proliferation of cassette players, particularly those installed in cars, was to encourage the solitary use of spoken word recordings, as opposed to the "spirited group discussion" described as a key part of the experience of hearing spoken word LPs in the home.

The books on tape market should be placed in the context of what Frederick Wasser calls the "harried leisure phenomenon" of the last decades of the twentieth century. An increase in the number of families with two working parents and a suburban lifestyle that required more commuting in cars fed consumer desire for media products such as the VCR, which provided more choices about when and what to watch: "The combination of product choice and time flexibility was sufficient to make [the VCR] ideal for a new lifestyle of more work and shifting schedules."[142] Books on tape could be made to fit with what Wasser calls the "fragmented patterns of family life" in a way that phonograph records could not. We should note that postwar discourses surrounding spoken word LPs reveal the home to have already been a site of "harried leisure" for many housewives. Surveying the rise of the books on tape market, Barbara Holdridge stated that the spoken word industry had "changed to suit the automobile culture that snatches its reading on the road, just as it does its soft drinks and burritos." She took "pleasure and pride," however, in Caedmon's having been "the progenitors, the mothers, if you will," of the spoken word industry.[143] Holdridge and Mantell were also trailblazers as female senior-level executives in a record industry that, even at the end of the 1990s, still had few women in decision-making positions and frequent incidents of sexual harassment in the workplace.[144]

Dylan Thomas, of course, did not fare as well as Holdridge and Mantell. At his second Caedmon recording session in 1953, the poet's appearance caused alarm: he was bloated, his arm in a sling, a cut over his eye, and his suit was smeared "with what looked like vomit." In the studio he was morose, and the reading of his "Poem on His Birthday" caused him trouble, particularly the last line, "As I sail out to die," which he could not read in a way that satisfied him.[145] Holdridge stated later that the line, which he had repeated again and again, still sounded "a little strange" when she heard the record years later.[146] Throughout this chapter, I have returned to Thomas's reading at the Kaufmann Auditorium as an emblematic event, one that can help us to understand some of the cultural forces shaping the market for postwar spoken word records. Thomas's last recording session is equally suggestive of the richness and complexity of spoken word records as modern performances. Recordings of Thomas's intimate readings were part of a revival of Victorian era discourses of domestic recitation as an antidote to popular culture but also helped to create new forms of media celebrity for poets as readers. Caedmon's recordings captured one of the most celebrated poets of the postwar era as he lingered in front of the microphone, doing multiple takes to find the right vocal nuance to convey the essence of a line like a movie actor, aware perhaps that he would be remembered as much via the long-playing record as by the written word.

In an insightful discussion of poetry recitation, Charles Bernstein points out that, where writing is typically understood to stabilize oral poetic traditions, authorial poetry readings destabilize poetic practice by making it "fluid and multiform": "a poem understood as a performative event and not merely as a textual entity refuses the originality of the written document in favor of 'the plural event' of the work . . . to speak of the poem in performance is, then, to overthrow the idea of the poem as a fixed, stable, finite linguistic object."[147] Here, then, is another example of the threat of hi-fi midcult records: they destabilized traditional protocols of text-based poetry and allowed the incantatory style of poetry recitation to take on new forms in the studio and new functions in the home. But Thomas's second and final Caedmon session suggests that something else is happening here as well. Thomas's attention to the line "as I sail out to die" reveals his awareness that record making was not only a matter of destabilizing poetic practice but also a means of restabilizing or fixing it; in other words, recording could also be a form of poetic writing.

CHAPTER 3

33 ⅓ Sexual Revolutions per Minute

In 1966 a man named Joe Davis was convicted by a federal jury of sending obscene materials through the mail. Davis was fined one thousand dollars and given a suspended sentence of six months in jail, despite the fact that the items that Davis had mailed contained no explicit images of bodies or sexual activity and, in some cases, no discernible verbal content at all: Davis had been dealing in erotic phonograph records. In historical surveys that discuss the role of the media in the sexual revolution, mention has been made of films (the fall of the Hollywood production code, sexually explicit European imports, the rise of the porn feature), books (the Kinsey reports, Masters and Johnson's *Human Sexual Response* [1966], Alex Comfort's *The Joy of Sex* [1972], Shere Hite's *The Hite Report* [1976]), magazines (Hugh Hefner's *Playboy*, Larry Flynt's *Hustler*, Al Goldstein's *Screw*), and television programs (*The Love Boat, Three's Company*, and *Charlie's Angles*). Little thought has been given to sexually explicit phonograph records, despite the fact that the recording industry enjoyed unprecedented prosperity and cultural influence during the decades of the sexual revolution. As we have seen, beginning in the late 1940s, a lively home market developed for long-playing recordings not only of music, but of poetry readings, children's entertainment, theatrical dramatizations, and comedy performances. Adult-themed records made between the 1950s and mid-1970s provide an overlooked case study of mass media erotica meant for home consumption before cable television or the explosion of porn on videocassette.

Under-the-counter recordings of erotic material—referred to as "blue discs" in 1930s and 1940s—attained a new degree of cultural visibility in the 1950s and 1960s. Postwar "party records" were often intended for a culture of male hi-fi aficionados, but during the same era, records made by female comics such as Rusty Warren presented bawdy material from a female perspective and reached legions of female fans. Warren's records were intended for mixed-gender social gatherings, but long-playing phonograph albums also functioned as a form of family sex education and home sex therapy for couples. Rudy Ray Moore and his collaborator Nancy "Lady" Reed were, along with Warren, among the most successful recordings artists working in this area.[1] Moore and Reed's LPs, which entered the *Billboard* soul chart in the early 1970s, presented an African American perspective both on blue discs of a previous era and on the best-selling sex manual *The Sensuous Woman* (1969). By placing Moore and Reed's work in a larger genre of erotic records, we can appreciate the ways in which it functioned to critique performance styles and attitudes heard on white erotica and provided an African American voice in the media discourse that constituted the sexual revolution. In all of these cases, the LP was well suited to the frank discussion and performance of sexuality, a point that performers often made by contrasting party records with network radio and television.

An examination of party records can fill a gap in the historical record of media consumption from this era and also illustrate different approaches to the vocal performance of erotic material. As such, one of the concerns of this chapter will be to examine the different ways that were found to "speak sex" for various home listening audiences. Indeed, one of the larger goals of this book is to explore the connection between performance and reception. Scholars of film reception such as Robert C. Allen have argued that cinema audiences are discursively constructed by such things as industry advertising and the design of movie theaters.[2] Styles of performance also play a role in constructing the intended audience. In her study of audiences in Africa, Karin Barber describes the role of performance in the formation of audiences: "Performances do not just play to ready-made congregations of spectators which are out there awaiting address; they convene those congregations and by their mode of address assign them a certain position from which to receive the address. Thus performances, in the act of addressing audiences, constitute those audiences as a particular form of collectivity."[3] Following Barber, I take the performances heard on party records as one form of evidence in the study of their reception. Before I begin a discussion of specific artists and LPs, however, I will situate party records in a post-war debate about "obscene" phonograph records: a topic that was the source of growing concern for law enforcement officers and legislators throughout the 1940s and 1950s.

The *New York Times* reported on November 1, 1942, that a campaign against "dealers in indecent phonograph recordings" was ordered by a police judge in Newark, New Jersey, after four owners of radio and music shops were charged with possessing obscene records. The fact that the judge also ordered a warrant for the arrest of a record distributor alleged to have "10,000 objectionable records in stock" reveals the extent of mass production and distribution in the operation.[4] Press coverage suggests that distributors of risqué records were increasingly at risk of prosecution toward the end of the 1940s. The *Lincoln Journal* reported on October 1, 1948 that the FBI had arrested a Kansas man on a charge of "illegally transporting obscene phonograph records between states." An FBI special agent stated that this was "the first case of its kind handled by the bureau." The arrested man was the operator of the Kansas City Music and Sales Company and had sold the records to "select customers on an under-the-counter basis."[5] As in other cases during the 1940s, law enforcement officials targeted music shops and record distributors who sold adult records to an exclusive clientele.[6]

Such was the case with Alexander L. Alpers, a San Francisco "record-shop operator" who was fined $200 by a district court in December 1948 for sending packages of allegedly indecent records out of state.[7] Alpers's conviction was overturned in June 1949 by the Ninth Federal Circuit Court, which stated that the law forbidding the shipment of obscene "matters" did not apply to phonograph records.[8] That ruling was overturned by the United States Supreme Court on February 7, 1950. In the *United States of America v. Alexander L. Alpers,* the court held that obscene phonograph records were within the prohibition of the United States code. In the wake of this decision, President Harry Truman updated federal law to include "obscene phonograph recordings and electrical transcriptions" in the ban on the interstate shipment of obscenity.[9] An article in the May 3, 1950 issue of *Variety* indicates that arrests continued after the new legislation: in a case called "the first of its kind" in Philadelphia, Albert L. Miller, owner of Palda Records, was indicted by the Federal Grand Jury on charges of "shipping pornographic recordings."[10] Although reports in the popular press suggest that the peak of law enforcement activity relating to obscene phonograph

records was in the late 1940s, the pursuit of obscene records continued. For example, the *Syracuse Herald-Journal* reported in 1958 that
six Queens music shops and a Manhattan record distributing house
were raided and eight men were arrested on charges of selling "obscene
phonograph records": "Hundreds of records, some selling as high as
$50 each, were seized."[11]

Press coverage thus indicates a thriving market for under-the-counter
risqué recordings in the 1940s and 1950s. But who was buying and
listening to these records? Under what social circumstances were they
played? What kinds of erotic performances did they contain? How did
party records fit into broader postwar discourses about gender and
sexuality? How did the content of adult records change during the
era of the sexual revolution? Information about these records is difficult to find, but one way we might begin to answer questions such
as these is by reference to the Joe Davis court case mentioned previously. One of the records that Davis sent through the mail was *Erotica:
The Rhythms of Love* (Fax Records). Later on, I will have occasion to
describe the performances heard on this record, but first consider the
dust jacket, which can provide some clues as to the nature of the audience for "obscene" records. The liner notes explain that *Erotica* was
"the culmination of more than two years of research, utilizing today's
most advanced electronic techniques and the talents of sound engineers
who have pioneered a host of technical achievements." The notes go on
to explain that a portion of the record was made "on a Magnecorder
PT6AH, using an RCA 77DX microphone, and taped at 15 ips (inches
per second)," with the help of an "Ampex 300 tape recorder." Perhaps
these esoteric technical facts were included to fend off obscenity charges
by demonstrating that the record held some kind of scientific merit. But
reference to such minutiae also suggests an address to a certain type of
audience: male hi-fi audio enthusiasts.

HI-FI HARD CORE

Many American men developed an interest in high-fidelity audio equipment after World War II, in part because of the extensive electronics
training they received in the armed forces. Writers such as Keir Keightley, Pamela Robertson Wojcik, and Barbara Ehrenreich have connected
the "masculinization" of hi-fi audio equipment at this time to larger
trends in postwar consumer culture. As men began to question their traditional role as breadwinner, the home hi-fi stereo became a male status

symbol to rival more traditional status objects that men had consumed vicariously, such as the family home and car: a notable shift from the female discourse surrounding the phonograph described in chapter 2. Ironically, while the hi-fi became an emblem of a new kind of male consumer spending, magazines marketed to audio enthusiasts often defined their own media consumption as a "high, masculine, individualistic art," in contrast to watching television, which was glossed as a "low, feminine, mass entertainment."[12]

Similar arguments can be heard on party records made during the era of high fidelity. Consider *Stag Party Special Number 1* (Fax Records), one of a series of records released in conjunction with the 1950s men's magazine *Adam*. Comic Buzzy Greene begins his burlesque club act by announcing, "You are now about to be the recipients of the last form of show business in the world today that has not been seen, or probably never will be seen on television—unless you have a very vivid imagination, and can picture Dr. Ross Dog Food or Texaco Gas sponsoring something like this, man! Huh, that'd be something wild!" Greene's comments illustrate how stag party records—like the audio tech magazines discussed by Keightley—presented hi-fi as an alternative to "the synthetic conformity of a society brainwashed by mass advertising."[13] In fact, risqué records might have held a particular appeal to hi-fi enthusiasts because they so bluntly transgressed the standards of network broadcasting.

Risqué records could also provide a means of bringing frank discussions of sex and the rough language traditionally associated with men into the home. I have described elsewhere how 78 rpm "blue discs" were heard in homosocial spaces such as the tavern and often featured joking traditions associated with male organizations.[14] Similarly, some postwar LPs advertised their ability to capture the language used by men in homosocial spaces such as stag parties, military barracks, and burlesque clubs. The liner notes for Fax Records' *Wild Party Songs Number 1: Saturday Night Riot* state that the "bone-tickling ditties of sin, sex and seduction" found on the album were "an important manifestation of our cultural heritage": "They are the lusty songs of men under stress, men who fought the wilderness, men who fought our wars, men protesting against tyranny and kings and poverty, men relishing the delights of their native customs and women. In army barracks, in ships at sea, at rotarian smokers, campus dormitories, now in 'polite' society, we hear these lusty refrains." Fax advertised some of its Stag Party records as documenting "private club dates and 'smoker' specials," where comedians could unleash "scorching gems of heavily-spiced ribaldry" that were "too bold for large night club audiences."[15] These records were thus representations of exclusive male social spaces as much as of a certain kind of language. In fact, *Saturday Night Riot* is among several Stag Party records to feature an ambient soundtrack running between musical numbers that includes the sounds of coughing, laughter, the clinking of glasses, and conversation. These ambient sounds make one wonder if "party records" were so named because they were meant to be played at parties or because they simulated a party atmosphere for isolated, suburban men.

Recall that the liner notes to *Wild Party Songs* had mentioned army barracks as one of the places where one could hear such "lusty refrains." In fact, military themes are prevalent on postwar party records, from Fax's series of Wild Service Songs albums to blue discs that dramatized the experience of American soldiers. For example, a record from the late 1940s entitled *Lt. Rudder* features a routine that circulated amongst soldiers during the final years of World War II. The routine was described in a 1945 Associated Press article: "Someone got weary of reading the honeyed accounts of America's returning air warriors and wrote a parody account of the homecoming of such a gay, cocky, young flier that has half the European theater of operations in stitches. The pilots, themselves, think it is wonderful, because they think the acclaim that greets their exploits is sometimes false and foolish and smacks of mock heroics."[16] The newspaper article could only reprint what it called a "heavily censored" version of the routine, with apologies to the original anonymous author, "in whatever pub or opium den he lies dreaming." The under-the-counter recording of the routine, however, was free to unleash Lt. Rudder in all his gay, cocky glory.

The Lt. Rudder skit articulated soldiers' ambivalent feelings about reintegrating into civilian life, where very different social rules held sway than in the homosocial context of the military. The record begins as an elaborate send-up of radio: following a fake commercial, we hear an earnest announcer declare that he is taking us to LaGuardia Airport for a special broadcast to welcome home Lt. Ronald Rudder, one of "America's leading aces" overseas. During a long build-up to the hero's arrival, we are introduced to Lt. Col. Eager Beaver, an army public relations man and liaison to Lt. Rudder. As side one of the record spins to a close, a crowd cheers and Rudder steps to the microphone. "How do you feel on being back in the United States again?" the reporter asks at the start of side two. Rudder replies in a matter-of-fact tone: "Uh, pretty damn pissed off." The army PR man anxiously interjects: "Lt. Rudder means his eyes were misty when the outlines of the States and Statue of Liberty—symbol of American faith and the fight for freedom—loomed into sight." The reporter comes back with a second question: "What's the first thing you're going to do in New York?" Rudder replies: "I'm going to go out and get laid." Again, Lt. Col. Beaver hastily cuts in to translate the flier's words into language fit for broadcast radio: "Uhh, he intends to say, he will fly back to his home and see his mom and all his folks." The record continues in this manner until Rudder announces: "Well, I'm sorry fellas, but I gotta get outta here before the bars close and line up a piece of ass, ya know?" Making one last attempt to clean up Rudder's statements, Lt. Col. Beaver quickly adds, "Yes, uh, Lt. Rudder can't wait to get back to a piece of his mother's apple pie, the girl he left behind, and, and, the old Main Street where he played Indian as a small boy."

The *Lt. Rudder* record mocks the platitudes and clichés of "false and foolish" accounts of male wartime experience—accounts that are associated both with feminized domestic life and broadcasting. Unlike radio and television, bawdy phonograph records such as *Lt. Rudder* and *In Hawaii* (a blue disc that dramatizes the adventures of two "lovable Marines" on leave in Honolulu) could present the rough, frank talk of soldiers while also providing a means of virtual escape from a postwar domestic space increasingly devoted to family togetherness.[17] We have seen that party records simulated spaces such as the burlesque club and the army barracks for a male audience. Party records were also released that represented another postwar male space: the "playboy" bachelor pad.

The Sweetest Music, an anonymous LP released circa the mid- to late-1960s, begins with a monologue by a man named Phil: "She worked on my staff at the office for several months. Cute little chick; nice shape; well-dressed, but very, very naïve. Dedicated? Uh! Last bird to leave the office almost every night. You know, babes are a dime a dozen for a swinging bachelor with a decked out pad. But Sheila played hard to get. 'No time for guys,' she said. She was strictly the career-girl type." Phil invites Sheila to help him celebrate his twenty-sixth birthday with "dinner and a night on the town." When she arrives at his apartment, Phil greets her with, "Come on right in, doll." "Hi, handsome," Sheila answers in a breathy whisper. "Hey, dig that sexy purple bathrobe." Phil whistles appreciatively and says, "My, aren't we dolled-up and lookin' groovy." After toasting to his birthday ("Here's cheers to our birthday boy. May the next twenty-five swing as madly as the first"), Sheila asks, "What are all those knobs sticking out of the wall, Phil?" "Little thing

I had installed a few months ago," Phil boasts, "stereo, FM, AM, the whole hi-fi bit. Music in every room in this pad, baby."

The Sweetest Music thus provides an audio representation of the playboy apartment that indicates the centrality of the hi-fi to the sexual arsenal of men like Phil (or the men who fantasized about being like Phil).[18] Steven Cohan has described the playboy apartment as a "theatrical backdrop" for the performance of male sexuality, a "fantasy playpen" that used modern technology for the single purpose of seduction.[19] Scholars such as Cohan, Osgerby, and Ehrenreich have emphasized the importance of the playboy apartment as a site of male consumerism.[20] Indeed, we should note how seduction and consumerism are combined in the *Sweetest Music* LP, since it offers a commodified enactment of sexual seduction to be consumed via the preferred medium of the playboy apartment: the hi-fi.

The Sweetest Music dramatizes seduction with a type of erotic vocal performance that distinguishes adult LPs made during the era of the sexual revolution from their predecessors. After treating Sheila to the "electronic pleasure provider" on his sensual reclining seat and dancing to music from his hi-fi, Phil lights a Tibetan candle and orally pleases Sheila, signified by the smacking of kisses, sighs, moans, and heavy breathing. This is a type of verbal performance that Rich Cante and Angelo Restivo have called porno-performativity.[21] Blue discs of a previous era only rarely attempted to depict the sex act with that kind of unrestrained vocalization. Instead, 78 rpm blue discs typically featured double entendres, riddles, and short burlesque sketches that suggested but did not explicitly state erotic ideas and situations. The extended porno-performativity heard on *The Sweetest Music* is made possible in part by the introduction of long-playing 33⅓ rpm records, first widely produced by Columbia Records in 1948. LPs provided the time to develop longer erotic narratives and to enact extended sessions of hard-core sexual action. During the moments of porno-performativity on *The Sweetest Music,* however, we are often unable to distinguish who is vocalizing, or even who is doing what to whom. We are left with only the vague outlines of a sex scene, as if the action were obscured by the pungent smoke of Phil's Tibetan candle.

A similar attempt at long-playing hard core can be heard on *Erotica: The Rhythm of Love,* one of the records involved in the 1966 Joe Davis obscenity trial. The recording is comprised of two overlapping tracks, one featuring an erratic bongo drum performance punctuated by occasional nonsensical vocal exclamations, and the other the sounds of a squeaking bed over which we hear a woman's periodic gasps and grunts. The jibberish of the bongo player seems meant to signify the primal quality of sex. Consider the liner notes: "The sounds you will hear in this recording will delight you. They express beauty and meaning that can be admired and understood by the primitive native and the sophisticated cosmopolitanite, by members of any society, past, present or future." As with *The Sweetest Music,* the effect is more disconcerting than erotic. In fact, the legal discussion surrounding *Erotica* reveals considerable ambiguity about whether the record was obscene at all. In a 1959 U.S. Post Office investigation of the Fax Record Company, it was stated that the "exclamations, cries, moans, sighs, words and other sounds" heard on *Erotica* captured "every possible sound made by the parties or by the bed on which the act of sexual intercourse takes place" and so left "no doubt in the mind of any listener" as to what was being recorded. The post office declared the record to be obscene because it left "nothing to the imagination as to what is going on, [and] set forth the act of sexual intercourse in its most lustful aspect."[22]

Circuit judge Sterry R. Waterman, however, said that the records in the Joe Davis case failed to appeal to his prurient interest, adding: "I must say that they bored me." Likewise, Supreme Court justice Potter Stewart, in his dissenting opinion, called the title *Erotica* a "gross misnomer."[23] We might understand these comments as evidence to support Linda Williams's claim that "there can be no such thing as hard-core sound."[24] Unlike the visual depiction of male orgasm, vocalizations such as those heard on the *Erotica* LP did not count as irrefutable proof that sex had taken place. The attempt to produce indexical audio evidence of intercourse in the case of *Erotica* was deemed by some listeners to be ridiculous. Ironically, it was when phonograph records were purporting to capture hard-core sexual action that they became less threatening to the prosecutors of obscenity. At a time when hard-core visual images in magazines and theatrical films were becoming more prevalent and when 8 and 16mm adult films made for home consumption were a growing concern of the U.S. Post Office, the content of these records must have seemed comparatively less prurient, not the pressing legal concern that obscene records had been a decade earlier.[25] The trade in small-gauge home movies and erotic LPs shared a site of intended reception in the home, and so both of these enterprises would have been encouraged by the Supreme Court's 1969 *Stanley v. Georgia* decision, which distinguished between public exhibition of pornography and home consumption. If, in the words of Justice Thurgood Marshall, the state had no business telling "a man, sitting alone in his own house, what books he may read or what films he may watch," neither did it have any business telling "a man" what records he could listen to on his hi-fi.

The sexist language in Marshall's statement is, of course, a product of its time but also points to gendered assumptions about the consumers of adult material. I have been arguing that *The Sweetest Music* and *Erotica* were intended primarily for a home audience of men that overlapped with a culture of hi-fi audio buffs. Records such as these experimented with the LP as a means of erotic escapism and audio voyeurism for male enthusiasts in the 1950s and 1960s. As we have seen in the previous chapter, postwar phonograph culture was not only the province of men.[26] In fact, other party records released during the early 1960s—records whose popularity eclipsed that of *Erotica* and *The Sweetest Music*—featured a female perspective on adult material and were made for a largely female audience.

KNOCKERS UP

During the 1950s, female performers such as Belle Barth, Pearl Williams, and Ruth Wallis delivered bawdy material in nightclub appearances and on live recordings of their acts. In the early 1960s, the most successful female performer in this style was Rusty Warren. Born Ilene Goldman in New York in 1931, she graduated from Boston's New England Conservatory of Music in 1952 and began playing in upstate New York lounges. By the end of the decade she had developed a risqué act and was selling records of her club performances. "At that time those records were not sold in stores," she said in a 1994 interview. "I was constantly touring in cities and towns, working in little lounges. After the show people would come up and I'd sell them an album, take a card and put them on a mailing list."[27] Her first record, *Songs for Sinners,* was released in 1959, followed by *Knockers Up!* a year later, and both *Bounces Back* and *Sin-Sational!* in 1961. We might gauge her popularity in the early 1960s by looking at the *Billboard* charts. *Knockers Up!* debuted at number thirty-one on November 7, 1960. It was still going strong at number twenty-six on April 7, 1962. In fact, Warren had four LPs in the charts that week: in addition to *Knockers Up!*, *Bounces Back* was at number thirty-five, *Sin-Sational* was number seventy-nine, and *Songs for Sinners* was number one hundred twenty-eight. As these chart positions indicate, she was certainly selling records: an advertisement in *Parade* magazine in December 1961 claimed that she had sold two

FIGURE 4. LP cover: one of Rusty Warren's popular recordings of the early 1960s. Used by permission of GNP Crescendo Records (gnpcrescendo.com).

million albums, and a 1963 newspaper ad stated that "in recordland she's a living legend—3,000,000 LP sales in little over a year."[28]

Warren was even featured in *Time* magazine in January 1963, albeit with an unfavorable review. "She is just another dirty comedian who deprives sex of all its grace and sophistication," wrote the reviewer, "while she claims to be helping inhibited females to enjoy themselves." That statement indicates an important fact about Warren's audience: it consisted to a large degree of women.[29] In fact, the *Time* review focused more on her audience than her act:

> The incredible thing about Rusty Warren is the crowds she draws. She has just left Mr. Kelly's in Chicago, where Greyhound buses arrived every day from assorted plains cities full of jolly, plump, graying matrons dying to see their goddess. Car pools came in from Iowa and far Missouri. "The women

are usually 40 to 50 or more, and hefty," she says. Many women regularly bring their husbands to hear her, blue-suit and brown-shoe types that have never seen a nightclub. Like Rusty, they all seem at home in a barnyard. They sit there and roar happily as Rusty expresses her desire to become the first woman to make love to an astronaut in space. The women fans wear Knockers Up buttons. They know her first LP albums by heart (more than 3,000,000 sold so far). They have made her a $5,000-a-week nightclub star, outdrawing Mort Sahl and Shelley Berman.[30]

The *Time* author clearly has disdain for Warren's audience members because of their age and social class, but most of all because of their gender.

Warren was very aware of her appeal to women, as can be gauged by the manner in which she addressed her audience. For example, on *Knockers Up!* she begins by stating: "As I look around I see a lot of married couples in the audience tonight, so if I may, I would like to talk to the wives, about what they brought with them." Furthermore, her material often pointed out male sexual inadequacies. On *Bounces Back,* Warren talks about men's loss of sexual vitality after marriage: "He was young, insistent, vital, strong, passionate. Yes, he was a youthful sex maniac! And ladies, here we sit; ten, twelve, fifteen years later, with *him.* Where did he go? Where is the mad sex maniac today when we want it? Have we not had our basic training? Did he not teach us all he knows? Oh, great white father! And now that we know what we know, *where the hell is he?*" At another point, Warren describes a newlywed couple in their honeymoon hotel suite. The bashful wife emerges, wrapped in a towel. "My dear," the husband says, "we're married now, you can drop the towel." He is so struck by the sight of her naked body that he asks if he can take a picture of her, saying, "I want to carry it close to my heart for the rest of my life." The wife then asks the husband to remove *his* robe, after which she asks, "May I take your picture?" The husband flexes his muscles and says, "Yes. What do you want to do with it?" Warren delivers the punch line: "Have it enlarged!" This joke was dramatized on an earlier 78 rpm blue disc called *Newlyweds*: an indication of how a frank discussion of male inadequacy was always present on blue discs. Warren brought that type of bawdy humor to a more mainstream and largely female audience.

But although Warren deflated male pride and made female sexual desire explicit, the showcase of her act was a burlesque of female social action. At the close of her set on *Knockers Up!,* Warren adopts a serious tone and delivers this recitation: "We girls figure that we have a lot to project in this world today. . . . These men are campaigning to give the best they have. Then we, of course, must campaign to give the best that *we* have. So if I may, I would like to do a number for the young ladies to prove that we *do* have something to give. Are you girls ready?" What follows is a military march on drums and piano, with Warren shouting: "Knockers up! Come on girls, throw those shoulders back and get your knockers up!" Apparently, some women did in fact march through the room when Warren played this song: she stated, "Women used to march outside, around buildings and all over the place!"[31] On the follow-up LP, *Bounces Back,* Warren presented a spin-off of the successful *Knockers Up!* routine. Again, she takes on a mock serious tone, shifting from a sexual to a political register: "These men, their ancestors have given us our political freedom. There is no reason today why we should not have sexual freedom." Patriotic music swells as Warren explains, "You know girls, it's great to live in a democracy today, where freedom is everywhere. But girls, we often take this freedom for granted. . . . Proclaim your freedom! Stand at attention! Pledge allegiance, and . . ." On cue, a jaunty musical number begins, with Warren singing: "Bounce your boobies, get into the swing!" "Loosen the bra that binds you," she shouts, "take it off if you feel like it!"

These ridiculous spoofs of female empowerment can make contemporary listeners a bit uncomfortable, as they seem to both objectify and condescend to the women in her audience. It is as if the critical moments in her act needed to be defused, laughed away as the harmless expression of female silliness. Nonetheless, we shouldn't dismiss the transgressive pleasure that Warren's routines clearly provided to her female fans. In fact, Warren's conflation of "knockers" and politics simply exaggerated the prevailing national obsession with large breasts. On *Bounces Back,* Warren quipped, "You have to have big knockers to be a star," and listed Jayne Mansfield, Gina Lollobrigida, Marilyn Monroe, and Elizabeth Taylor as evidence. The fact that Warren's "Knockers Up" and "Bounce Your Boobies" routines equate breasts with power, freedom, and social agency ("we *do* have something to give") draws attention to prevailing standards concerning the female body and so perhaps registered as a subtle social critique.

We should note that Warren's transgressions were counterbalanced by her tendency to portray herself in a grotesque manner: she often referred to her less than ideal sex life and sadly inadequate "knockers." In this, Warren was similar to "unruly" female burlesque performers such as Mae West, Sophie Tucker, and Bessie Smith: performers whose transgressive power "was channeled and defused through their con-struction as grotesque figures."[32] Warren also disregarded standards of femininity with regard to her voice. This is not the place for an exhaus-tive history of female vocal etiquette, but suffice it to say that since at least the turn of the century, American women were encouraged to consider their voices as a potential problem and urged to keep their voices low and free from a raspy or nasal tone.[33] We might note that the most iconic "erotic voice" of the era belonged to Marilyn Monroe, who presented a breathy whisper similar to Sheila's on *The Sweetest Music*. By contrast, Warren presents erotic material not with a demure, sensual whisper but with a loud, full-voiced rasp.

Warren's approach was influenced by earlier bawdy female comics who transgressed the cultural rules of female vocal production: Pearl Williams, for example, delivered her jokes with a harsh, raucous laugh. In an insightful essay on female comics, Michael Bronski argues that Williams and Belle Barth were part of "a distinct Jewish show-biz cul-ture" descended from "Yiddish shtetl culture," which he argues had "long appreciated publicly assertive women": "After all, while men were expected to stay at home and study the Torah, women were in the public sphere, the marketplace, and the street. Such publicness often lent itself to outspoken candor—especially after immigration to the US."[34] The bold, brash voices of these female comics served to project their bodily presence and assert themselves as sexual subjects. More than this, Warren conveys a remarkable sense of freedom through her gym-nastic vocal ability: one minute she has the exaggerated high-pitched tone of a child, the next she delivers a salty punch line in a throaty rasp, and later she belts out a song with a deep, powerful chest voice. Warren said in an email interview that she "played an androgynous role, yell-ing, shouting, being unladylike," but added that she "had to be careful not to cross over into vulgarity. I was extremely careful never to veer into that zone at all. My worst words were hell, damn." Here we find an indication of the importance of vocal inflection as a means of managing the risks involved in delivering erotic material as well as a rejection of certain codes of femininity and heterosexual intimacy.

For now, we should note that, despite the fact that Warren's "unlady-like" vocalizing added to her self-presentation as a grotesque figure, many of Warren's fans still perceived her act in socially progressive terms. In fact, Warren was sometimes billed in the later years of her career as the "Mother of the Sexual Revolution," a claim that we might understand in several ways. First, Warren's records were an early example of an increasingly frank discussion of sex by women in the mass media, a trend that would become more pronounced later in the decade. Consider that David Allyn begins his history of the sexual revolution with the release of Helen Gurley Brown's 1962 book, *Sex and the Single Girl,* arguing that the American public adored Brown's "breezy style, forthright manner, and pragmatic attitude about premarital romance."[35] Barbara Ehrenreich, Elizabeth Hess, and Gloria Jacobs note that Gurley Brown's book was a best seller at a time before "feminism" existed in "the American political vocabulary" and demonstrated that "extramarital sex did not have to mean ruin."[36] We should note Warren's presence on the American entertainment scene in the years immediately before and during the release of *Sex and the Single Girl* as well as the fact that she presented a similarly "breezy" and "forthright" message about female sexual desire and the limitations of traditional courtship and marriage.[37]

Warren stated that women in the early 1960s were "admitting that they liked sex, and that they liked men looking sexy. They were coming out of their shell of sexual inhibitedness—the way they'd been trained. That's why I was titillating them; they were trained not to talk this way, and here I was doing it!"[38] On a fan website dedicated to Warren, an anonymous essayist argues that the comedienne "used humor to deliver her message that women do have sexual appetites" and did so at a time when female sexuality was "extremely repressed." Note how the author describes the nightclub audiences heard on Warren's 1960s records:

> These couples are the heads of suburban households, the mom and pop of nuclear families—or they are on the path to being such. The women sit in clothing that today seems glamorous, at least to me, but underneath their cocktail dresses, their lives are more restrictive than their foundation garments. They chafe not from underwires and rubber, but from the reality of being "Mom" even to their husbands. They dressed that night with hopes that "Daddy" would see them, once again, as a woman. They hopped the alcohol would loosen inhibitions just as they had when they were dating—and that they'd find themselves steaming up the backseat of the car, or at the very least, they'd get some action once they got home. Oh, pray that he wouldn't drink too much and the only activity she'd see would be removing his clothing as she tucked him in.[39]

The author of this passage understood Warren's records as historical documents of a time when women were waking up to the consequences of cultural double standards relating to sex and marriage. The author even goes on to offer Warren as the female answer to Hugh Hefner and *Playboy:* "Rusty exposed male hypocrisy, gender stereotypes, and the female libido to a conservative American public." These are dramatic claims, and authors such as Michel Foucault have taught us to be wary of the suggestion that sexuality has been repressed. Nevertheless, accounts of her legions of female fans, sell-out performances, and chart-topping LPs indicate that Warren did undoubtedly strike a nerve with a generation of women.

It is in generational terms that we might understand the claim that Warren was the Mother of the Sexual Revolution: she was literally entertaining the *mothers* of the generation that would become sexually active in the 1960s. Consider that on her LP *More Knockers Up!* Warren tells the parents in her audience not to worry about their children. "It is now 9:15," she says, "and all your teenagers are home in front of the television set watching the Beatles. So mothers, don't even call home for the next hour, because if the phone rings, they won't answer it." Indeed, the boisterous female audience members who can be heard on Warren's LPs should be placed in the history of popular culture beside the screaming female fans at performances by rock bands such as the Beatles. Ehrenreich, Hess, and Jacobs argue that the screams of female Beatles fans were a form of cathartic release from sexual repression: "Adulation of the male star was a way to express sexual yearnings that would normally be pressed into the service of popularity or simply repressed. The star could be loved noninstrumentally, for his own sake, and with complete abandon. Publicly to advertise this hopeless love was to protest the calculated, pragmatic sexual repression of teenage life."[40] Though she had a much different relationship with her female fans, Warren served a similar function for an older generation of women who were, in their own way, obliquely protesting the calculated repression of married life. Here, then, is an explanation for the dismissive portrayal of the middle-aged female audience at Warren's club appearances found in the *Time* magazine review cited earlier. Beatles fans and "single girls" were carving out a cultural space for the expression of a certain female sexual agency, but this was confined to "girls." Warren's misbehaving middle-aged audiences did not fit with that emerging cultural script and so seemed aberrant and troubling in the eyes of the article's author.

Warren's quip about the kids at home watching the Beatles on television can also be heard as another instance of a rhetoric that contrasted adult phonograph records and broadcast entertainment. In fact, Warren's *Banned in Boston* LP contains a musical number called "Pay As You See TV," in which she imagines a future where viewers would be able to "put a dollar in the slot for the shows that [they] want to see."

Warren suggests that the "password" for such a service would be "sex." "They say there'll be no boring commercials, a little more zest and zip," she sings, "if we could see what we want to see without any censorship." She goes on to describe how she would be a "rising star" on this "naughty network," which would also include such programs as "lusty lurid scenes from confidential magazines" and "an hour of bawdy songs on *Sing Along with Mitch.*" This gag points out the restrictions of broadcasting: as we have seen, a recurring theme of party records of this era.

Warren's records were intended for social gatherings that were an adult alternative to the television "family circle."[41] Warren wrote in an email interview that her fans were mostly young suburban couples who were "busy building their families." "You first caught my show at your local lounge," she wrote, "took the record home, and that weekend you had the neighbors over for a barbecue." In fact, Warren stressed in another interview that her records were "always a shared experience": "You never sat alone and listened with headphones like people do today," she said. "I was a 'party record' concept—you shared my records with friends at a barbecue or party."[42] The use of the home hi-fi by groups of young suburban couples for titillating entertainment represented a marked contrast to both the television family circle and the hi-fi as means of escape for male audio enthusiasts. Later in the 1960s, sexually explicit LPs were marketed to serve yet another function: home sex education for families and sex therapy for couples.

THE SENSUOUS PHONOGRAPH

David Allyn has referred to the 1960s and 1970s as the "Golden Age of Sexual Science" due to the many influential books on sex published at that time. LP records provided a medium for bringing the changing content of sexological literature into the home during this period and can reveal the different ways in which listeners to such material were constructed as audiences. Before the "Golden Age" to which Allyn refers, those seeking information about sex often turned to marriage manuals and advice books for teenagers that provided a mixed message of "sexual conservatism and enthusiasm," while reinforcing traditional marriage and gender roles.[43] Some LPs made in the 1960s presented lessons in sex education that worked in a similar manner.

The Illinois State Medical Society released a record entitled *Sex and Your Daughter* in 1965 that featured one side for parents only, and another to be heard with both parents and children present. *Sex and*

Your Daughter was concerned with enforcing traditional gender roles as much as discussing sexual science: for example, parents are told on side one that their daughter's sexuality should be defined in terms of her future role as a mother. "Above all, emphasize the importance of being able to have children," the narrator states, "for the young woman approaching womanhood, it is essential that she fully understand the process she will experience in preparation for this sacred responsibility." The side to be played in the presence of the daughter features a dramatization in which "Dr. Sims" visits a family to speak to the daughter "Betty" about growing up. Dr. Sims explains to Betty that the meaning of love is best illustrated by her mother and father: "Father works hard to earn a living . . . so you can have food, clothing, and a home," while "Mother takes care of home [and] shopping." The record thus illustrates the mixed message provided by many marriage manuals: parents are encouraged to be more open with their children about the "sacred responsibility" of sex, but only in the context of the traditional family ideal.

Although the content of the Dr. Sims record was meant to train children to be the parents of the future, the act of listening to the record was intended to fortify the family of the present. Parents were given suggestions on side one as to how to structure the listening event. The child was to be seated between the parents, with all three looking at diagrams that accompanied the LP. The sexual content of the record was thus experienced within the context of a family gathering: "During the playing of the record, do not hesitate to put your arms around her with affection," parents are told. "When the record has been played, it should be a natural impulse of the child to turn to you and kiss you. The record has been worded in such a way that she will follow this natural impulse. So don't hesitate to encourage this display of affection." Parents were also told how to structure the time immediately after playing the record: "You might have a little snack with ice cream and cake. Let the conversation flow normally and naturally. This time is extremely important, so put her at ease and act normally." The record was thus intended to function as the focal point in a ritual of postwar family "togetherness" at the same time that it conveyed traditional values about sex and gender to the next generation.

The narrative of a doctor's intervention in the sexual development of a child can also be heard on Stanley Z. Daniels's *Sex for Teens (Where It's At)* (Carapan 1969), a record that has become a camp classic, famously sampled by alternative rock hipster Beck on his 1996 track "Where It's At." *Sex for Teens* was part of a series of sex education LPs released by

Daniels, one of which—*Sex Explained for Children*—was nominated for a Grammy in 1971. On the 1969 LP for teens, we hear a dramatization featuring Sue, her hysterical brother Bill, and their unnamed and all-knowing therapist father. Much of the record's camp appeal stems from its strained attempts at using the slang of the counterculture. For example, Bill is outraged that Sue is "hung up" on her phony new boyfriend: "Wow, what a loser!" While Sue thinks he's groovy, Bill says he's freaky. "That guy doesn't relate to anything," Bill complains. "Man, did you see his hair? My hair's long, but it's all washed and combed." Beneath Bill's long hair resided the mind of a conservative ideologue, as demonstrated by his concerns about the welfare state: "If he doesn't find out where it's at, I'll probably have to support that slob and some dumb chick that he's knocked up and their kids, all on welfare, living off the establishment. He doesn't have what it takes to make it on his own."

In fact, despite cosmetic concessions to the counterculture and some frank discussion of contraception, the introduction of Bill and Sue's father quickly makes the record resemble television sitcoms of the 1950s, with sage advice delivered by the basso-voiced patriarch. After hearing Bill's rants, "Dad" describes how his medical practice has taught him that the "greater freedom among young people" is linked to a high frequency of "bad relationships" where sexual pleasure is taken selfishly: "Those who give a damn and are not afraid to relate . . . they are the beautiful people." "You're right," Sue responds. "Dad, that's beautiful." Besides such warnings, it becomes clear that Dad's enthusiasm for the sexual revolution is limited to the heterosexual couple. When Bill confesses that he finds homosexuals to be "freaky," his father laments, "Unfortunately, some homosexuals may make you feel uncomfortable in their presence. Many are social misfits because they're often psychologically unstable. In my practice I've rarely treated a satisfied or happy homosexual man or woman. Although one may occasionally come across some who seem to have adjusted into this type of life and make the best of it." Later, Dad explains that, with the help of therapy, homosexuals can be converted and "attain" a heterosexual life, where they have "more of a chance for happiness and emotional maturity." Homosexuality, it seems, was not "where it's at." As was the case with the Dr. Sims record, *Sex for Teens* illustrates how the hi-fi could bring a patriarchal and heteronormative perspective akin to marriage manuals into the home, perhaps in a context of reception similar to that suggested on *Sex and Your Daughter*.

That style of sex literature met with new competition in the mid-1960s from sexologists who attacked the credibility of marriage manuals and offered their therapeutic services as a more scientific alternative. William Masters and Virginia Johnson's *Human Sexual Response* (1966) and *Human Sexual Inadequacy* (1970) were at the forefront of an expansion in the development of clinical programs designed to "inform, educate, and actively assist couples to overcome sexual problems."[44] In contrast to the mixed messages that came before, this new sex therapy was "positive and enthusiastic about sex," conveying what Janice Irvine calls an ideal of "hypersexuality—a 'more is better' model of performance"—that helped to make sex therapy a "viable and valuable product" in a consumer culture where sex had become increasingly commoditized.[45] LPs that offered advice on sexual technique were one commodity outlet for the new sex therapy.

Consider an LP called *The Art of Sexual Lovemaking,* which was released by Helicon Enterprises in 1967. The record's liner notes refer to its creator, Frank S. Caprio, M.D., as "a world renowned authority on sex and marriage," formerly on the staff at the Walter Reed Hospital in Washington, D.C. The record is said to provide "a frank discussion of the love relationship in all its beauties and pleasures" as well as "the secrets of successful lovemaking": "For the first time, in the privacy of your own home, you will be able to: listen to intimate case histories, learn numerous sex techniques, become a better lover." *The Art of Sexual Lovemaking* presented that information in the form of a male announcer whose polished, antiseptic delivery resembles the narrator of the social guidance films of the 1950s and so feels awkwardly out of sync with the intimacy of the material: "Be mature in your behavior and thinking," he intones, "and keep yourself well groomed."

Two years later, Atlantic Records offered a very different approach to the recorded sex manual with its release of an audio version of the best-selling book *The Sensuous Woman* (1969). *The Sensuous Woman* was released anonymously, with the author known only as J, but the publisher quickly succumbed to pressure and revealed J to be Joan Garrity, a thirty-one-year-old former advertising copywriter. A 1970 *Chicago Tribune* review described *The Sensuous Woman* as "a steamy little sex manual" whose contents were "so sexily far out" that it had "girls gulping, guys gaping and husbands bringing it home to their wives tucked into the folds of their newspaper—after they [had] read it themselves."[46] Ehrenreich, Hess, and Jacobs claim that *The Sensuous Woman* offered an "iconoclastic" style that represented a "radical departure" from mainstream sexual technique in its discussion of topics such as oral sex.[47] Instead of sober moralizing about the hazards of premarital sex or homosexuality, Garrity presented a cheerful discussion of techniques such as the "butterfly flick" and the "Hoover."

The book became a runaway best seller and was released in LP form by Atlantic Records in 1971. *The Sensuous Woman* LP features a solo monologue by "Connie Z," who recites some of the most memorable passages from the book as well as additional material that took the form of vocal enactments of sexual excitement. These added sections of porno-performativity demonstrate how Garrity's book blurred the lines between instructional manual and hard-core porn. In fact, the LP found some success on the latter front, judging by a *Screw* magazine review that concluded that it was "a jerk-off product disguised as an instructional guide." "The record is so good that you are guaranteed at least three erections (I had six and one intercourse)," wrote the reviewer. "The language is clear, forceful, and very straightforward. You will find yourself leaning back against a chair, and you suddenly have an uncontrollable urge to seduce the sexy voice, or almost anything you can get your hands on or around."[48] Although *The Sensuous Woman* LP was ostensibly marketed as a sex guide for women, here is evidence that the album could succeed where the *Erotica* LP had found only mixed success and stimulate the prurient interest of men.

There was thus an underlying uncertainty about the intended addressee of *The Sensuous Woman* LP: is it an instructional guide for women or a "jerk-off product" for men? In 1974 the *Chicago Tribune* reviewed a new LP that had avoided that kind of confusion by presenting sexual information emphatically to a couples audience. The review argued that, unlike books such as *The Sensuous Woman* and Alex Comfort's *The Joy of Sex* (1972), in which "an individual gathers new insights alone," this new LP allowed two people to "listen together and share observations."[49] The record was *The Pleasures of Love* (Life Workshop) and was largely the work of Don M. Sloan, M.D.[50] Trained as a workshop fellow at the Masters and Johnson Institute in the early 1970s, Sloan went on to become the codirector of sexual therapy at New York Medical College as well as the first president of the Society for Sex Therapy and Research from 1975 to 1976. Sloan claimed in an email interview that *The Pleasures of Love* was an outgrowth of his approach to therapy, which he described in the 1983 article entitled "The Dual Therapy Approach to the Treatment of Sexual Dysfunction."

Originally conceived by Masters and Johnson, the dual therapy, or St. Louis, approach to sex therapy consisted of two therapists, one male and one female, working with a committed couple. Sloan stressed that sex was to be understood as a form of communication, with sexual problems best seen as a "breakdown in communication between two people": "Sex is looked upon as a means of 'speaking' . . . [one] that is as descriptive and as pointed as any communication can be despite its subtlety."[51] Thus it was the communication between the couple that became the entity for healing, and the goal of therapy was to "remove the barriers of communication" that had been set up by the couple. After an initial phase of interviews, therapy began with a series of "sensate focus exercises," in which the sense of touch was used as "a means of animal communication."[52]

Sloan's first sensate exercise involved "nongenital body touch," where the couple took turns in the roles of "doer" and "receiver." The doer was to "actively proceed through various manipulations on the nude body of the receiver," while the receiver remained passive but was instructed to verbalize acceptance or rejection of the doer's touching.[53] The second sensate continued turn-taking bodily touch but added the genitals. After this came the first guided coitus between the couple, with the female in the top position, followed by a second session of coitus, in which more positions were allowed. *The Pleasures of Love* LP enacts the stages of the dual therapy approach, presenting the voices of a male and female actor who describe the sensate and coitus exercises. On side one, the actors describe their bodies while looking at themselves naked in a mirror. The couple takes turns getting to know the intimate anatomy of their partner in the sensate exercises on side two, with the genitals included by side three. By side four, the two are engaging in guided sex, their verbal descriptions of the act accompanied by wah-wah guitar, reminiscent of soft-core porn soundtracks of the time.

The LP medium was particularly well suited to communicating both an understanding of sex as a form of speaking and as a therapeutic technique in which erotic sensation was to be translated into verbal utterances. Indeed, Sloan's LP is a vivid illustration of the Western compulsion to "speak sex" that has been discussed by scholars such as Michel Foucault and Linda Williams. *The Pleasures of Love* also represents the exploration of a type of media interactivity akin to a dance instructional record, where the actions of home listeners are meant to coincide with the spoken words of prerecorded performers. Sloan's record is thus an inversion of karaoke: instead of supplying the backing tracks for a live vocal performance, listeners are invented to synchronize the movements of their bodies with a prerecorded voice. As such, *The Pleasures of Love* represents a vivid example of Angela Carter's oft-quoted assertion that pornography "has a gap left in it" so that the reader may "step inside it."[54] The therapeutic strategy of Sloan's record is short-circuited, however, by the fact that the actors end up speaking *in place of* at-home listeners. Since the actors on *The Pleasures of Love* must constantly verbalize their experiences, there is never enough of a gap left for the at-home couple to complete the verbal component of the exercises. To step inside the prerecorded therapy session, listeners had to let the LP do the talking for them.

A satiric illustration of a record-led sex therapy session can be found in *Kentucky Fried Movie* (1977), the first film written by Jim Abrahams, David Zucker, and Jerry Zucker, who would go on to mainstream success with *Airplane!* (1980), *Top Secret!* (1984), and *The Naked Gun* (1988). The film is a collection of short comedy sketches, many of which are parodies of television. In one scene, we find an attractive young couple enjoying a candlelight dinner. The woman (Nancy Steen) leans back on the couch and praises the man (Jack Baker) on his "delicious dinner." "Well, I do my best," he replies and then whispers something in her ear. She smiles and nods in approval. He gets up and walks to the stereo, takes off the mood music that has been playing, and puts on a new LP. We hear soft, romantic music, and then the deep voice of a male narrator who says, "Welcome to the wonderful world of sex, where together we will achieve a new and exciting level of sexual fulfillment. After dimming the lights give your partner a reassuring smile, and a gentle kiss. Then, move to opposite areas of the bedroom to disrobe." We see the couple attempt to follow these instructions, but the man proves unable to finish removing his clothes at the proper time, and in his haste to catch up, knocks over several pieces of furniture. They rejoin each other sitting on the bed, as the voice on the record announces, "at this time the male may whisper to the female, (a) I love you, (b) I need you, or (c) I want you." During the short pause provided by the record, the man smiles and says, "b." The absurdity of the scene is amplified when, as the woman leaves the room to attend to birth control, the record abruptly shifts to circus big-top music as the man looks on expectedly and prepares the bed. Once the woman returns, the couple begins passionately kissing, but just as the LP narrator warns that "one of the most frequent problems encountered during the sexual act is that of premature ejaculation," the man's pained expression indicates that he has followed the LP's script all too closely. The sketch ends when the record assures its listeners that "the *Joy of Sex* album" has come equipped with "Big Jim Slade, former tight end for the Kansas City Chiefs," who bursts through the door and displays his impressive physique before whisking the woman away.

This skit indicates a familiarity with the sex therapy records I've been describing as well as an awareness of the shortcomings of their technique. The LP in *Kentucky Fried Movie* becomes comical because, like *The Pleasures of Love,* it does all the talking; its attempts to regiment the stages of lovemaking only serve to highlight their often clumsy and awkward nature, and in the end, it cannot really address the common problems of sexual dysfunction. But this sequence is also notable due to the fact that, in the otherwise almost completely white context of *Kentucky Fried Movie,* all the performers in it are African Americans. The association of African Americans with sexually explicit records had some basis in the record culture of the time. Thus far I have been describing ways in which LPs took part in constructing the sexual revolution. Records from this time also provided a venue from which some African American performers could critique aspects of that revolution.

BLACK AND BLUE DISCS

In a 1966 *Ebony Magazine* article, Kermit Mehlinger stated that the media were allowing sex to be "discussed more intelligently with less feelings of shame and guilt." As an example, Mehlinger pointed to the fact that "party records" by comics like Redd Foxx no longer had to be "played in a soundproof room."[55] Besides this reference, little thought has been given to the role played by sexually explicit spoken word phonograph records made by African American comics during the 1960s and early 1970s, despite the fact that this was a time when, as we have seen, the recording industry enjoyed considerable prosperity and cultural influence. This was also the era of the sexual revolution, and Mehlinger's statements suggest that long-playing records were a significant factor in media discourses of sexuality in the African American community at this time.[56] Indeed, Mehlinger's *Ebony* article ran adjacent to an advertisement for the Dooto company's explicit comedy albums, which included not only the work of Redd Foxx but also a record called *Below the Belt* (1961) by Rudy Ray Moore. Moore is best known for his starring role in the Dolemite blaxploitation films of the mid 1970s, but he first achieved media notoriety as the creator of a series of party records that featured recitations such as "The Great Titanic" and "The Signifying Monkey." Indeed, Moore's films were financed by money from LP sales. Much has been written about the African American tradition of oral folk poetry, or "toasting," to which recitations such as "The Signifying Monkey" belong, but Moore's records also made reference to the sexually explicit blue discs or party records I have been discussing.[57]

Despite being largely overlooked by media scholars, spoken word LPs like Moore's were an important medium for diverse African American performers such as Bill Cosby, Moms Mabley, Flip Wilson, Dick Gregory, Richard Pryor, and George Kirby (whose career I will discuss in chapter 4). In fact, phonograph records arguably offer the best vantage point on many of those influential performers who, in the 1950s and 1960s, were breaking new ground for African American comics in the mainstream entertainment industry. It is beyond the scope of this chapter to cover all of these performers in the depth that they deserve, but it is important to note that explicit material of the kind released by Moore and Reed was not the only genre of spoken word phonography to which African American performers were making important contributions.[58] Although I do not want to reinforce stereotypes that have associated African Americans with the display of sexuality, I hope to reveal the cultural critique and formal innovation that can reside in what may be too easily brushed aside as simply "blue" material. To begin that critical work, Moore's and Reed's records need to be placed within a larger context both of spoken word LPs and of postwar developments in radio and television broadcasting. Along with radio, sexually explicit phonograph records provided an important media outlet in the precable era for African American performance styles, serving as an alternative to network broadcasting and the Hollywood film studios.

THE FORGOTTEN FIFTEEN MILLION

The rise of network television in the 1950s had a profound effect on American radio. As advertisers moved their accounts to the new visual medium, radio went from network to local programming, and from national to local advertising. Philip Ennis points out that while the total radio advertising budget rose between 1940 and 1955, this was due to the growth of local accounts: "As network advertising declined from almost half (46 percent) of radio's total advertising in 1940 to less than a tenth (9 percent) in 1956, local radio advertising doubled its share (from 29 to 61 percent)."[59] The number of local radio stations more than doubled during this time, and American radio became dominated by small, independent stations that featured disc jockeys spinning current phonograph records in place of live network entertainment.[60]

Stations such as these had to cater to narrowly defined local markets to survive, and one of the results of these changes was an increase in radio stations targeted to the African American community.[61]

Spurred by research that suggested that radio was a key medium for African American consumers, the radio industry turned decisively toward the black market in the 1950s.[62] A pivotal event in the growth of "black appeal" radio was the publication in October 1949 of an article in the radio and television trade journal *Sponsor* entitled "The Forgotten 15,000,000: Ten Billion a Year Negro Market Is Largely Ignored by National Advertisers." For historian William Barlow, that article helped to revise industry assumptions that African Americans were "too poor and too socially marginal to be considered a viable market" and so represented a crucial breakthrough for black appeal stations in their "quest for inclusion and respectability in the radio industry."[63] Though still marginalized by film and television, African American audiences were actively courted by local radio stations, and a "black" approach to music and performance style found a prominent place on America's airwaves.

Phonograph records played a central role in the programming of many small independent radio stations: Barlow notes that radio shows featuring disc jockeys playing records were "particularly popular" among the black audience.[64] The records getting airplay at this time were frequently made by small, independent companies that were—like local radio stations—exploiting niche markets such as middle-class teenagers and the African American population in northern industrial cities. Scholars such as Andre Millard and Richard Peterson have described how companies like Apollo, Jubilee, Savoy, Modern, Stax, Specialty, King, Sun, Chess, Verve, and Atlantic became important industry players through their release of rhythm and blues, bebop, and electric blues records.[65] Independent labels challenged the big four record companies—Columbia, RCA Victor, Decca, and Capitol—in record sales between 1954 and 1958.[66] Local radio stations, the disk jockey, and independent record labels have often been noted as factors in the rise of rock and roll in the 1950s, with radio DJs like Allen Freed and indie labels like Sun and Chess combining to create an alternative media synergy for a generation of American teenagers. I would only add that, while independent labels released records by postwar bebop and rhythm and blues musicians, they also released records by African American comics. Take, for example, the Los Angeles record company formed by Walter "Dootsie" Williams.

Williams grew up in the Watts section of Los Angeles, where he became first a jazz trumpeter and later a bandleader. After working as a record company talent agent, Williams formed the company that would become Dooto Records in 1946, thirteen years before Berry Gordy Jr.'s Motown Records. Though not as well known as Motown, Dooto was an important black-owned company of this era, with the *Chicago Defender* calling it "the largest Negro-owned recording company in the nation" in 1963.[67] Dooto received extensive coverage in hometown paper the *Los Angeles Sentinel,* which boasted in 1967 that not only was the company the "largest Negro-owned recording firm long before Motown was ever dreamed of," but that Williams himself made "all the important decisions for his enterprises. You don't see Caucasians calling shots in his businesses the way you do if you visit Motown in Detroit."[68] Williams stressed his desire to champion the "wealth of talent among Negroes," which he asserted had not "been given an opportunity to express itself to capitalize on its value in the open market of American competition. We have striven to remedy this situation."[69] Dooto first emerged onto the national entertainment scene via the doo-wop group the Penguins, whose single "Earth Angel" was released in 1954 and reached number eight on the *Billboard* singles chart. Dooto would find its most enduring success however, through its pioneering approach to comedy. Williams hit on the idea of marketing records of nightclub comics in the mid-1950s and soon had Billy Mitchell and Redd Foxx under contract, with the latter's first LP released in 1956. Since black records of the 1950s have often been associated with the singles market, it is notable that Williams claimed that his company was the first "Negro-owned company" to give albums great attention, adding that in 1959, 70 percent of Dooto's production was albums.[70]

We should also note that Dooto's comedy releases came several years ahead of more celebrated white comedy LPs in the late 1950s and early 1960s, discussed in chapter 5. Indeed, in a feature article about Williams's company, the *Chicago Defender* stated that "long before the Mort Sahls, Shelly [sic] Bermans and Bob Newharts," Dooto had sold millions of albums by the likes of Mitchell, Foxx, Allen Drew, George Kirby, and Scatman Crothers.[71] Though the *Chicago Defender* wrote in 1962 that comedy records were "the current rage in homes," Williams had aspirations to expand Dooto beyond records and spoke to the press about his plans for a Dooto film production company and Dooto television and radio stations to serve the Southern California black community.[72] In December 1962 Williams opened the $300,000 Dooto Music Center in South Los Angeles–Compton, which served as an auditorium that could hold more than a thousand people, recording studio, film and television production facility, and civic center. Williams also used this space for closed-circuit television telecasts of boxing events in the 1960s. "It is unlikely," wrote the *Los Angeles Sentinel*, "that any Negro-owned center of this kind is to be found anywhere else in America."[73]

That the multimedia Dooto empire was built on LPs is reflective of an era when African Americans still had a limited presence in Hollywood film and network television production. Donald Bogle argues that in the mid-1950s, American television "remained locked in a time warp; not yet ready to present—on a regular weekly basis—dramatic or more complicated African American characters."[74] Though Bill Cosby's role on *I Spy* in 1965 and Diahann Carroll's series *Julia* in 1968 signaled significant change, Bogle notes that primetime television in the 1960s "still failed to present African American cultural references and perspectives."[75] By contrast, radio and records offered an alternative avenue to media production and representation for African American performers and audiences. In his history of African American comedy, Mel Watkins writes that records provided "a less sanitized sample of early twentieth-century black humor than did black genre films" since "the recording industry was not subjected to the rigid censorship imposed on motion pictures": "Although often banned on radio, comedy routines and songs presented on phonograph records could reflect risqué or earthy aspects of black humor that were taboo in films."[76] Dooto's comedy LPs were an important part of that development, and records of risqué material that could not be broadcast supplemented the achievements of "black appeal" radio. Indeed, because the LP allowed discussion of topics not allowed on radio or television, they became a significant channel for the discussion of the sexual revolution. Kermit Mehlinger's reference to party records in the 1966 *Ebony* quote cited previously therefore becomes less quirky than it might at first appear: records, along with radio, were an important part of the postwar African American media-scape, and comedy records by Dooto artists such as Rudy Ray Moore were a significant medium for the frank discussion of sexuality during the era of the sexual revolution. Moore's LPs thus deserve to be considered as significant media texts in their own right, not simply as ancillaries to his films.

Moore was born in Fort Smith, Arkansas, one of seven children of a coal miner. He grew up in Cleveland, but after a discharge from the army, he resettled in Los Angeles, where he managed a record store. According to some accounts, his entrance into record production was the result of an encounter with "an aging freeloader who begged change from the customers by reciting the traditional 'blue' humorous stories that have been handed down in the ghettos for years." According to his publicity, Moore took note of the enthusiastic response garnered by these "traditional tales" and decided that such "ghetto expression" could "find an audience in a black audience divided among the older people who would remember the tales fondly and the younger people who could pick up the tradition."[77] After making records for Dooto in the early 1960s, Moore released several nationally successful LPs of such "earthy humor" with Kent Records.

Like Dootsie Williams, Moore used the revenue from his records to move into other forms of media production, in this case, applying LP profits to making his first film. The importance of Moore's records is gauged by the visual style of his films, which served to showcase the routines found on phonograph records. For example, in *Dolomite* (1974), Moore is stopped in a parking lot by a group of men who ask him if he is really the film's eponymous hero. "Yes, brother," he replies. "I'm Dolomite." The men ask Moore to prove his identity to settle a bet, and he reluctantly agrees, launching into his version of "The Great Titanic," found on the record *Eat Out More Often*: a literal enactment of African American toasting as a form of street theater.[78] Toward the end of the film, Moore (Dolomite) appears in a club where, after a tribal dance routine, he recites "The Signifying Monkey," which opened his record *This Pussy Belongs to Me*. The importance of these verbal performances is indicated by the visual style of the film. Moore is presented in a static medium close-up, interrupted only by occasional shots of the applauding audience. In essence, the films become "visualized" phonograph records. As stated above, "The Great Titanic" and "The Signifying Monkey" are well-known examples in a repertoire of African American toasts. But Moore's recorded output included his own versions of other forms of recorded erotica that both provide further evidence of the prevalence of records in African American cultural life and also comment on discourses of race and sexuality in the early 1970s.

SIGNIFYING GEORGE

As an example of the ways in which Rudy Ray Moore and Lady Reed's records intervened in a tradition of recorded erotica, consider their version of a blue disc entitled *Silent George*. The source text of Moore and Reed's adaptation was released anonymously on a 78 rpm record circa the 1930s and begins with a man's half-whispered voice, who sets the scene. "Hey folks, gather around. Here's a pip of a story about a man known to his many girlfriends as Silent George. Now, the time is midnight, and Mary Jones, a beautiful young girl, is in her bedroom asleep." There is a knock on the door. Mary whispers, "Oh my goodness, a burglar. But it might be . . . Gosh, I hope it isn't who I think it is." Further knocks, and then the door opens. "George, what on earth!" Mary states. "What are you doing out here? You know how Daddy feels about us keeping late hours. No, George, you cannot come in this time of night." For the rest of the record, George remains silent, but his increasingly brazen sexual advances are revealed through Mary's half-whispered statements and protests. George becomes more aggressive, kissing her breast, fondling Mary ("no, please don't put your hand down there on me"). Mary's protests become more desperate: "George, you're forcing me. Why do you have to be so rough?" Finally, Mary cries out, "Daddy, Daddy, oh Daddy," but these calls for help become the moans of ecstasy, and the record ends when Mary delivers the punch line: "George, I'll give you just four hours to take that big thing out of me."

Silent George stands out among pre-1950s blue discs because of its female narrator and breathless performance of passion. But equally notable is the record's subsequent appearance in African American culture. Swing bandleader Lucky Millinder released a musical version in 1950, where we hear vocalist Myra Johnson sing, "I heard somebody knocking on my front door. Know I heard that knock before." "It was George," she exclaims, and the band answers, "Silent George!" "I hollered 'Daddy, Daddy! Come here quick and make George stop.'" Johnson sings during the refrain, "I believe George is blowing his top!" Millinder and Johnson tone down the punch line ending of the earlier blue disc but retain the troubling premise that although the woman says "no," she means "yes": "George, I'm giving you just twenty-four hours to get out of here." Johnson lets out a sigh and moans, "Uh, love that George." Millinder and Johnson's record suggests that the "Silent George" routine was known by at least part of the postwar African American audience.

Rudy Ray Moore's version of "Silent George" was released approximately twenty-five years after Millinder's, on the album *The Rudy Ray Moore House Party Album: The Dirty Dozens,* volume 1 (Cherry Red Records) and takes advantage of the extra time provided by long-playing records to expand the narrative of the skit.[79] Moore's record begins not with an address to the listener or a knock on the door, but with an unnamed man and woman (played by Moore and Lady Reed) who discuss the whereabouts of their friend George. "That motherfucker done ate and slipped out," Reed complains. "He gone down the street to fuck." Moore is shocked by Reed's claim that George is with a woman named Clotia: "Clotia's a cherry girl!" he says. Reed replies that Clotia has been feigning her sexually naiveté, adding that she should wear a veil when she gets married: "That bitch oughta wear black for all the dicks she done buried." Moore and Reed come upon Clotia's room and secretly observe George enter. In what follows, Moore and Reed stick closely to the earlier version of "Silent George," another indication that the record was familiar to African American audiences. But Moore's remake does more than duplicate the blue disc. Note that it is Moore in the role of Clotia, narrating the sexual action in an exaggerated falsetto voice: both an instance of female impersonation and vocal whiteface that "signifies" on white performance.[80]

Meanwhile, Lady Reed complicates the listener's engagement with the interaction between George and Clotia by making sardonic comments as she secretly watches the amorous couple: an example of overlapping dialogue I will discuss with regard to the Firesign Theatre's comedy albums in chapter 5. By simultaneously presenting a recording of a past era and Reed's sly commentary on it, Moore's "Silent George" feels a bit like an audio version of *Mystery Science Theater 3000*. But more than nostalgia or cynical irony, Moore and Reed's performances send up mainstream white erotica and by extension certain white sexual preoccupations. To best appreciate Lady Reed's performance, note that a common trope of blue discs was the depiction of female characters that were unaware of the sexual dimensions of the dialogues in which they participated: recall Mary Jones's wide-eyed innocence in the face of George's lascivious acts. Further, blue discs typically only provide verbal descriptions of female bodies. Take for example the introductory framing material on the blue disc version of "Silent George," in which a male speaker colludes with the audience ("Hey folks, gather around . . .") and asks that we visualize "a beautiful young girl." These performance norms were shaped by the sexual double standard in white American society that allowed premarital and extramarital sexual expression for men but denied them to women.[81] In such a social context, feigning sexual ignorance in the manner of Mary Jones or Clotia would be an important way for women to remain viable marriage partners.

Notably, African Americans did not always place the same premium on female sexual inexperience. Eugene Genovese writes that in the culture of the American slaves, "virginity at marriage carried only small prestige," adding that "that particular pretension, staunchly adhered to by the whites . . . the slaves found slightly ridiculous."[82] Robert Staples makes a similar point writing about the black community in the 1960s, stating, "The nonvirginal Black female is not excluded as a future prospect for marriage."[83] We might note, then, that Lady Reed is quick to refute Clotia's performance of sexual naiveté. When Clotia gasps, "George! What are you going to do with that jar of Vaseline?" Reed very matter-of-factly states George's intentions. What is more, Reed's commentary on "Silent George" displays an open and unabashed appreciation of George's body: it is Lady Reed who colludes with listeners and encourages us to visualize George's body ("Look at that dick!" she says, "Look at his ass!").

The double-voiced structure of Moore and Reed's record can be heard as a vivid example of the African American expression known as *signifying,* which transforms preexisting material by "trifling with, teasing, or censuring it in some way."[84] Signifying is typically associated with creative indirection, and yet Reed's blunt commentary makes the erotic content of the situation between George and Clotia crystal clear, working in effect to defuse a regime of double entendre humor meant to suggest but not explicitly state erotic content. In one sense, then, Moore and Reed critique the ham-fisted job of indirection through double entendre heard on so many blue discs. But more than this, Moore's broad portrayal of Clotia mocks her pretensions to sexual ignorance, and Lady Reed's earthy asides provoke laughter at Clotia's ridiculously ritualized denials: both of which work to make the logic of the double entendre *and* the sexual double standard appear ridiculous.

Where the blue disc of "Silent George" ends with Mary Jones's calls for her "Daddy," Moore and Reed's record returns to the introductory narrative frame, as the two friends leave the lovemaking couple to walk back to the party. "George was supposed to be my date!" Reed says, while Moore complains, "I asked Clotia to come, she talking about 'I can't come to your house, cause you got all those . . . nasty people there,' and that bitch lay down and have a dick like that, and talkin' bout she's a nice girl!" This dialogue suggests that Moore and Reed's characters are not upset by the morality of George and Clotia's act, but instead are irked by the social dimensions of their coupling.[85] Further, this framing narrative depicts a platonic male-female friendship that contrasts with the ridiculously empurpled George and Clotia and so broadens the scope of the routine beyond the heterosexual couple.[86] John D'Emilio and Estelle Freedman have argued that for the many black Americans who had to struggle against the "burden of poverty and unemployment," sexual relations developed within a "network of kinship obligations" against which the "nucleated couple" often had to compete. By contrast, the discourse of "sexual liberalism" that came to prominence during the second half of the twentieth century spoke most directly to the middle class, "whose incomes, socialization, and style of living made possible the intense focus on the privatized couple of the companionate ideal."[87] Moore and Reed reframe the sexual encounter on the "Silent George" disc, placing it within a larger social context, another technique that highlights the social assumptions that shaped the conventions of mainstream white erotica. To put it another way, Moore and Reed's revisions make us hear blue discs such as "Silent George" in a considerably whiter shade of blue—that is, they make us hear the white, middle-class origins of much "blue" material.

MR. AND MRS. BIG

If Moore and Reed's "Silent George" comments on the representation of white sexuality heard on blue discs, their remake of a record entitled *Mr. Long Dick* does the same for representations of black sexuality. To best appreciate Moore and Reed's adaptation, we should again begin by examining the anonymous, 78 rpm blue disc source text *Mr. Long Dick,* which begins with a knock on the door. "Now who in the god- damn hell can that be?" says a woman, whose vocal inflection suggests that she is African American. A man enters, announces that his name is "Long Dick," and says that he has come to see the woman's daughters, who he has heard are "well-educated in fucking." He announces that he is offering five hundred dollars to anyone who can have sex with him until they count up to five. "Well, come in, Mr. Son-of-a-Bitch," the woman says. "Your long journey is over." The woman asks why he is called Long Dick, and he responds by showing her his "identification card." She whistles in frank appreciation: "Goddamn! What I couldn't do with a dick like that!" The woman asks Mr. Long Dick to work his "big black ass this way" and leads him to her first daughter's room. "OK, Mr. Dick," she says. "You may enter this room. But remember, I will be right outside of this door, listening to every goddamn count my daughters make. And don't forget, Mr. Dick—before you leave, make damn sure you stop by me."

The man enters the room and tells the daughter, "OK, start count-ing, baby." After various moans, groans, and much heavy breathing, the first daughter is only able to count to two before the mother enters and says: "Goddamnit! Just listen to those motherfuckin' whores, running out of breath on the count of three. As hard a time as I had teaching them how to fuck. I believe they're going to let me down." The same chain of events follows with the second daughter, although her vocalizations indicate that she has received more pleasure from the encounter than her sister. Again, the mother enters to scold her daughter, and then turns to Mr. Long Dick: "Goddamn it, you're going to fuck me before you leave this house!" "All right madam," he replies. "You asked for it . . . start counting." The mother, however, refuses to follow Mr. Long Dick's peculiar instructions: "Not so goddamn fast, Mr. Dick. I'll tell you when." For the rest of the record, the two sigh and moan, while the woman gives instruction: "You've got it over too far to the right. Put it back to the left. . . . Slowly, slowly, slowly. There! There! Ooo, Daddy!"

As indicated by its title, this record is concerned with the expression of male sexuality. The strategy taken here is similar to that found on "Silent George": male sexual prowess is depicted through the female voice. Mr. Long Dick's strange insistence that his sexual partners count to five is a demand that his potency be represented: the female voice literally becomes a measurement of the male organ we cannot see. My reading of this record differs from the description of the female voice in film pornography, which becomes what Linda Williams describes as an aural fetish of "the female pleasures we cannot see."[88] The particular formal properties of sound-only erotic media require the female voice to operate as an aural fetish for both male and female pleasures. The presentation of male potency on *Mr. Long Dick* stands out among the genre of blue discs, which frequently joked about male sexual inadequacy. We should note, then, that *Mr. Long Dick*'s portrayal of a superpotent man and sexually savvy woman is achieved by placing the action in an entirely black milieu and, in that respect, is representative of the ways in which blue discs have conflated race, gender, and sexuality.

As I have discussed elsewhere, on the rare occasions when African American women were depicted on 78 rpm blue discs, they were presented as being aware of the erotic dimensions of the proceedings—a knowledge most of their white counterparts lacked.[89] Blue discs continued a tradition of racist exploitation by offering depictions of hypersexual African American women and "pure" white women who were comically unaware of the sexual nature of the proceedings, both for the entertainment of presumably male and largely white listeners. But we should notice how this racist logic paradoxically allowed the black women depicted on blue discs a certain circumscribed agency denied to their white counterparts, albeit an agency that restated troubling stereotypes. That is, black female characters such as the woman on *Mr. Long Dick* are allowed to take a certain degree of control over the sexual situation, even while they become sexual objects. Such ambiguities in racial stereotypes about sex have long been a source of material for black humorists who, Lawrence Levine argues, have been aware that "the pervasive stereotype" of African Americans as "oversexed, hyper-virile, and uninhibitedly promiscuous was not purely a negative image; that it contained envy as well as disdain, that it was a projection of desire as well as fear."[90] With this in mind, consider Rudy Ray Moore's remake of *Mr. Long Dick,* which maintains the earlier blue disc's depiction of black sexual potency while reconfiguring its dynamics of verbal performance.

Moore's track "Mr. Big Dick" appeared on *The Second Rudy Ray Moore Album: This Pussy Belongs to Me* (Kent 1971) and begins with a soliloquy by the eponymous hero: "Oh, it's so goddamn hot tonight. I guess I've walked all over this damn town, looking for a woman to satisfy me. Everywhere I've gone, every whorehouse in town, these bitches start hollerin' 'too big, too big.' There's one more place over there: Queen Bee. I think I'll knock on her door and see if she's got a thing to offer." The story then unfolds in a similar manner as the blue disc version, except that the female characters speak in a very different way. In contrast to the first daughter's quiet passivity on the blue disc, here she brags: "Mother, you and sister just go and simply relax, because I am going to destroy this dick! Let me tell you something, Mr. Big Dick. You might be big in size, but I'm big otherwise. Yes, Daddy, and fuckin' is my game. And I'm layin' to make this pussy drive you insane." Nonetheless, both daughters fail to count to five, and the mother enters (played by Lady Reed), saying: "I got a pussy so good it made a lame man walk, a blind man see, and a dumb man talk. Daddy, fucking is my business and I got this pussy to sell. It'll make you come from just listening to the good fuckin' tales it'll tell. It's so good it tickles my legs when I walk. It's travelin' good news that asks but never talks. So come on Mr. Big Dick to my beck and call. I'm a damn good wrassler. Never lost a fall." Unlike the blue disc version, the mother agrees to Mr. Big Dick's request to count to five, but her counting becomes a further demonstration of her own verbal skill: "One. This looks like it'll be some fun. Two. Come on Mr. Big Dick, let me see what you can do." Not only does she make it to five, but she continues all the way to eleven as the record fades out, suggesting that the couple continue their lovemaking indefinitely.

Moore thus transposes the Mr. Long Dick routine—with its conflation of sexuality and verbal performance—into the register of African

American toasts, which often depicted sex as a contest of verbal agility between a heroic "pimp" and a "whore." But while Moore and Reed borrow the toast's dynamics of agonistic verbal contest, they do not replicate their typical outcome. Toasts typically depicted the pimp as the victor, "superfucking" his competitor into "adulating respect."[91] However, the couple on "Mr. Big Dick" are equally matched in bed, and Queen Bee clearly outshines Mr. Big Dick in terms of verbal skill. While the 78 rpm blue disc had utilized the female voice to index male potency, Reed's voice is more explicitly a vehicle for the display of her own verbal and sexual expertise. Moore and Reed thus revise the depiction of African Americans on white adult records, retaining themes of sexual potency while amplifying the element of verbal artistry and, in the process, transforming the representation of the sexual couple.

SENSUOUS BLACK

We have thus far seen how Moore and Reed reinterpreted white erotica of a previous era, but equally notable were their recorded rejoinders to one of the best-selling sex manuals of their own historical moment. Recall that one of the most successful of the publications on sex from the "golden age of sexual science" was Joan Garrity's *The Sensuous Woman,* and that Atlantic Records released an LP version of Garrity's book in 1971, featuring a solo performance by Connie Z.[92] Perhaps irked by mainstream record companies moving into their adult LP turf, Moore and Reed released records entitled *The Sensuous Black Man* and *The Sensuous Black Woman,* responses to Garrity's book that coincided with the publication of articles in the popular press by African American writers who felt that the black experience had been left out of the golden age of sexual science. In his 1971 *Ebony* article, Alvin Poussaint observed that neither Alfred Kinsey nor Masters and Johnson had made much mention of blacks in their work, and he wondered why white social scientists, "who ordinarily rush to study all types of black behavior (especially if it's socially deviant or titillating)," had avoided the study of "black sex."[93] In this light, Moore and Reed used *The Sensuous Woman* as a rhetorical prop that allowed them to address the "great neglect" Poussaint had identified and, in so doing, add their own sexual science to the media marketplace.

The Sensuous Woman had been praised in the popular press for having a direct, down-to-earth tone. Similarly, Ehrenreich, Hess, and Jacobs note that Garrity used "a language that middle-class housewives would easily understand," making sex sound "as ordinary as cleaning house."[94] Moore and Reed, however, asserted that Garrity's language was not their own. "We're not going to bullshit about it," Moore says at the beginning of *The Sensuous Black Man*. "We're going to tell it just like it is." Moore goes on to explain that he won't be using "those old high-class 'falutin words like penis and vagina": "We gonna use plain words like dick, tongue, and pussy, because baby, that's where it's at. We're gonna do it that way so everybody can understand." Moore's statement reminds us that distinctions about what are "proper" or "profane" terms for sexual anatomy are class distinctions. In addition to contrasting their style of speech to Garrity's, Moore and Reed held that black men and women did not have to follow Garrity's program of practical exercises to become "sensuous."

Note that Garrity begins her book by declaring that she was "not particularly pretty": "I have heavy thighs, lumpy hips, protruding teeth, a ski jump nose, poor posture, flat feet and uneven ears." And yet she claimed that, through her "intelligence and hard work," she had become a "Sensuous Woman" who was "getting and keeping men."[95] In fact, "work" was an important part of Garrity's rhetoric: she offered the enticing suggestion that sexual allure and fulfillment were available to anyone who would put forth the necessary effort required to become "sensuous." Such a discourse of "work" should be understood in terms of Mark Jancovich's arguments about class distinction and the sexual revolution. Jancovich claims that the lower middle class has traditionally distinguished itself from the working class by "emphasizing its respectability," which in turn make it a convenient target for a new middle class of symbolic goods and service workers who rejected the old and embraced an "ethic of fun." In this view, the sexual revolution represented a means of class distinction that involved a new kind of self-discipline: "The new petite bourgeoisie displays its distinction from the old through its 'liberated' sexuality, but it is a 'liberation' that is only ever achieved through education, discipline and intense self-surveillance. The 'liberation' of the body from its 'repression' is therefore experienced simultaneously as the rediscovery of a natural self and as the enactment of a carefully controlled performance. It is both a liberation from alienation and a whole new mode of alienation."[96] It was that "new mode of alienation," as represented by Garrity's sensuality regime, that Moore and Reed rejected.

Rudy Ray Moore declares on *The Sensuous Black Man* that "after hearing all that shit about becoming sensuous, I decided to tell the brothers just where it's really at. And fact about it, most brothers are born sensuous." At another point, Moore tells his listeners that they are "the master of the most sensuous body of any race." Similarly, Lady Reed told black women that "being black, you were born hot-cock, and you know how to fuck." Later, Reed mocks "those other girls" who are taking lessons to become sensuous "under the camouflage of exercise and belly-dancing": a reference to one of Garrity's practical suggestions. Black women, according to Reed, had a "natural gift." Moore and Reed's suggestion that blacks are more "naturally" sexual is problematic because it seems to repackage or ratify certain racist stereotypes.[97] But Moore and Reed's assertion of the natural sensuousness of the black body also functions to critique the class-based rhetoric of work at the heart of Garrity's *Sensuous Woman.*

At one point, Reed dismisses one of the more memorable elements in Garrity's sensuous training program: a tongue exercise involving an ice cream cone. "Make circle and swirling patterns with your tongue on the ice cream," Garrity wrote, "lap at it delicately like a kitten with milk, put all of your mouth over the ball of ice cream, sliding down until your lips touch the cone and then s-l-o-w-l-y withdraw it."[98] Reed quipped that "this ice cream bit was not geared for the black woman per se. . . . We don't have time to be fucking with those double-dips." Much like the way she disdainfully puts down Clotia's performance on "Silent George," Reed mocks moments of white sexual "transgression" as laughably prudish and misdirected. Reed did not have much time for female masturbation either, a topic that takes up a good portion of Garrity's sensuous workout regime. At one point Reed defines "this sensuous shit" as "getting yourself ready to fuck—bustin' your own nuts." "Now you know girls," she continues, "this ain't never been your bag. Playing with your own pussy? Oh no, no, never, never, never." The only sexual exercise a woman needed, Reed suggested, was heterosexual coupling.

It is easy to see the limitations of Reed's comments—if read as advice and not parody—since they seem to deny female sexual pleasure except through men. *The Sensuous Black Woman* was certainly not offering a utopian vision of female empowerment: "Do it when he wanta, how he wanta, for as long as he wanta," she advised. "Drop your drawers at the door if necessary." But note that Garrity's emphasis on female masturbation in *The Sensuous Woman* was not reflective of a progressive feminism either.[99] Garrity stated that women had to learn about masturbation to allow men to continue to be selfish in bed: "The reason you have to teach yourself to come alive is that men don't have the patience to explore your body thoroughly while they are sexually excited themselves."[100] Indeed, at one point Garrity decries the recent emphasis on female sexual satisfaction, stating that it had made women "greedy, selfish, and dumb": "We forgot what females have been taught since time began: that as women we should be ardent conservationists of our most important natural resource—man—instead of heedlessly using him up. Pin up on your bed, your mirror, your wall, a sign, lady, until you know it in every part of your being: *We were designed to delight, excite and satisfy the male of the species*" (italics in original).[101] Passages such as these suggest that the success of both *The Sensuous Woman* book and *The Sensuous Woman* LP was due in part to how Garrity offered women a route to more sexual enjoyment without any progressive political commitments. By rejecting Garrity's rhetorical connection between sexuality and work as well as her emphasis on individual gratification, Moore and Reed also rejected a therapeutic view of sex as—to borrow Foucault's words—something that "called for management procedures" and "had to be taken charge of by analytical discourses."[102]

Perhaps the clearest illustration of the different approaches to sexuality heard on the *Sensuous Black* LPs and *The Sensuous Woman* LP is not in what the performers say but in how they say it. Note that Connie Z lowers her voice to a breathy whisper for the hard-core moments of the *Sensuous Woman* LP. This approach to the delivery of erotic material is overdetermined. We might understand Connie Z's performance in terms of Linda Williams's observation that film pornography has tended to privilege the depiction of spontaneous, "dark, secret" sex, or Foucault's discussion of the Christian tradition of confession, what he called "the general standard governing the production of the true discourse on sex" for Western societies.[103] We might also hear Connie Z's collusive whisper as an index of what Michael Warner has described as the ideologies and institutions of heterosexual intimacy. "Heterosexual culture," Warner writes, is closely tied to "the ideologies and institutions of intimacy" through which "personal life" is structurally differentiated from "work, politics, and the public sphere."[104] For Warner, the link between heterosexual intimacy and the "institutions of personal life" serves to "conjure a mirage," "a home base of pre-political humanity from which citizens are thought to come into political discourse and to which they are expected to return in the (always imaginary) future after political conflict."[105] What is clear is that Connie Z's vocal inflection frames her sex advice as secret, intimate knowledge delivered to an imagined individual listener.

Such aspects of Connie Z's performance become easier to perceive when compared to Lady Reed's approach on the *Sensuous Black Woman* LP. Reed often moves from a full voice to a shout ("Fuck me! Fuck me! FUCK ME!"), a style of delivery that suggests the open declaration to a group, a vocal index of a more social view of sex. In fact, note that Moore and Reed's records were party albums in a very literal sense: they were recorded not in a studio or nightclub—as was the convention for comedy LPs at that time—but in Moore's house, with an audience of his friends.[106] On Moore's *House Party* record, audience members even take turns stepping to the microphone to exchange stylized insults. We might understand Moore and Reed's interaction with their audience as a form of call and response: a trope that Samuel Floyd argues is representative of "the dialogical, conversational character of black music."[107] The *Sensuous Black* LPs embody call and response in another way as well: side one is a monologue by either Moore or Reed, and side two is a question-and-answer forum with the audience. The use of a full-voiced delivery and the interactive nature of call and response stand in stark contrast with the confessional, intimate whisper as a technique for the performance of erotic material. In short, Moore and Reed not only talk about sex in social terms, they do so using particularly social forms of talk.

Many of the points I have been making about Moore and Reed's work can be summarized by reference to Lady Reed's remarkable solo record, *Queen Bee Talks*. As the title of the LP indicates, this record is a showcase for female speech, and Reed subverts the tendency on blue discs to use women's voices only as a gauge of male sexuality. The male organ here is verbalized not with breathless awe, but with playful insults: at one point she categorizes the different types of male members she has known, from "parlor peters" ("it's not worth going to the bedroom . . . it's too small") to "attic dicks" ("pat it and shove it out the window"). We also find the fluidity between performer and audience typical of Moore and Reed's call-and-response approach: a woman in the audience stands to complain, "I'm sick and tired of that dirty, low-life, dog-ass pimp of mine. I'm not giving that motherfucker another dime!" "Talk, sister!" Queen Bee shouts. In fact, Reed plays the role of a guest speaker at a gathering of prostitutes who are organizing a union: a clear indication of how Moore and Reed's social perspective on sex could have political resonance, of how rejecting an "ideology of intimacy" could trouble the view of sex as a prepolitical mirage.

Reed's choice of narrative theme is particularly resonant in light of Angela Carter's suggestion that although prostitutes have been favorite heroines of pornographic literature, the economic aspects of a prostitute's activity tend to be dealt with "only lightly": "To concentrate on the prostitute's trade as trade would introduce too much reality into a scheme that is first and foremost one of libidinous fantasy, and pornographic writers, in general, are not concerned with extending the genre in which they work to include a wider view of the world."[108] At one point, Carter wonders about the possibility of restoring the "context of the world" to the "shadows of pornographic representation," an act that could provide a fresh perspective on the world and perhaps even transform it.[109] By stressing the social dimensions of sex in their remakes and parodies, Moore and Reed exposed the tendency to elide the context of the world in some of the most seemingly excessive and unrestrained expressions of white sexuality: erotica and explicit sex manuals. As such, their records provide a fresh perspective on the shadows of pornographic representation as well as on the LP record's role in delivering vocal performances that provided a vehicle for competing definitions of sexuality during the era of the sexual revolution.

In the four sections of this chapter, I have suggested that sexually explicit records convened the home audience in different configurations and so played a part in four overlapping sexual revolutions: stag party records were used by postwar men seeking to preserve homosocial forms of talk and find escape from the spaces of suburban life; the records of sexually explicit female comics on the periphery of second-wave feminism were heard in mixed-gender social gatherings of the early 1960s; LPs helped bring new forms of popular sexology to couples in the early 1970s; and Moore and Reed commented on those developments from a black perspective and in social forms that rejected an ideology of intimacy. We might note the tendency of many of these records to frame sex as a private, therapeutic endeavor.[110] Hilary Radner has argued that the sexual revolution articulated a "new cultural arena" around the assumption that individual fulfillment rather than reproduction was the goal of sexual activity.[111] That new cultural arena was shaped in part by a new sexology popularized by Masters and Johnson—and heard on Dr. Sloan's LP—that failed to address larger social relations: "Sensate focus and the squeeze technique are potentially important therapeutic tools, but they don't touch the source of the most intractable sexual problems of heterosexuals: fear, anger, boredom, overwork and lack of time, inequality in the relationship, prior sexual assault on the woman, and differential socialization and sexual scripts. . . . In sex therapy, the 'cure' is orgasm, not social change. And this is vital, because orgasms can be marketed in a profit-making system, while social change cannot."[112] As we have seen, LPs played a role in that profit-making system, often by marketing the vocal performance of orgasm.

The release of sexually explicit LPs by mainstream record labels and the discussion of them found in the popular press indicate the changing status of the home hi-fi during the late 1960s and early 1970s. By that time, home stereos were no longer primarily the domain of affluent professional men or a culture of male hobbyists.[113] Throughout the 1960s, high-fidelity stereo components and LP records reached a growing number of households due to technological developments and the record industry's realization that LPs provided a more dependable source of income than the pop singles market.[114] The proliferation of affordable stereo sets during the late 1960s has been linked to the success of post-Beatles progressive rock bands such as Yes, Emerson, Lake and Palmer, and Pink Floyd. Sloan's gatefold double album would not have seemed out of place beside similarly packaged rock records of this period. Progressive rock LPs—with their long, complex narratives, fantasy themes, and high production values—would have lost much of their impact if heard on the 78 rpm monophonic record players of a previous era. In fact, such studio-driven conceptual LPs were often consumed from beginning to end in a "cinematic" manner, suggesting that the stereo phonograph player was an important precursor to the VCR as a form of home media consumption. I have argued that party records were often defined in opposition to radio and television broadcasting, but ultimately adult LPs such as *The Sensuous Woman, The Pleasures of Love,* and *The Sensuous Black Man* represented early experiments with home media erotica aimed at the same couples audience that would become a market for cable television services with explicit content and adult films on videocassette by the end of the 1970s.[115] It is fitting, then, that one of the latest examples of an adult LP I have discovered is *Erotic Aerobics* (1982), which offered a half-baked attempt to ride the coattails of one of the earliest and best-selling videotapes of the 1980s: *Jane Fonda's Workout* (1982).

Though the material heard on adult-themed records became more sexually explicit during the postwar era, that material was increasingly performed in ways suggestive of intimacy. Where once risqué material was accompanied by the ambient party track heard on Fax's stag party records, the sounds of Rusty Warren's boisterous audience, or even Dr. Sims's enactment of family togetherness, the vocal performances on records such as *The Sweetest Music, The Sensuous Woman,* and *The*

Pleasures of Love were dominated by what Michel Chion calls the "I-voice": a dry, clear voice implying subjectivity and the address to an intimate interlocutor.[116] Moore and Reed's LPs represent notable exceptions to that trend and, along with the discourse surrounding Rusty Warren's work, suggest a connection between styles of erotic performance and class. The fact that the LP circulated such explicit and often intimate performances in the public marketplace stands as a demonstration of the media's role in the destabilization and recalibration of public and private space that characterizes the era of the sexual revolution. What is certain is that sexuality could be performed and consumed in the home on LPs in ways that it could not on network radio and television during this era and in ways that reveal the interplay between the performance and consumption of erotic material. In fact, erotic records stand as a powerful example of how media performances convened and constituted audiences around discourses of sexuality at this time and, in so doing, helped to convene and constitute the sexual revolution itself.

CHAPTER 4

Mimetic Moments

In the autumn of 1962, a small record company released an LP that was soon selling more quickly than any phonograph record that had come before it. Two weeks after it went on sale, 1.2 million copies had been shipped. In four weeks its sales topped 2.5 million, and by eight weeks, it had sold 4 million copies, topping the former best seller, the *My Fair Lady* soundtrack, which had taken six years to sell 3.5 million. A Chicago record store owner claimed that it was the hottest selling item he had seen in fourteen years in the business, and a distributor in Atlanta was said to be greeting airplane shipments at 2:30 in the morning.[1] That blockbuster disc was not recorded by Elvis Presley, Ricky Nelson, Frank Sinatra, or Bobby Darin but by an unknown twenty-six-year-old lounge entertainer, and his record did not contain show tunes or popular hits, but a spoof of President John F. Kennedy and his family. The phenomenal success of Vaughn Meader's *The First Family* (Cadence Records) marked an early peak in the rise of the postwar market for comedy records but was also a high–water mark in the history of a specific type of comedic performance: the vocal imitation of media celebrities.

This chapter is concerned with a subgenre of comedy records made by celebrity impressionists between the 1950s and 1980s, but more broadly with what imitation as a form of media entertainment can tell us about media performance and celebrity. Richard Bauman has defined *performance* as the "assumption of responsibility to an audience for a display of communicative competence," and *imitation* as a form of communication in which "the manner of speaking is to be interpreted as utterances that are being modeled after that of another person or persons."[2] I am interested in modes of entertainment that are hybrids of imitation and performance, of instances when imitation is framed as performance, or when audiences interpret performance as imitation. That hybrid form, which I will refer to as imitative performance, has been an important part of comedy performance in the twentieth-century media, most notably during a postwar "renaissance," during which time performers frequently took advantage of the phonograph record to capture and distribute their acts.

Media, performance, and imitation have often been discursively intertwined: consider the narratives connecting mimicry and technologies of reproduction described by Michael Taussig; or the fact that the early phonograph was frequently understood as an "artful mimic"; or the discourses of sound "fidelity" that have consistently surrounded the phonograph; or the perception of the cinema as a "mimic stage," whose audiences were dangerously prone to imitate the behavior they saw on the screen.[3] Frequently understood in terms of social imitation, the modern media also encouraged and disseminated new forms of imitative performance. Sound films, phonograph records, radio, and television made it possible for far-flung audiences to recognize celebrities by their unique voices and gestures and thus encouraged a shift from the ethnic caricature of the nineteenth-century American stage to what Susan Glenn calls the "comedy of personality": "The imitation, sometimes in a satiric vein, of the particular style and repertoire of *specific individuals*." Glenn has argued that female mimics on the vaudeville stage between the 1890s and the 1920s represented a "significant break" from the ethnic impersonation of the past.[4] Glenn connects this "mimetic moment" to the emerging phonograph industry, noting that writers sometimes compared the stage mimic Cissie Loftus to a phonograph player.[5] The phonograph industry continued to play an important role in the cultural life of imitative performance as a key medium for a postwar mimetic moment: phonograph records made by celebrity impressionists provided an outlet for an act that was regulated on network radio.

The LPs of postwar impressionists took part in the social construction of media celebrity, since professional mimics functioned both as unofficial Hollywood studio publicity and as a rationale for expanding the legal rights that celebrities held over representations of their personae. Imitation also provides a lens through which we can perceive the construction of cultural hierarchies of performance during the postwar era, both in terms of dramatic acting and the acts of comedians in the 1970s who sought to critique a previous generation of entertainers. In these and other ways, the LPs of postwar mimics illustrate how phonograph records offer a fresh perspective on American media history. The form that this chapter takes is itself an imitation of the routines of postwar impressionists, who often moved in rapid succession through a repertoire of famous personalities. Such a structure allows me to speak to many aspects of imitative performance while tracing a history of the "comedy of personality" in the postwar American media.

FRANKLIN D. ROOSEVELT (DEAN MURPHY)

In the 1944 MGM film *Broadway Rhythm,* a supporting character named Trixie Simpson (Nancy Walker) falls into a haystack while visiting a farm. To her surprise and ours, an actor pops out of the haystack next to her. Though dressed as a farmhand, he does not attempt to present a coherent character. Instead, he performs a series of rapid-fire imitations, including Joe E. Brown; Edgar Bergen's Charlie McCarthy and Mortimer Snerd; actors Ronald Colman, Clark Gable, and Jimmy Stewart; and finally President Franklin D. Roosevelt. The performer who played this eccentric farmer was Dean Murphy: a stage and radio entertainer renowned for his ability to imitate media celebrities, his signature shtick being Roosevelt. Murphy's eclectic act featured personalities from film, stage, and politics, but the presence of radio performers is notable. Murphy was working at a time that has come to be known as the golden age of radio, when that medium was a powerful force in American cultural life. Network radio greatly increased the public's familiarity with the voices of specific individuals, and in so doing created an audience that could quickly recognize the personalities in an act like Murphy's. Leo Braudy has even argued that performers who made careers out of "becoming a succession of specifically recognizable others, could hardly have existed before radio."[6] The work of Steven Connor, Susan Glenn, and Matthew Solomon on precinematic popular performance has shown that the imitation of "recognizable others" existed before radio. Nonetheless, radio offered performers such as Murphy both an outlet for their vocal talents and a national audience increasingly adept at recognizing specific famous voices.

Murphy's imitation of Roosevelt is an apt way to begin a history of imitative performance in the media, since FDR has become a key figure in studies of modern celebrity.[7] As is well known, Roosevelt received an unprecedented degree of media exposure during his time in the White House, becoming familiar to radio listeners through his famous Fireside Chats.[8] Though radio proliferated FDR's voice and helped to create his media celebrity, it also provided an outlet for vocal mimics. In fact, FDR imitators were carefully regulated on network radio. The *New York Times* reported in 1937 that presidential impersonators had been banned by NBC and CBS except during "news dramatizations" such as *The March of Time,* on which there was less chance that the audience might believe it was actually the president speaking.[9] Larry Nixon, a representative of New York radio station WMCA, defended the decision to take Arthur Boran—a "professional imitator"—off the air at the Press Photographers Association dance, stating that radio was "no place to mimic the voice of the President of the United States." Nixon added that broadcasters had adopted the rule that President Roosevelt should not be impersonated on the air because "ghosted" voices confused listeners: "Too many in the unseen audience might think it was actually Mr. Roosevelt at the microphone, whether the mimic delivers a serious speech or mere nonsense. Furthermore, mimicking is not good broadcast entertainment and by eliminating it we protect the listener from confusion."[10] Even *The March of Time* had to obtain special permission from a presidential secretary to imitate Roosevelt's voice. Dean Murphy and Art Carney were among performers who supplied sanctioned imitations of FDR for programs such as *The March of Time.*

The regulation of presidential mimics on the radio encouraged performers to find other outlets for their vocal talents, and phonograph records became an important component of the careers of many impressionists in the decades that followed. It would be a mistake, however, to view mimics such as Murphy as inherently oppositional, underground, or transgressive artists. In fact, Murphy gained the enthusiastic endorsement of the president himself.[11] It was often noted in Murphy's press coverage that FDR had requested the mimic's appearance over twenty times at White House functions, and that the pince-nez used in his act were a gift from Roosevelt.[12] One way to understand this cozy relationship between imitator and imitated is by reference to the work of Harvey Sacks, who wrote that seeing something as an imitation inevitably leads to related questions about "who owns reality."[13] Sacks stated that we perceive one person's actions as an imitation only in relation to our judgment that there is another person who is "entitled" to take that action. For that entitled person, it is quite irrelevant "to find out how *they* came to do it."[14] For example, if we see a child imitating what we consider to be adult behavior, we look for the source of the action, but when we see the adult involved in the same action we do not. Likewise, when Dean Murphy squints and speaks in slow, melodic phrases, we look for a source, but when President Roosevelt does the same, we do not. We might extend Sacks's argument to say that imitative performance can retroactively define the subject of an imitation as an original. That is, when we see a person's action as imitation, we subtly ratify who was imitated as authentic. Here, then, is one reason for the White House's cautious embrace of presidential mimics, from the 1940s to the present day.

Dean Murphy's presence at the White House illustrates how imitative performance became part of the process through which a modern sense of media celebrity was constructed. Warren Susman has described the emergence of a culture of personality, in which individuals strived to distinguish themselves from others in the modern urban crowd.[15] Susman points to a tension at the heart of this project: one had to present a striking individuality to be distinct from the crowd, but at the same time had to appeal to that crowd.[16] The relationship between celebrity and impressionist reveals a similar paradox: to become a media celebrity—the paradigmatic "authentic" individual in the era of the mass audience—one needed to display distinctive and idiosyncratic mannerisms that, in turn, made one easy to imitate. Professional imitators such as Dean Murphy used the mannerisms of public figures as raw materials to gain entry into the media and, in the process, helped to create and sustain the media celebrity of figures such as Franklin D. Roosevelt.

BETTE DAVIS (ARTHUR BLAKE)

Dean Murphy was not the only comedian to become famous in the 1940s for an impression of an inhabitant of the White House. Other comedians, such as Arthur Blake, also impersonated political figures. Blake was best known, however, not for his imitation of the president, but for his imitation of the first lady, Eleanor Roosevelt. Erving Goffman has pointed out that a speaker is typically allowed to mimic another only within certain limits and that the "rules of mimicry" concerning the kinds of copying that are appropriate vary from culture to culture. Goffman illustrates this by pondering the rules of gender imitation: "If a speaker quotes a person of the other sex, how far can gender expression be mimicked without the mimic becoming suspect?"[17]

Arthur Blake's cross-gender performances were a notable exception that can illustrate the rules of gender mimicry in the postwar American comedy of personality.

The professional imitation of celebrities was a predominantly male pursuit during the postwar era. This had not always been the case. Susan Glenn has demonstrated that female mimics were an important presence on the vaudeville stage in the first decades of the twentieth century, where they imitated famous female stage performers. Glenn argues that the prevalence of female mimics was partly the result of the widespread belief that women were linked to hysteria and an unstable self.[18] One way to explain the subsequent male domination of the act is in terms of Susman's "culture of personality": the desire to make oneself stand out from the crowd would certainly have had different implications for men and women, with the latter generally less able to project an idiosyncratic or attention-grabbing manner in public spaces. As a consequence, women were less able than men to mobilize performative strategies for gaining the media spotlight. With fewer distinctive and recognizable female personalities in the media pantheon, there would be fewer female mimics to imitate them.[19] Further, male imitative performance might have held a certain fascination for middle-class men in the postwar era: a time when white-collar work in large, impersonal corporations was thought to be encouraging "other-directed" behavior.[20]

Whatever the causes, celebrity imitation had, by midcentury, become primarily a matter of men imitating other men. Arthur Blake's imitations of female celebrities such as Hedda Hopper, Louella Parsons, Bette Davis, Barbara Stanwyk, Carmen Miranda, and Katherine Hepburn during the 1940s and 1950s were thus notable for the way in which they pushed against prevailing rules of mimicry. Despite, or perhaps because of, the flaunting of these rules, Blake enjoyed significant success in mainstream show business. Press coverage often described his "terrific impersonation of Bette Davis" and provided anecdotes about Blake's encounters with the Hollywood star: "The other night they met at a party, and Blake unconsciously started mimicking Bette's gestures and voice as they talked. It got so bad one of the guests turned to Blake's manager, Irvin Cohen, and asked, 'Which is which?'"[21] Blake's impression of Davis can be heard on an LP recorded in 1957 entitled *Curtain Time: The Satirical Impressions of Arthur Blake* (Star-Crest). The LP features monologues, skits, and songs delivered in the voices of male stars such as Raymond Burr, Peter Lorre, Jimmy Stewart, Frank Morgan, Lionel Barrymore, Orson Welles, and Clifton Webb as well as female personalities such as Zazu Pitts, Sophie Tucker, Barbara Stanwyck, Bette Davis, Eleanor Roosevelt, Louella Parsons, and Tallulah Bankhead. Blake's much-discussed Bette Davis bit is largely a matter of emphasizing the final consonant of her words, as in "to the lef-T," "someone I want to mee-T," and "would you like a cigare-TTE?"

Curtain Time illustrates both how familiar the quirks of film stars were to audiences at this time and how Blake's act served as de facto publicity for the Hollywood studios. In 1948 the *Oakland Tribune* explained that the film community had taken Blake to their heart when "the box office stopped tinkling so loud . . . and the stars began looking around for good publicity": "Now they love me," Blake said. "I'm just a million bucks worth of free plugs to them."[22] In another article, Blake stated that "movie stars don't mind being imitated—in fact, they love it," and went on to describe how Barbara Stanwyck had provided him with recordings of her voice so that he could get her inflections right: "The secret is kinda talking through your teeth," Blake explained. Blake also claimed that Lana Turner had confided to him, "I wish I were important enough that you could do me," a fact that was offered as proof that nightclub mimics had become "a good barometer of stars' box-office popularity."[23] As with Dean Murphy's FDR, Blake's imitations retroactively defined film stars as authentic, helping to confirm their status as vivid and distinct personalities.

Returning to Blake's 1957 LP, note that the record begins with a knock on the door. "Mr. Blake! Mr. Blake!" a voice announces. "Onstage, Mr. Blake." The comic responds, "Yes, yes, I'm ready Joe." After a few moments Blake says, "All right, bring up the curtain," and we hear the applause of a nightclub audience. Note that there is a certain ambiguity as to the type of club in which Blake is appearing. Indeed, Blake's imitation of female stars allowed him to move between mainstream venues and gay nightclubs. Blake's career indicates a certain fluidity between impressionists and female impersonators who imitated Hollywood stars such as Mae West, Bette Davis, and Marlene Dietrich. The boundaries between the traditions of drag performance and celebrity mimicry seem to have been permeable at this time, and some have claimed that both Dean Murphy and Arthur Blake were in fact gay.[24] Regardless of Blake's sexual orientation, the use of female figures in his act caused some confusion among critics. In a *Variety* review of Blake's 1946 act, *Symphony in Satire*, at the Embassy Club in New York, the author writes that although "Blake's impressions fill the bill admirably," he had gone "overboard in the number of femme takeoffs."[25] Or consider a 1971 article in *Gay* magazine that described Blake's appearance at the Loading Zone bar in New York: "To refer to Mr. Blake as a 'female impersonator' would be inaccurate," the review noted, "since his repertoire includes impressions of just as many men. For every Louella Parsons, there is a Noel Coward; for every Tallulah Bankhead, a Jimmy Stewart; for every Gloria Swanson, a Charles Laughton, in short, for every man there's a woman."[26] Blake's range of impressions enabled him to appear in different contexts of performance, but it could also confound audience expectations.

Blake moved across categories of imitative performance during the 1940s and 1950s, but the rules of mimicry for most postwar impressionists limited the act to male performers imitating male stars.[27] Rich Little, one of the most successful impressionists of the 1960s and 1970s, once said that the hardest people to imitate were "big, strong guys without any easy mannerisms. And a masculine, deep voice is the hardest one to do." As examples of stars who were difficult to imitate, Little listed Robert Redford, Rock Hudson, and Gene Hackman. By contrast, Little stated that he had "learned his Truman Capote imitation in 10 minutes."[28] We might return here to Sacks's idea that seeing an imitation has to do with "who owns reality." Perhaps Little had difficulty imitating figures like Redford or Hudson because they so effectively embodied cultural norms of masculinity, creating a performance that was difficult to see as a performance at all, and so was difficult to imitate.[29] Impressionists became adept at locating and representing those aspects of male media personalities that deviated from cultural norms. Here we find another manifestation of Susman's paradox: celebrities had to make themselves distinctive to stand out from the crowd but not stray too far from the accepted codes of performed identity. Postwar mimics helped to calibrate and police the boundaries of those cultural norms but also had to police their own performances according to the rules of mimicry.

ED SULLIVAN (WILL JORDAN)

Dean Murphy and Arthur Blake helped to pave the way for other celebrity imitators that followed, although the residents of the White House during the 1950s were not as widely aped as were the Roosevelts. Peter Robinson argues that the office of the presidency was felt to be off-limits for many comedians in the immediate postwar era: "Americans were generally unprepared to laugh in ways that might provoke suspicion or poke fun at the institutions they considered the bulwarks of their freedom."[30] It is telling, then, that the most important addition to the repertoire of celebrity imitation during the 1950s was not President Truman or Eisenhower but television host Ed Sullivan. The originator of the Sullivan imitation was Will Jordan, and his routine can help us to address some important aspects of imitative performance.

Will Jordan first appeared on Sullivan's *Toast of the Town* in 1953, which is coincidentally also the first year that the Oxford English Dictionary has an entry for the word *impression* used to describe "an imitation or impersonation of a person or thing, done by a comedian as a form of entertainment." Jordan's initial Sullivan impression did not connect with audiences. According to a *Washington Post* article from 1958, Jordan's act began as a true-to-life, accurate imitation of Sullivan and produced little response. When Jordan appeared on Sullivan's show the following year, he gave his imitation of the host "a whole new personality": "Ed says 'Show' with a kind of drawl; I made it 'Shew.' Ed likes to draw out the word 'big'; I made it 'r-e-a-l-l-y big.' Ed has a very mobile face, but he never moves his body. I added the shoulder shaking bit, the knuckle cracking bit, and rolled my eyes upward so the audience saw the whites." In the wake of these changes, the Sullivan act became a huge success, and Jordan was able to triple his pay, make more than six hundred appearances on radio and TV, and release several comedy records.[31]

Following his success on television, Jordan released a 45 rpm single called *Roast of the Town* on Jubilee Records, written and produced by Kermit Schafer. Jordan's disc featured imitations of the television personalities of the time: Dean Martin and Jerry Lewis, Liberace, Groucho Marx, Desi Arnaz, Arthur Godfrey, Wally Cox (star of the show *Mister Peepers*), and Jackie Gleason. Jordan's vocal impressions were placed in the context of a ceremony for the "Shnook TV Awards," hosted by Sullivan. Dean Murphy's act had relied heavily on radio personalities, but Jordan's *Roast of the Town* indexes the arrival of television personalities into the celebrity pantheon. Notably, the disc demonstrates the rules of gender mimicry prevalent at the time. At one point in the sketch, Jordan has Desi Arnaz and Lucille Ball take the stage to accept their award for TV's Best Husband and Wife Team. Although both Arnaz and Sullivan address her, Ball's voice is not heard. The record ends as all the celebrities are brought back to say their names: a virtuosic, rapid-fire change of identity that ends with Jordan speaking as himself. The voice Jordan uses to say, "and this is Will Jordan," betrays a strange kind of flatness: the "real" voice, his own identity, struggles to emerge in contrast to the idiosyncratic celebrities that came before it.

FIGURE 5. Ed Sullivan and Will Jordan give their performances of "Ed Sullivan." Courtesy of Photofest.

Though Jordan was clearly adept at a range of male voices, his Sullivan act became so successful that, despite being appropriated by countless other comics, he achieved a certain degree of authorship over it. In fact, Jordan asserted that he had not exaggerated Ed Sullivan's mannerisms but had "invented" them.[32] In his history of postwar American comedy, Gerald Nachman argues that Jordan's Sullivan bit had demonstrated the creative possibilities of the impressionist and revealed how "a truly inspired mimic could go beyond reproducing a voice, reshaping himself into the personality itself."[33] One commentator even argued that Jordan had "created a new character which is based on Ed Sullivan," and that other comics who did the routine were imitating Jordan, not Sullivan.[34] Will Jordan's Ed Sullivan reminds us that the goal of comedic imitation is not the creation of a perfect reproduction of the celebrity, since the audience must always perceive the labor of the imitator.

Consider a category of expression that Goffman calls "mockeries and say-fors," which involve the projection of "an image of someone not oneself while preventing viewers from forgetting even for a moment that an alien animator is at work."[35] Imitative performance is similarly double-voiced: it conveys both the subject of the imitation and the authorial intentions of the "alien animator." Who, we might then ask, is the author of Will Jordan's Ed Sullivan? To what extent can authorship reside in the voice and mannerisms of a speaker as opposed to their verbal utterances? Where are the boundaries between the imitation, exaggeration, and invention of a celebrity persona? Modern media technologies have allowed nuances of voice and gesture to become central to our experience of performance, but to what extent do these aspects of self-presentation exist in the public domain?

During the same decades that the postwar celebrity impressionist was prominent in American show business, similar questions regarding media performance and authorship were being asked in regard to American publicity law. Rosemary Coombe writes that, though the right of publicity had originally developed to deal with the "unauthorized use of a person's name or picture in advertising," it grew over the course of the twentieth century to include a person's physical pose, singing style, vocal characteristics, frequently used phrases, performance style, mannerisms, and gestures.[36] Coombe refers to comedian Burt Lahr's 1962 suit against the Adell Chemical Company, which had hired a "sound-alike" performer to imitate Lahr's voice in television ads: a job often undertaken by professional mimics. The court found that Lahr did in fact have rights over his "distinctive and original combination of pitch, inflection, and comic sounds."[37] The Lahr case points to the widespread use of vocal sound-alikes in broadcasting at this time and the related need to legally recognize the significance of voice and gesture in media performance. Recall Will Jordan's pleas for his originality ("I did not exaggerate Ed Sullivan's mannerisms. . . . I *invented* them").[38] In light of developments in publicity law, such claims to authorship can be seen in part as legal protection, since they distinguished the labor of the impressionist from that of the mere look-alike or sound-alike.[39]

As the Lahr case illustrates, imitative performances played a significant role in the legal construction of media celebrity. Coombe points out that the attributes of performance that became legally protected as an individual's "persona" were those that could be proven to be "publicly identified" with a given performer: "It is the degree to which the particular attribute is socially distinctive or publicly recognizable that determines its protection against unauthorized use." Public recognition of the elements of a celebrity persona became the rationale for proprietary claims over those elements: in short, "social knowledge and social significance" were "expropriated as private properties."[40] Impressionists such as Will Jordan circulated and to some degree created the "distinctive and original" attributes of media celebrities, and in the process, their acts of imitation helped to create the ownership of those attributes.

JOHN F. KENNEDY (VAUGHN MEADER)

The same year as the Bert Lahr case, the art of the impressionist received a significant boost with the phenomenal success of Vaughn Meader's *First Family* album. Mimics such as Arthur Blake and Will Jordan had made phonograph records before Meader, but none had enjoyed success on the scale of *The First Family*. Besides its remarkable degree of cultural visibility, Meader's record is also notable for the ways in which it constructed a characterization of Kennedy from a range of disparate media intertexts. Meader's record was, from the start, an intertextual and intermedia hybrid, since it represented the collaboration of former disk jockey Bob Booker and television writer Earl Doud, who had worked for Jack Paar, Johnny Carson, Ernie Kovacs, Steve Allen, and Jackie Gleason. After having their demo record rejected by most of the major record labels, they secured backing from Cadence Records and recorded the LP in New York City on the night of President Kennedy's October 22, 1962, speech to the nation explaining the Cuban missile crisis.[41]

As was the case with Dean Murphy's FDR routine, Meader's LP gained its first mass exposure on the radio. Producer Bob Booker's radio savvy was an important part of the LP's success. Booker had structured the record to "maximize air play" by including segments that were short enough to fit between commercial breaks as well as a few longer tracks intended "for the late night disk jockeys who needed to put something longer on to let them run out to the bathroom."[42] In fact, radio airplay of *The First Family* led to White House concern about mimics similar to that shown by the Roosevelt administration in the 1930s. Just after the LP's release, the *Los Angeles Times* reported that some radio listeners had mistaken *The First Family* for the actual voice of the president: "Many people started to write the White House, asking what in the world the President was doing talking that way right on the air for all to hear." The article went on to note that the White House was "quietly advising" disc jockeys to preface the record with announcements that clarified that it was "mimicry, intended as humor."[43] Though the White House could to some degree control the reception of Meader's record on the radio, there was little to be done about the millions of LPs being played in American homes.[44]

The success of Meader's Kennedy imitation is partly attributable to the growing popularity of comedy LPs at this time, as discussed in the previous chapter. Another obvious factor was the distinctive quality of the president's voice. "If the good citizens of the United States had elected someone with the flat diction of the Great Plains," wrote the *Los Angeles Times,* "maybe [Meader's record] never would have happened." "Then add a pretty wife who sounds half Brahmin and half Broadway," the article continued, and "basking in these inflected glories was inevitable."[45] We should also note that the Kennedy presidency—like FDR's—represented a quantum leap in the degree to which the American public experienced the president as a media celebrity. Besides his famous television debates with Richard Nixon, Kennedy was also the first president to hold televised news conferences; he appeared in TV specials that gave Americans "an unprecedented view" of the president at work; and First Lady Jacqueline Kennedy led a televised tour of the White House in February 1962.[46] Michael Curtin describes Mrs. Kennedy's White House tour as "the highest-rated program of the season" and noted that, with global syndication of the program, its total audience was several hundred million.[47] Television appearances such as these furthered JFK's image as "a celebrity politician" who could inspire confidence and loyalty while simultaneously attracting huge television audiences.[48] "Like a true film or television performer," Leo Braudy writes, "Kennedy combined the desire to be seen and the desire to be desired with an impalpable distance, an abstract immediacy. A child of his era, the first president to have grown up entirely with the movies and the twentieth century, he was steeped in the awareness that being seen on the screen can heighten desire even as the solitude of the image also distances it into something timelessly appealing."[49] JFK's distinctive voice and the proliferation of his media image made him a prime target for imitators.

Meader's *First Family* LP often took as its subject the incongruities of the president's media presence, making connections between the array of Kennedy's media intertexts in unusual and humorous ways. In the LP's most famous skit, a presidential press conference is turned into a comedy routine. "When will we send a man to the moon?" a reporter asks. "Whenever Senator Goldwater wants to go," Meader replies as Kennedy. On another track, President Kennedy conducts family business as a press conference, applying his precise style of public oratory to questions from his family concerning allowance, preferences for salad or coleslaw, and the distribution of bathtub toys. Jackie Kennedy's televised tour of the White House is also spoofed on a track featuring Naomi Brossart, who plays the first lady with an exaggerated, zombie-like whisper. Also consider the opening track of the LP, which takes aim at network advertising in a manner similar to Bob Newhart's comedy albums popular at the time. In a short skit intended to fit seamlessly into radio playlists, we hear the voice of a broadcasting pitchman, who announces, "Ladies and Gentlemen, I'm speaking to you from a typical American home in Hyannis Port, Massachusetts. Since January of 1960 this family of smiling and happy people have undergone a change. You might say they've been engaged in a new and different type of experiment. Sir, as head of this average family, what was this new experience undergone by you and the members of your household?" Then comes Meader's unmistakable JFK: "Well, after ah, two years of brushing with ah, Crest toothpaste, our group had 21 percent fewer cavities with Crest." The humor in all of these cases is as much about television as about the Kennedy family.

Meader also played with the president's television presence by casting the high-brow first couple in a narrative reminiscent of a television sitcom. The track begins with the Kennedys at home on a weekend evening, having this discussion:

> *Jackie*: Isn't it nice being here alone on a Saturday night, just the two of us for a change?
>
> *JFK*: That's what you said last Saturday and the Saturday before that and the Saturday before that. Don't you want to see a movie?
>
> *Jackie*: Fine. There's a wonderful abstract Swedish picture playing.
>
> *JFK*: I knew you'd say that.

The president goes on to suggest a "good Italian film playing, seeing as you like foreign films." The film turns out to be *Hercules* (1958) starring Steve Reeves. Later, the Kennedys try to order a pizza and call Secretary of State Dean Rusk and his wife to convince them that they are in the midst of a wild party. In Meader's skit, JFK's television persona blurs into Kennedy-appointee Newton Minnow's "Vast Wasteland" of American network television: Camelot meets the Clampetts.[50] In this and other instances, Meader's LP condensed or recombined a range of Kennedy's media appearances and so suggested that behind the president's fractured media celebrity existed a coherent, imitable persona.[51] I would argue that such a dynamic holds for this variety of imitative performance more generally: in the celebrity impression, an array of intertextual material is compressed into a densely packed, embodied performance.

Meader's vertiginous fall from the heights of success after Kennedy's assassination is perhaps better remembered than his meteoric rise: pithily summed up by Lenny Bruce's first words upon taking the stage, just four days after Dallas: "Boy, did Vaughn Meader get fucked!"[52] It is striking to witness Meader's erasure from primetime television as broadcasters began a "hurried examination" of their programming to eliminate material that would be "out of place" after the assassination. Meader had appeared on an episode of the *Joey Bishop Show* scheduled for broadcast in February, but because it had revolved around Meader's Kennedy impression, the tape was erased.[53] ABC postponed his appearance on *Hootenanny*, CBS "put off" his five-day stint on the daytime show *To Tell The Truth*, and his LP was removed from the shelves of record and departments stores. Meader soon announced that he would never do his Kennedy act again.[54]

Although the nation had apparently lost interest in hearing Meader's impression, Kennedy's actual voice proliferated on a glut of tribute and memorial records released in the years after his death.[55] *Redbook Magazine* wrote in 1964 that within days of the assassination, "the first recordings designed as memorials to him had been issued and were finding a huge audience. More than a dozen such albums are now available, and additional ones are in preparation." The records were being embraced, the article continued, by "many millions of us who have been left with a feeling of deeply personal bereavement by John F. Kennedy's death, and they will help to keep his spirit alive in as many homes." Publisher Norman Cousins was quoted as saying, "Nothing was more remarkable or characteristic of JFK than his voice and his ideas. Both are preserved [on LPs]."[56] JFK tribute records would win the Grammy award for Spoken Word LP in 1965 and 1966. Kennedy continues to be remembered largely as a voice: a testament perhaps to the cultural resonance of the LP during the era of his presidency.

Vaughn Meader's career may have been over, but his record inspired a new mimetic moment in American entertainment, or, as one writer put it, "the mimic gimmick" enjoyed a "raucous renaissance" in the 1960s and early 1970s. Following Meader, this "renaissance" found an important outlet on LP records. The moral of Meader's career for other aspiring mimics was to avoid becoming too closely associated with one contemporary public figure, and the new wave of impressionists frequently relied on a stock repertoire of the Hollywood stars of a previous era. Another performer active in the 1950s and 1960s built a career on the imitation of a single American celebrity of an even earlier vintage.

MARK TWAIN (HAL HOLBROOK)

Impressionists have often been perceived as a debased or amateurish breed of actor. For example, note that Dean Murphy's only line as "himself" in *Broadway Rhythm* is to announce that he wants to go to acting school. Nachman writes that mimicry was never considered a "high show-business calling" but instead a "fluke talent, a mere trick, a technical skill, a kind of comic special effect."[57] A critic in the *Los Angeles Times* wrote in 1972 that impressionists were often considered freaks and "looked upon as a dog act."[58] Will Jordan described impressions as a dead-end career move: "Nobody wants to be a mimic," he said. "I never met a mimic yet who wants to do it. We all want to be ourselves, but the public loves mimics. You do it because you get the instant recognition."[59] Postwar impressionist Frank Gorshin often expressed his desire to be considered an actor rather than a mimic: "I want to be thought of as an actor. In doing impressions I'm not playing myself but different roles, and try to become these people as I do them."[60] He even wrote an editorial for *Variety* in which he reminded readers that, although known as an impressionist, his act also consisted of singing, comedy, and "a lot of straight, dramatic acting."[61] All of these comments reveal a prevailing cultural hierarchy of performance in which acting trumps celebrity mimicry. We may ask, however, just how different are the performances of the actor and the impressionist?

James Naremore has defined acting as "a special type of theatrical performance in which the persons held up for show have become agents in a narrative."[62] Though impressionists have sometimes embedded their bits of mimicry within rudimentary narratives, we will do best to consider the issue from another angle. Note that although actors embody characters in a narrative, they also typically animate a script. Richard Schechner provides a way to understand this dynamic of "animation" in his discussion of performance as "restored behavior": "Performance means: never for the first time. It means: for the second to the *n*th time. Performance is 'twice-behaved behavior.'"[63] Victor Turner glosses Schechner to the effect that performance behavior is always practiced behavior; it is "either rehearsed, previously known, learned by osmosis since early childhood, revealed during performance by masters, gurus, elders, or generated by rules that govern the outcomes as in improvisatory theatre or sports."[64] If all performance is restored, "twice-behaved" behavior, then we might distinguish the labor of the actor from that of the impressionist by comparing the kind of material each restores and how.

In the tradition most pertinent to this discussion, actors are given scripted words and stage directions that they restore using their voices and gestures. The latter then constitute the performer's own distinctive interpretation of a role and hence the recognizable aspect of their identity as performers. Impressionists, on the other hand, take as their script the particular voices and gestures of media celebrities. We might say, then, that they do the inverse of the actor: for them the voice, mannerisms, and gestures are given, and they must provide the words.[65] It is worth noting that the impressionists of the 1950s and 1960s were not imitating "actors" so much as "stars." As Barry King has pointed out, film acting has tended to involve what he calls "personification," in which "the range of the actor is limited to parts consonant with his or her personality."[66] This has meant that film stars "begin to conduct themselves in public as though there is an unmediated existential connection between their person and their image," making clear that "the persona is in itself a character, but one that transcends placement or containment in a particular narrative."[67] Not only do stars tend to perform their persona even when not in front of the camera, but they often end up restoring their own mediated behavior, essentially becoming professional impressionists with one routine: themselves.[68] Leo Braudy tells an anecdote about the time that the impressionist Rich Little met John Wayne, whom he had been imitating for years: "Worried that Wayne had been offended, Little was cautious until Wayne welcomed him heartily and thanked him for keeping Wayne's own career afloat by reminding the audience of his image. Then he asked Little for a favour. He was doing a show that night and hadn't had time to read the script. Could Little read it with Wayne's voice and Wayne's gestures so that Wayne could see if it was right for him?"[69] This story provides another example of the utility of the impressionist to the star but also suggests that, cultural hierarchies to the contrary, the two performers are very nearly in the same line of work: both Little and Wayne make a living animating "John Wayne."

It becomes less obvious, then, that actors should be automatically considered superior to impressionists, and we can investigate the discursive construction of such distinctions through the career of a performer who developed an act of elaborate imitation on the stage during the same years as the postwar mimetic moment, and yet who was never considered an impressionist but always an actor of the highest caliber. Hal Holbrook's *Mark Twain Tonight!* a stage show that was released as an LP by Columbia Records in 1959 (later nominated for a Grammy), can reveal some of the discursive work that went into distinguishing actors from impressionists at this time.[70]

Holbrook began performing as Twain with his wife Ruby in 1947 while they were attending Denison University. Ed Wright, the head of the Theater Department at Denison, offered the Holbrooks a job appearing as famous personalities at school assemblies, women's clubs, and small colleges around the country.[71] In 1953 Holbrook developed a one-man Twain show while also appearing on the daytime radio and TV serial *The Brighter Day*. He took his Twain act to New York nightclubs in 1955, where he was seen by Ed Sullivan and offered a slot on *Toast of the Town*. Holbrook called his appearance on Sullivan's show "the break I had been waiting for," and he soon received other television jobs and even offers from Hollywood.[72] The Sullivan appearance also helped Holbrook acquire backing for the Broadway debut of *Mark Twain Tonight!* which opened at the Forty-first Street Theater in 1958.[73] Though continuing to appear on stage, Holbrook's Twain act achieved its cultural apotheosis as an Emmy Award–winning prime time CBS television special in 1967, produced by David Susskind.

Holbrook's CBS broadcast was both a critical and commercial success, seen by an estimated 37 percent share of the available audience, which represented more than thirty million viewers.[74] *Mark Twain Tonight!* was perceived as the antithesis of typical network television, and Holbrook was not bashful about his distaste for television. He wrote that Twain's humor was lost when "the percentage of television addicts in the audience is major": "I suppose if we watch television for five or six more years, without discarding it in disgust," he continued, "the whole nation will be asleep." Holbrook concluded that television had "done more to soften the backbone of America than any single thing, even Joe McCarthy."[75] It is in this light that Holbrook stated his hope that his CBS show would "broaden the range of what can be presented on television."[76] *Mark Twain Tonight!* was produced as an exceptional television event and received by television critics in the same vein. One critic wrote that it was "a poetic portraiture hardly ever attained by any medium of communication" and "went a long way in saving a sorry TV season from almost complete oblivion."[77] Another critic claimed that "there is more fun and certainly more laughs in Twain's work than ten TV shows."[78]

One aspect of Holbrook's special that critics found to be most distinctive was the relationship between Holbrook/Twain and the audience. Holbrook's stage performances and LPs had reached a different demographic than that typically associated with television viewing. The *Washington Post* described how Holbrook had toured "many of the Nation's top universities," where he had found a receptive audience. "The foundation of my audience is in colleges," Holbrook stated. "The minds of the students have not been closed shut and that group, along with professors, is a fine audience. Commercial audiences are not as used to listening as college groups are."[79] Those watching Holbrook in the studio audience at the 1967 CBS broadcast were perceived as being quite different from the typical audience of television comedy.[80] For one thing, the *Chicago Tribune* noted that laugh track was not used: "Standard TV gimmicks weren't needed, because the audience, most of it made up of people who'd written to the network for tickets, took Holbrook both to its heart and to its funny bone."[81] Indeed, some critics felt that Holbrook's pace allowed for a more thoughtful audience response: "This venture is a form of audience participation in which the observers are given many opportunities to stop a moment and think while they are being entertained."[82] Holbrook's appearance on CBS seemed to critics to be a refreshing moment of quality television. When we recall that high-culture LPs released by Caedmon records had been framed in opposition to television, it is notable that Holbrook's show had been widely available on LP for eight years at the time of the network broadcast.

Though associated with comedy records of the time and active at the height of the vogue for celebrity mimicry, Holbrook was almost never described by critics as an impressionist. An examination of the press discourse surrounding Holbrook can reveal some of the salient factors that distinguished acting from other forms of imitative performance. Press discussion of *Mark Twain Tonight!* focused on Holbrook's physical transformation and painstaking historical research in his animation of the famous author. Readers were often told of the three hours of makeup required to transform the thirty-year-old Holbrook into the seventy-year-old Twain, with many articles featuring photos of Holbrook before, during, and after his makeup was applied. Holbrook even claimed that he had to "shrink three and one-half inches" onstage through a process of "actual body shrinkage" to accurately play the part.[83] Besides makeup and adjustments to his body, the popular press frequently described Holbrook's dedication to research, described as a "quest for authenticity," in animating Twain. Holbrook spent "years studying the legendary humorist's mannerisms," a typical article noted: he had "studied old newspaper reports of his appearance, as well as Twain's own commentary on his platform method . . . [and] interviewed many people who knew the author personally or saw him on the platform."[84] It was the "thoroughness" of Holbrook's preparations, wrote another author, that made him "unique among our young stars."[85]

All of this exhaustive research could make Holbrook's imitative performance difficult to define. A *New Yorker* reviewer wrote that to find a suitable parallel to Holbrook's "uncanny resurrection" of Twain, "one would have to go to Colonial Williamsburg."[86] In his discussion of performance as restored behavior, Schechner distinguishes between the "restoration of a historically verifiable past," as in the case of historical reenactments like Colonial Williamsburg, and the "restoration of a past that never was," as is the case in most acting, in which a fictional character is "restored" via a script.[87] Schechner notes that the former is "very unstable" and tends to turn into the latter.[88] Such was the case for the *New Yorker* reviewer, who found Holbrook's technique to be intrusive into the accurate restoration of the historical figure of Twain: "It is impossible not to admire [Holbrook's skill]. And that, paradoxically, is the difficulty with the performance. For one cannot simultaneously admire an actor's methods and wholly believe in the illusion he is trying to create . . . it is a dazzling display of virtuosity, but one that calls attention to itself so emphatically as to baffle its own intention."[89]

The visibility of Holbrook's labor made his performances similar to Method acting, an approach that King argues refers back "to the person of the actor, the consistent entity underlying each of his or her roles."[90] In Schechner's terms, the Method actor tends to restore not just a written script but also his or her subjective, emotional memory. Similarly, Holbrook likened his acting process to a well: "From it [the actor] draws up experiences that have come to him along through life, and he uses these in translating the experiences in the life of the character he plays."[91] Holbrook described some of the experiences from the "well" of his life that had become part of his construction of Twain. These included observations of his grandfather, from which he learned "how an old man handles a cigar": "I learned many other things from him, too, which I have incorporated into my characterization of Mark Twain."[92] We would not hesitate to consider this kind of imitation "acting," perhaps indicating an underlying assumption that restoring behavior gleaned from one's memory of copresent interaction is the authentic work of actors, whereas learning behavior from film and television programs is the inauthentic work of impressionists. What becomes clear is that Holbrook's labor, as expressed through physical transformation, research, and the framing of his performance in terms of emotional memory and direct observation, helped to establish his imitative performance as acting rather than the "dog act" or "comic special effect" of the impressionist.[93]

We might also note that Holbrook animated a written script—Twain's oeuvre—and not the mannerisms of a living celebrity whose "original" persona could be easily crosschecked.[94] As a result, the nuances of Holbrook's stage business are easier to read as his own actorly choices. As one reviewer put it, "He has a talent for quiet, for age, for fiddling with his coatsleeves, for winking and not winking with the selfsame eye, for holding a lighted match in one hand while shaking out a handkerchief with the other, for touching things he has no intention of using but seems only to want to remember, for putting down one foot after another on a threadbare stage carpet as if it was the carpet and not his feet he didn't consider wholly trustworthy."[95] These actorly flourishes and attention to detail clearly displayed Holbrook's authorship and added to the rationale for defining his imitative performance as acting.[96] Though Holbrook's virtuosity prevented reading his performance as historical restoration along the lines of Colonial Williamsburg, it also made clear his status as an actor and artist. Critic Richard Schickel wrote that Holbrook offered "a selective, artist's vision of Twain, not an impersonation": "He is most assuredly true to the known biographical facts about his subject, but his greatness springs from the fact that he is, above all, true to his own vision of the man."[97] For Schickel, Holbrook's performance left the viewer "speculating on the most tantalizing enigmas": "Where, one must wonder, does the subject's identity end and the actor's begin? At what point does historical truth cease merely to support the higher truth of artistic invention and actually to yield to it? At what points has some eerie transmigration of Twain's spirit and Holbrook's taken place? At what points can such a transmigration never occur? What, in short, is the exact nature of the reality we have witnessed?"[98] Not only did Holbrook take part in the "mimic gimmick" of his time, but his act made explicit some of the most "tantalizing enigmas" of imitative performance, and his career demonstrates both the pervasiveness of that mode of performance in the postwar era and some of the ways in which distinctions were made about it.

PEARL BAILEY (GEORGE KIRBY)

One section of *Mark Twain Tonight!* that critics frequently singled out for praise involved Holbrook/Twain reciting excerpts from *The Adventures of Huckleberry Finn* (1884) as the eponymous hero. Holbrook described how, to sustain interest in a one-man show, it was necessary to find ways to periodically shift the tone of the act. One method was to portray other characters, in "a sort of double impersonation." Holbrook settled on a technique in which he first created the character to be played in a given episode and then animated that character while "thinking" Mark Twain: "The voice quality immediately changes when I do that and the physical movements acquire a different pace and quality."[99] We can see in the 1967 CBS special that when animating Huck in *Mark Twain Tonight!* Holbrook's voice remained in the register of the seventy-year-old Twain, but the movements of his feet on the carpet and flashing eyes belonged to the twelve-year-old Huck: a performance within a performance that was an unmistakable display of virtuosity. There was, however, yet another layer to this performance not mentioned by critics at the time. Shelley Fisher Fishkin has argued that Huck's voice in the novel was modeled on several African American children whom Twain had encountered and that it was experiments in African American dialect that led to the famous author's breakthrough approach to narration: "The voice with which Twain captured our national imagination," she concludes, "is in large measure a voice that is 'black.'"[100] Holbrook's performance thus becomes a Russian doll of nested imitations: he animates Twain, who animates Huck, who animates African American speakers. During the moments when he portrays Huck, then, we find mimicry subtly crossing racial lines: a notable occurrence in a postwar context in which white impressionists did not imitate black personalities.

The postwar era marked the end of two long and troubling American stage traditions: blackface minstrel performance and the ethnic caricature of the vaudeville stage. Nevertheless, writers such as Eric Lott and Krin Gabbard have argued that white performers such as Elvis Presley and Marlon Brando developed new forms of racial mimicry appropriate to the post-blackface era. It is notable, then, that both Presley and

Brando were frequently imitated by white impressionists. In a fascinating essay on Elvis Presley impersonators, Lott argues that the "blackface tradition" lived a "disguised, vestigial life" in Elvis's imitators: "Elvis impersonators impersonate the impersonator, a repetition that nearly buries this racial history even as it suggests a preoccupation with precisely the blackface aura of Elvis. . . . It is as though such performance were a sort of second-order blackface, in which, blackface having for the most part overtly disappeared, the figure of Elvis himself is now the apparently still necessary signifier of white ventures into black culture— a signifier to be adopted bodily if one is to have success in achieving the intimacy with 'blackness' that is crucial to the adequate reproduction of Presley's show."[101] Lott's insights have numerous implications for an analysis of imitative performance in the postwar era, but at this point, I want to suggest that Mark Twain, a figure elaborately dressed in a distinctive white suit not unlike the latter-day Elvis Presley, provided a "necessary signifier of white ventures into black culture," enabling Hal Holbrook to enact a "second order" blackface performance. Twain was thus a useful avatar that enabled a wider range of ethnic impersonation than was typically allowed to white performers.

Hal Holbrook's Twain can thus reveal some of the rules of racial mimicry that held for white performers during a time when long-standing norms concerning ethnic and racial caricature in American popular entertainment were in flux. How did these rules apply to African American performers? Harvey Sacks took racial difference as his primary example of the power dynamics inherent in the designation of an act as imitation. Sacks described how "pre–Civil War literature on slaves" often declared that "Negroes and children" were great imitators. For Sacks, the notion that an adult African American was a "terrific imitator" implied that "what he's doing can hardly be distinguished from that thing which, if someone else were to be doing it, would be seen as the real thing": "The adult Negro slave does something, it's seen as an imitation, and it's explained by virtue of the fact that he learned it from the masters. How it is that his same-age master learned it is no issue."[102] Homi Bhabha makes a similar point concerning colonialism, stating that racial difference prompts seeing the behavior of the colonized—those who are "almost the same but not quite," or, as he puts it, "almost the same but not white"—as mimicry of the colonizer.[103] Judgments about racial mimicry are thus an important index of larger questions about who owns reality.

Repressive hierarchies of social power were certainly a factor in the prominence of mimicry in some genres of African American vocal performance. Lynn Abbott describes an African American quartet singing tradition that featured "many onomatopoeic effects," including the imitation of banjoes, boat whistles, church bells, locomotives, brass bands, and steam calliopes."[104] We might also note the African American expression known as *marking*: a form of verbal performance that Claudia Mitchell-Kernan defines as the depiction of characters through the use of direct quotation, in which the narrator "affects the voice and mannerisms of the speakers." The marker attempts to report "not only what was said but the way it was said, in order to offer implicit comment on the speaker's background, personality, or intent."[105] For African American performers, then, mimicry was both a prominent part of the traditional repertoire and a potentially troubling category of performance, one associated with long-standing stereotypes and yet one at which African Americans were thought to excel.

George Kirby was an African American impressionist active during the postwar mimetic moment whose act suggests that African American performers had access to a broader repertoire of imitative performances than many of their white peers. Kirby got his start working as a porter at the Club Delisa in Chicago, where he worked his way up to bartender, all the while developing imitations of "the various stars of the radio," such as Amos and Andy, Jack Benny, Bing Crosby, and Louis Armstrong. In 1947 he was booked into a career-making run at the 845 Club in New York.[106] Duke Ellington caught his act and took him out on tour. Stints followed with Cab Calloway, Earl Hines, Lena Horne, Stan Kenton, Count Basie, Sarah Vaughan, and Billy Eckstine.[107] According to the *Pittsburgh Courier*, Kirby became the "first Negro comedian to be featured at the Copacabana in New York" when he appeared on the bill with Bobby Darin in 1962, as well as being the first black comedian to play the "main room of a major Los Vegas hotel" when he joined Harry Belafonte at the Riviera Hotel.[108] Kirby's act can be heard on an LP entitled *A Night in Hollywood* (1959), released on Walter Williams's Dooto Records. The album reveals that Kirby imitated many of the same white media stars as other mimics: James Cagney, Edward G. Robinson, Ed Sullivan, and Cary Grant. Indeed, Kirby was hailed in the press as "the first black comic to venture bold impressions of whites."[109] On his Dooto LP, the "boldness" of Kirby's racial mimicry is manifested by the way in which he placed some of his impressions of white stars against the backdrop of a cool jazz number. When Cagney and Robinson are made to recite the lines of a smooth version of "I'm Shootin' High," the listener is immediately struck by Kirby's skill at mimicry, but also at how flat and rigid the stars sound in that musical idiom.

Perhaps more notable than his impression of white stars, however, was the fact that Kirby also imitated black celebrities like Louis Armstrong, Nat King Cole, and Joe Louis. Consider Kirby's appearance on a 1972 ABC comedy special, where he performed a monologue as boxer Joe Louis. An expressive single blue spotlight immediately establishes a different tone than the typical variety show comedy routine. The voice of an announcer states, "One of the highlights of the early days of television was a program called *Greatest Fights of the Century*. No fighter provided more thrills to the viewers of that show than this man, Joe Louis, heavyweight champion of the world and one of the greatest fighters of the century." Kirby then speaks as Louis, describing his father, a sharecropper in Alabama: "He really knew what it was to be hurt. He died when I was four years old. The poor man never got the chance to find out what it feels like to win . . . I had glory, fame, and respect. I fought a lot of people, but I never hated anybody . . . at least I knew what it was to win." Note that the announcer identifies the subject of the imitation before the act begins, meaning that Kirby needs to provide few overt mannerisms to signal "Joe Louis." Indeed, in animating Louis, Kirby presents an understated, low-key delivery that stands in stark contrast to a century of what Robert Toll has called a "grotesque," "wild," and "seemingly compulsive" style of racial caricature derived from the minstrel stage.[110] What we see here is celebrity mimicry as homage, not parody, and based less on distinctive quirks of personality than on the celebrity as an embodiment of shared social experience.

Kirby's subdued performance as Louis differed from many of his more flamboyant imitations. In fact, Kirby was as adept at crossing lines of gender as he was of race. Kirby often imitated the voices of black singers in musical numbers, and on the Dooto LP we hear his impressions of Louis Armstrong, Nat King Cole, Ella Fitzgerald, and what was often called his "classic" bit: Pearl Bailey. The *Chicago Defender* described how, when Bailey was starring in *Hello Dolly* at the St. James Theatre in New York, she asked the audience to close their eyes and brought Kirby onstage to sing the title song in her voice.[111] Note that on an ABC *Comedy Hour* broadcast in 1972, Kirby utilized split-screen technology to perform duets with himself: as Louis Armstrong and Pearl Bailey, and as Nat King Cole and Ella Fitzgerald. At another point in the program,

Kirby appeared in elaborate drag as Pearl Bailey and sang a duet with Frank Gorshin, who sang in the style of Dean Martin. Kirby's cross-gender mimicry went against the grain of trends in postwar imitative performance, and though at times—as in his scene with Gorshin—such a performance could come uncomfortably close to racial derision, nonetheless it allowed Kirby a wider range of celebrity subjects than many of his contemporaries.

Kirby's act crossed lines of race and gender, but his mimicry went further still to include the imitation of musical instrumentalists, musical instruments, and sound effects. In addition to animating famous popular singers, Kirby would sit at the piano and perform in the style of Duke Ellington and Count Basie. His act also featured vocal imitations of musical instruments, and on the Dooto LP Kirby takes solos as a standup bass and a trombone. Kirby was thus adept at animating nonanimate objects and, in fact, was referred to in the press as "a master of sound effects."[112] One critic wrote that Kirby did "the best impressions of a 747 taking off and four motorcycles roaring into a roadside diner that I have ever heard."[113] In an HBO special that captured Kirby's 1978 appearance at Grossinger's Hotel in upstate New York, we see him mimic the distant sounds of a World War II battle and a jet taking off. Kirby achieved these effects through the deft manipulation of a closely held microphone, a distinctly modern approach to vocal imitative performance that was taken up by subsequent performers such as Bill Cosby and Richard Pryor. For example, the New York Times described Cosby's "masterful use of the microphone": "It is an essential part of his presentation, much as a piano is for a singer. With it, he achieves effects of space and distance."[114] The Chicago Tribune stated in 1967 that Cosby used "the microphone like a musical instrument, not just to magnify his voice, but to deliver the sounds of explosions and door slams and barbers' shears and touchdowns and sore throats and thunder and swimming lessons."[115] George Kirby was an important and influential proponent of this modern use of the microphone. Kirby's act demonstrates the potential range of imitative performance and so reveals the rigid boundaries in which most entertainers worked in the postwar years. We might say that the racist configurations of social power in America created the stereotype of the African American as a "good imitator," which in turn made black performers like Kirby have to work all the harder. At the same time, the decline of ethnic and racial caricature on U.S. stages provided a certain freedom to black performers such as Kirby, who crossed racial lines with more ease than white impressionists.

ELVIS PRESLEY (ANDY KAUFMAN)

The mimetic moment set off by Will Jordan's Ed Sullivan and encouraged by Vaughn Meader's JFK crested with a series of shows called "The Kopykats" that aired on *The ABC Comedy Hour* in 1972. These programs featured impressionists such as Frank Gorshin, Will Jordan, Rich Little, George Kirby, David Frye, and John Byner. On one episode that featured guest host Debbie Reynolds, the LP became the central theme of a sketch. On an *All in the Family* parody with Reynolds and Shecky Greene, we see the two performers put on an LP record and begin to dance together, but voices on the record break the mood. The voices belonged to the Kopykat cast members, who performed as Cary Grant, Zsa Zsa Gabor, and President Nixon. Greene and Reynolds address the LP, asking, "Would you like a drink?" The voice of Nixon responds, "No, I must keep my mind perfectly clear," and the segment ends with a close-up on the spinning record. The use of the record player in this sketch provided an excuse for a few celebrity imitations, but it also signals the importance of the LP for the postwar mimetic moment.

More often than referring to the phonograph, though, the Kopykats programs took television as their topic. For example, "The Kopykats Kopy TV" featured a "TV Roundup" segment, with Rich Little as newsman Walter Cronkite; a morning exercises program hosted by Will Jordan as Ed Sullivan; a weather report given by David Frye as Richard Nixon; and a spoof of *The Honeymooners* with George Kirby as Ralph Kramden. The program also contained a segment on late-night movie broadcasts that featured John Byner as Humphrey Bogart and Little playing Fred MacMurray in *The Caine Mutiny* (1954); Will Jordan doing both Charles Laughton and Clark Gable in *Mutiny on the Bounty* (1935); and Byner as James Cagney, Little as Jack Lemmon, and Frye as Henry Fonda in *Mister Roberts* (1955).[116] These skits make clear that the Kopykats relied heavily on a pantheon of Hollywood stars from the studio era. As an illustration of both the prevalence of the Kopykats and their reliance on film stars, consider that Bob Booker, cocreator of the Meader's *First Family,* produced a record called *The New First Family* (Verve) in 1967 that featured the talents of Kopykats Will Jordan, John Byner, and David Frye. The gag of the LP is that it imagines a future in which Cary Grant is president, Ed Sullivan is vice president and speaker of the house, John Wayne is secretary of defense, and Dean Martin is secretary of state.

Critics sometimes wondered why impressionists weren't adding New Hollywood stars to their repertoire: "When was the last time you saw anyone do an impression of, say, Dustin Hoffman, Elliot Gould or Sonny and Cher?" one critic asked. "Is it that the new crop of celebrities are more actors than personalities?"[117] Performers such as Hoffman, Gould, Robert De Niro, Jack Nicholson, and Al Pacino were certainly personalities as much as actors and have been imitated by later comics, but perhaps insufficient time had passed in 1972 to allow audiences and impressionists to perceive the elements of their performances that transcended particular film roles, and so the intertextual personae of the new stars were not yet immediately recognizable. What is more, part of the appeal of doing impressions for the performer was the immediate audience response they could elicit. New Hollywood stars may have been well known to some segments of the population but lacked the universal recognition needed for a sure-fire routine.

Besides Hollywood stars, President Nixon was a recurring target of the Kopykats and became the particular specialty of David Frye, who updated Vaughn Meader's approach by releasing a series of LPs featuring his Nixon impression. As had been the case with Meader's *First Family,* Frye's *Radio Free Nixon* (Elektra 1971) was made with radio in mind: Frye's LP features station identifications for the fictional WNIX that are tailor-made to encourage FM radio airplay. Unlike the Meader LP, Frye's LP did not mock network broadcasting as much as aspire to it: a prominent laugh track accompanies each routine, lending them the atmosphere of a television sitcom. Frye's LPs featured the comic imitation of the sitting president, an act that had caused White House concern when done on the radio but which had become an established part of American broadcast comedy with the 1975 debut of *Saturday Night Live (SNL).* Early seasons of *SNL* featured Dan Ackroyd's impression of Nixon and Carter and Chevy Chase's Gerald Ford. Chase's abstract rendition of Ford, however, signaled a change in attitude toward celebrity mimicry. "Chase's technique here was characteristically and disarmingly crude," writes Tony Hendra, a writer for *National Lampoon* magazine and author of a history of postwar "boomer humor." "Looking nothing like Ford, and attempting nothing in the way of an impression, he simply announced himself in various ways as the President and proceeded to fall around."[118] Chase's performance was a rejection of the craft of the impressionist, a rejection of the labor of the actor (see Hal Holbrook's makeup and research), and a refusal to ratify a celebrity status above his own.[119] "Impressions of any kind," Hendra continued, "however uncanny, are parasitic—an acknowledgement of the superior talent or greater celebrity of their target. Unless they go further than mere impression . . . they become simply a debasement of the recognition factor that exists in all humor."[120] For Hendra, the rejection of the "parasitic" technique of celebrity mimicry was a key ingredient in the early *SNL*'s progressive comedy. In fact, imitative performance became a site of a struggle over the definition of authentic performance for comedians in the mid-1970s.

In addition to Chase's "anti-impression," the early years of *SNL* featured regular appearances by comics such as Steve Martin, Andy Kaufman, Albert Brooks, and Lily Tomlin who presented a style of "anticomedy" that, according to Philip Auslander, took "the failure of comedy, the impossibility of being a comedian in the postmodern world, as its subject."[121] If these performers announced the death of a certain kind of show business, then it is no surprise that their approach would seem antithetical to the nostalgic acts of the Kopykats.[122] It is more of a surprise, perhaps, that Andy Kaufman—the most celebrated of the "anticomics"—made imitative performance central to some of his most famous routines.

In one of his most repeated and iconic acts, Kaufman's "Foreign Man" character ineptly attempts a series of impersonations of various celebrities. Announcing himself as President Jimmy Carter, Foreign Man's voice and bearing remain stubbornly his own. We don't expect much, then, when he announces his next impression will be of Elvis Presley. However, after turning his back on the audience, Richard Strauss's *Also Sprach Zarathustra* blasts from the sound system, and he soon emerges transformed into a jaw-dropping Elvis. As Keller notes, while Kaufman never stepped out from "behind the mask of the Foreign Man to reveal himself," the Elvis impersonation made clear that Foreign Man was "not what he seemed to be."[123] Kaufman's act at once mocked old-school impressionists and attempted to beat them at their own game. As with Chase's portrayal of President Ford, Kaufman was clearly not concerned with a display of technique for its own sake: the virtuosic quick-change act of a Rich Little or Frank Gorshin is exactly what Kaufman mocks as hackneyed and amateurish. Although the Elvis routine is a startling display of physical mimicry, Kaufman seems more concerned with exposing the jagged layers of performance and identity that professional impressionists had tended to smooth over.[124] In short, after Kaufman's routine, the Kopykats seemed quite out of date.

Later in his career, Kaufman trailblazed another kind of self-reflexive imitative performance, one that prompts us to consider the spatial and temporal dimensions of the rules of mimicry. Kaufman's impersonation of "Tony Clifton" both on- and offstage prompts questions about how long imitative performance can be sustained and in what performance spaces an imitation can take place. Kaufman began appearing as an abusive nightclub entertainer named Tony Clifton: he dressed in a garish tuxedo, his face obscured by an elaborate wig and makeup. Kaufman did his best to confuse the public about the ontological status of Clifton, sometimes framing his performances as an impression of a real person: "Kaufman often stated that he had discovered Tony Clifton on some stage in Las Vegas, and that his subsequent appearances in Clifton's guise were just his poor imitations of that original singer."[125] At Kaufman's 1979 Carnegie Hall show, he announced himself as a Clifton mimic but was then joined onstage by the "real" Clifton, played by Kaufman's assistant Bob Zmuda.[126] As with the Elvis routine, the Clifton shtick brought the theme of imitative performance to the center of Kaufman's explorations of celebrity, identity, and performance. With Tony Clifton, Kaufman took his critique of the Kopykat generation of impressionists a step further, doing an impression of exactly the kind of slick Las Vegas entertainer who did impressions in his act. Clifton thus turned the mimetic moment back on itself, making the Kopykats copy themselves.

Kaufman's Clifton has been hailed as an example of postmodern performance art because of the way in which he transgressed typical performance space. Take, for example, the famous instance on the set of the television show *Taxi* when Kaufman/Clifton refused to identify himself to his co-stars and carried on the Clifton routine even when the cameras were off. Kaufman was pushing the spatial and temporal dimensions of the rules of mimicry. J.L. Austin made a distinction between pretense and more elaborate imposture: "In a pretense there is preference for an element of the extempore . . . if there is too much [elaborate pretense], with making-up and dressing-up like an actor rather than a mimic or a diseuse, we begin to prefer to speak of, say, impersonation or imposture or disguise. To pretend to be a bear is one thing, to roam the mountain valleys inside a bearskin rather another."[127] The Tony Clifton performance marks a shift in the magnitude of imitative performance from impression to impersonation. To appreciate this distinction, imagine if impressionist Vaughn Meader had appeared as President Kennedy in times and places not clearly defined as performative.[128]

At this point it will be useful to summarize some of the distinctions I have made between imitative performances over the course of this chapter. When a performer animates a nonhuman figure—an animal or a car, for example—then that person is a *mimic*. When the animated figure is a character in a narrative or script, then that performer is an *actor*. When the animated figure is the intertexutal star persona of a media celebrity, then that performer is an *impressionist*. If the celebrity figure is animated primarily by means of physical or vocal resemblance, then that performer is a *look-alike* or *sound-alike*. When the figure is not an individual but a social type, then the performer is an *ethnic caricaturist*. The term *impersonator* can designate those instances when a figure is animated for prolonged periods of time, animated outside of traditionally defined performance spaces, or both. Of course, all taxonomies "leak," and perhaps it would be useful if I more clearly identify those liminal cases that will immediately spring to mind. Johnny Depp's recent roles in the *Pirates of the Caribbean* (2003, 2006, 2007) and *Charlie and the Chocolate Factory* (2005) reveal him to be adept at combining the work of the actor and the impressionist. That is, his animation of Captain Jack Sparrow and Willy Wonka were widely read to involve the imitation of Keith Richards and Michael Jackson, respectively. Depp illustrates how imitations can be laminated between the actor's script and performance to form another layer of cultural meaning. As another example, note that part of the critical debate about the film *Borat* (2005) had to do with the extent to which Sacha Baron Cohen was either an ethnic caricaturist or impersonator. We might also observe that different eras have privileged different modes of imitative performance: ethnic caricature was dominant on the late-nineteenth-century American popular stage but was replaced by mid-twentieth-century impressionists and the "comedy of personality," which has subsequently been supplanted to some degree by various types of impersonation.

Indeed, Kaufman's exploration of imitative performance in the mode of impersonation has been extremely influential, inspiring Sacha Baron Cohen's *Da Ali G. Show* and *Borat* and many aspects of Comedy Central's *The Daily Show* and *The Colbert Report,* among others. In the wake of Kaufman and those he inspired, the acts of the Kopykats began to look hopelessly out of step, a relic of an earlier era.[129] The Kopykat generation made a final appearance on LP in 1981, appropriately enough with another remake of Vaughn Meader's *First Family* LP: Rich Little's *The First Family Rides Again* (Boardwalk), built around his impression of Ronald Reagan. Little's brand of celebrity impression was no longer fashionable by that time, and the LP was no longer a privileged medium for cutting-edge, uncensored comedy, having been supplanted by the rise of videocassette and cable television channels such as HBO. Little's record was a residual style on a residual medium.

Nonetheless, the casting of Ronald Reagan in a remake of Meader's *First Family* LP was apt in several respects. For one thing, note that Bob Booker claimed that it was Ronald Reagan's bid to be governor of California that inspired him to make the earlier *First Family* remake, *The New First Family*, which had played with the boundaries between media stardom and politics, as noted previously.[130] But further, some historians have argued that the Reagan White House represented a self-conscious attempt to recreate the aura of Kennedy-era Camelot: "Once more Hollywood came to Washington; once more conspicuous consumption and dazzling parties were the order of the day . . . once more a professed devotion to government thrift was combined with larger deficit spending; once more the United States sought peace by preparing war." For historian Hugh Brogan, Reagan was performing a Kennedy imitation in which "everything was overdone": "Reagan wanted to make the United States feel good about itself again (Kennedy had wanted to get it moving) and his method was to grin at every problem." Reagan's "appalling caricature" of the Kennedy style did however "contain a grain of truth": "Kennedy's leadership (and by implication all political leadership) could never have amounted to more than a glittering show."[131] The Reagan presidency, like those of FDR and JFK, represented a further blurring of the lines between media celebrity and American political life. For Cull, the humor of the original *First Family* LP had lay in the audience's ability to recognize the similarities between the real JFK and Meader's parody while remaining "secure in its certainty as to the differences": "So long as the President was more than a collection of catch phrases and poses, everyone knew that the institution was healthy."[132] Similarly, for the humor of *The New First Family* LP to work, the audience must find a certain degree of incongruity and ridiculousness in the premise that Hollywood stars are running the country. Perhaps the humor of impressionists lost some of its affect when audiences could not so easily distinguish between the real and the acted in the multimedia construction of celebrity, or between political life and entertainment.

It could also be the case that impressionists lost their prominence in comedy entertainment because audiences were increasingly able to enact their own imitative performances. James Naremore eloquently reminds us that we are all mimics, actors, impressionists, and look-alikes in our everyday interactions: "We are always copying other actors, never arriving at an unacted emotional essence, even though we become increasingly adept at noticing strains or inconsistencies in the performances of others. For that reason, professional acting could be regarded as part of

an unending process—a copy of everyday performances that are themselves copies. In turn, it induces members of the audience to add to the
chain of representation by copying what *they* see, adopting mannerisms for a personal repertory."[133] During the postwar era, professional
imitators became intermediaries in that "unending process." Note that
Frank Gorshin often told the press that he had gotten his start as a
mimic by working as an usher in a movie theater, a job that allowed
him the chance to revisit and study star performances: "Naturally, I'd
see the same movie many times," he said. "All at once, at parties, I found
myself doing impressions of the actors I saw on the screen."[134] Similarly,
George Kirby was said to have been able to see movies as a child before
his peers because his mother and aunt were vaudeville performers, and
that "each week his buddies would pool their pennies so that George
could go and then return to give them a blow by blow account."[135] By
the 1970s, new media platforms had emerged that provided audiences
with opportunities for repeated viewings of star performances in the
home, making it easier for all of us to find ourselves, like Frank Gorshin and George Kirby, doing impressions of performers we've seen and
heard, a topic to which I will return in the next chapter. In the decades
before the proliferation of home media, the LP was a means by which
dynamics of repetition were explored in home media consumption and,
not coincidentally, was also the medium that best captured the mimetic
moment of the postwar era.

CHAPTER 5

Blind Television

In his 2008 book on American comedians, Richard Zoglin describes an "obsession" with stand-up comedy that he shared with many of his baby boom peers. Zoglin states that his generation experienced stand-up comics through two media: audiences watched them on television variety shows and "communed with them in private on the all-but-forgotten medium of long-playing records."[1] Zoglin's book is one of several recent histories of postwar American comedy that make passing reference to the records made by the "new comedians" of this era but do not sustain an argument about the LP medium.[2] Bringing scholarly perspectives on recorded sound, the record industry, and media performance to an examination of the postwar comedy album provides new insights into the work of well-known figures such as Lenny Bruce, Mort Sahl, Mike Nichols, Elaine May, and Steve Martin and also brings other, less-discussed performers and groups such as the Firesign Theatre, the Credibility Gap, Albert Brooks, and Lily Tomlin into the picture. From an initial burst of chart success in the late 1950s to a resurgence of sales in the mid-1970s, the comedy LP was an important avenue for innovative performers and served as a niche medium for comedy entertainment in the broadcasting era. Comedy LPs were frequently understood in relation to network television: at the same time that comics banked on selling records through their television appearances, their records parodied television genres, presented material that the networks censored, imagined the future of broadcasting, and even represented modes of television viewing. Postwar comedy LPs were so intertwined with television that they were described by Philip Proctor of the Firesign Theatre as a form of "blind television."

Throughout this book I have been interested in the ways in which performances convened audiences around the phonograph and how records represented a variety of performance spaces. Postwar comedy LPs documented changes in the spaces of American comic performance at the same time that they showcased techniques used by performers to go beyond those particular spaces to create and sustain a wider public of listeners. By *public,* I refer to Michael Warner's notion of "the kind of public that comes into being only in relation to texts and their circulation," a "space of discourse organized by nothing other than discourse itself."[3] Warner argues that one of the challenges of creating and maintaining such a public is the need to address "indefinite strangers" and to place them "on a shared footing."[4] Warner makes the intriguing suggestion that "the development of forms that mediate the intimate theater of stranger relationality must surely be one of the most significant dimensions of modern history," though he adds that such a story has been told "only in fragments."[5] This chapter is an attempt to tell part of that story: to examine how comedians of the postwar era developed forms of address that could "mediate the intimate theater of stranger relationality." The comedy record is a particularly apt topic for such an investigation, since comedic performance hinges on the creation of a particularly tangible affective connection between performers and "indefinite strangers," and long-playing records circulated those performances to a national public.

This chapter is divided into sections that relate to the performance spaces indexed on comedy LPs: the nightclub, cabaret, studio, and stadium. LPs by nightclub and cabaret comics of the late 1950s and early 1960s featured a jazz aesthetic associated with a sense of spontaneous improvisation and closely connected to specific urban nightspots. Records preserved the innovative acts of a new generation of nightclub comics such as Lenny Bruce and Mort Sahl as well as a cabaret style descended from the Compass Theater in Chicago. In both cases, comedy records provide insight into approaches to improvisation, a key component of postwar American art.[6] By the end of the 1960s, the LP became the medium for a late flowering of audio theater, a recorded version of radio drama in the era of television. The work of groups such as the Firesign Theatre featured a rock aesthetic that utilized the possibilities of the multitrack recording studio to create dense, fantastic sonic spaces that encouraged and rewarded repeated listening. Where records of the jazz aesthetic had striven for a sense of immediacy through their representation of a live performance, Firesign's "hypermedia" representation of media history was symptomatic of a time when television was becoming an archive of both its own past and Hollywood films of a previous era. In the late 1970s, Steve Martin's comedy LPs hit the top of the charts, capturing a stadium rock aesthetic that included his signature catchphrases. Martin's success came at the end of the comedy album's largest cultural impact, and by the early 1980s, the LP was displaced as the home medium for edgy satire by NBC's *Saturday Night Live* and cable television. Though the comedy LP was prominent on the American cultural stage for only a few decades, they were the right decades, decades during which American comedy was re-created by innovative performers and, as Zoglin's assessment of his generation's "obsession" indicates, when the form had powerful cultural resonance for a broad audience. The first appearance of those comedic innovations, which would be experienced by many Americans through LP records, came in a handful of urban nightspots.

NIGHTCLUB

The years after World War II represented the apotheosis of the urban American nightclub. After the repeal of Prohibition, opposition to nightlife weakened across the country, and nightclubs became a more acceptable part of urban culture. Thanks to a booming wartime economy and the disruption of family life caused by army recruitment, the 1940s and 1950s represented "the biggest era" yet for the nation's niteries: "Uprooted from their homes with money to spend, ordinary soldiers from around the country for the first time had the chance to patronize nightclubs. Fueled by wartime expenditures, the nightclub achieved the height of its prosperity."[7] *Variety* wrote in 1946 that "the saloon business has never enjoyed a bull market as in the past four years" and explained that wartime restrictions were siphoning "the mass dollar" into both "class and mass saloons."[8] The fact that nightclubs became a frequent backdrop to the films noir of this era is, according to Vivian Sobchack, an indication of the cultural prominence of such spaces in American postwar cultural life.

Sobchack argues that the space of the nightclub in such films represented a dark alternative to the postwar suburban home.[9] Likewise, a handful of small urban clubs became strongly associated with a critique of mainstream American culture during the 1950s. Clubs such as the Purple Onion, the Hungry i, Ann's 440, Mister Kelly's, the Bitter End, and the Café Wha had originally appealed to the beat subculture but began attracting a culturally elite, sophisticated, middle-class clientele, in part by booking a new breed of socially aware comedians. In these nightclubs, comics such as Dick Gregory, Woody Allen, Jonathan Winters, Lenny Bruce, and Mort Sahl developed what David Marc describes as "a relatively didactic, politicized, sometimes even angry response to mass society, the cold war, the indignities of Jim Crow, the denial of free speech, and a hypocritical web of traditions and taboos that gratuitously valorized religion and vilified sexuality."[10] Nightclubs such as these fostered a discourse that was opposed to mainstream American life as depicted on network television. Marc argues that urban nightclub audiences demanded "something of the exotic, the naughty, the 'adult,' otherwise, why not stay home and watch TV?"[11] Though Marc contrasts the nightclub to home media, the acts of many of these comics were heard in postwar homes on long-playing records.

The first comic to gain national prominence through an association with both the urban club scene and the LP was Mort Sahl. Much has been written about how Sahl based his act on references to current political events, famously signified by his use of a rolled up newspaper as a prop onstage. Sahl's brand of topical humor was innovative in the late 1950s and early 1960s. As one theater owner put it: "McCarthyism had chilled everything, and comedy was a lot of mother-in-law jokes. There wasn't any political humor. All you had to do was go on stage and say 'Eisenhower,' and everybody had an orgasm."[12] Sahl's onstage newspaper was emblematic of the comic's commitment to what Stephen Kercher calls "liberal satire," but it was also metonymic of Sahl's solution to a key challenge facing comedians: the generation of new material to satisfy the requirements of the broadcasting era.

In moving from the stage to radio, comedic performers encountered a formidable challenge: weekly or even daily radio broadcasts devoured their material. Radio comedians had to meet "the continuous demand for new laughs," the *Washington Post* wrote in 1936. "One funny program isn't enough. Comedians frequently come in and create a sensation—for one broadcast. Then they're through. They've used up all the gags and situations that were their vaudeville stock for years. When these are gone, the entertainers have no more to offer. On the stage you can go on repeating lines indefinitely. On the air, a gag is dead immediately after it has been used and can never be repeated."[13] In 1942 the

New York Times wrote that a comedian's act on radio had to be "done over again next week," a fact that had "profoundly changed the pattern of radio comedy since the innocent time when comedians got off as many jokes as they could collect every seven days."[14] Network pressures such as these helped to shape a comedy format that consisted of a featured comedian who contributed a certain character or identity in addition to trademark gags, recurring situations, and a cast of humorous secondary characters. In other words, the sitcom became the preeminent approach to withstanding the demands for new comedic material in network broadcasting. In Warner's terms, the sitcom was a constellation of techniques meant to calibrate comedic performance to the frantic pace of network broadcasting. Mort Sahl met the challenge of broadcasting's "temporality of circulation" by another technique: mining the ceaseless creation and circulation of news to produce topical comedy. Note Warner's claim that the "key development" in the emergence of modern publics was the appearance of newspapers and newsletters: "temporally structured forms oriented to their own circulation."[15] Sahl's use of topical material turned the modern temporality of media circulation into an engine for the creation of comedy material and in the process placed the strangers in his audience on a "shared footing."

The use of ephemeral subject matter created a sense of spontaneity and engagement with the present moment, as did another of Sahl's comedic techniques: improvisation. Daniel Belgrade describes how a range of spontaneous art forms of the postwar era such as bebop jazz, abstract expressionist painting, and beat poetry all suggested that "the most significant art is exactly that art which is ephemeral, interpersonal, and speaks powerfully in the moment and situation for which it is created."[16] For comics, an improvisational approach provided a means of generating new material to be circulated by the media. Mort Sahl's topical monologues were understood as part of this larger cultural trend toward spontaneity, with critics often comparing Sahl to an improvising bebop jazz musician. Tony Hendra suggests that Sahl "probably invented" the comedic "riff," "that extended free-form metaphor that explores all the possibilities of a preposterous premise or paints the details of a verbal picture based on one" and claims that such a free-form approach "had much in common with a similar movement in jazz." "Sahl's method was to establish a theme as a jazz musician did and then wring changes on it," Hendra writes, "wringing every possible phrase or comment out of its inherent absurdity until the possibilities had been exhausted, very much in the same way that a jazz soloist would handle a solo."[17] On records such as *Mort Sahl at the Hungry i* (Verve 1960), we hear Sahl's riffs on current events in long, unbroken takes. Jazz scholars have described the importance of recording technology in capturing and dispersing unscripted improvisations as well as the long-playing record's capacity to capture the longer improvisations of performers such as John Coltrane. Similarly, Sahl's extended topical monologues could be captured and reproduced by the LP in a manner difficult in the era of the 78 rpm disc.[18]

Given the title of Sahl's 1960 album, we should note another similarity between nightclub comics of this era and bebop jazz: the close association between records and live performances in specific nightclubs. Besides Sahl's Hungry i session, compare comedy records such as *Dick Gregory: Live at the Village Gate* (Poppy 1970) and *Smothers Brothers Live at the Purple Onion* (Mercury 1961) to a few notable examples of postwar jazz records that reference their site of performance: Bill Evans's *Sunday at the Village Vanguard* (Riverside 1961); John Coltrane's *Live at Birdland* (Impulse! 1963); Sonny Rollins's *A Night at the Village Vanguard* (Blue Note 1957); and Eddie "Lockjaw" Davis and Johnny Griffin's *Live at Mintons* (Fantasy 1961).[19] Postwar bebop has long been associated with specific nightclubs such as Minton's Playhouse and Monroe's Uptown House, where musicians such as Charlie Parker or Dizzy Gillespie traded complex and elaborate solos for audiences of their peers after long stints with more commercial big bands.[20] Besides sharing a similar taste for extended improvisational riffing and nightclub ambiance, bebop and the new comedians were often on the same independent record labels. Sahl, for example, was on Norman Granz's Verve Records, which also released records by Oscar Peterson, Coleman Hawkins, Sonny Rollins, Lester Young, Ella Fitzgerald, and Dizzy Gillespie. As we can see, a number of industrial and aesthetic connections forged an association between new comics and adjacent forms of postwar spontaneous art.

Besides Sahl, the other comic of this period whose work was most often compared to jazz music was Lenny Bruce: for example, on liner notes to one of Bruce's live LPs, jazz critic Ralph J. Gleason described his comic bits as "modal improvisations à la Coltrane" and "verbal jazz improvisations à la Charlie Parker." Bruce also suggested to his nightclub and LP audiences that they were being allowed access to material that could not be broadcast on television. On a track from the LP *Togetherness* (Fantasy 1959) entitled "The Steve Allen Show," Bruce imparted an intriguing backstage account of his battle with television censors over whether he'd be allowed to tell a joke about Jewish burial practices. Bruce is frank about the restrictions placed on comics by the machinery of network television and so implicitly holds up the LP as a medium that allowed comics and audiences more freedom. But this bit also illustrates the importance of ethnicity in the comedy of this era: it is the "Jewishness" of Bruce's joke that is at issue in the "Steve Allen Show" incident. Kercher describes the central role played by Jewish Americans in postwar satire: "Coming from an ethnic background that was historically persecuted and excluded from positions of cultural authority, raised in a culture that prized wit and deflationary humor, these thoroughly assimilated, articulate, determined, politicized young Jews proudly maintained the perspective of detached observers. As many of them have remarked, their Jewish consciousness contributed greatly to their identities as cultural renegades and facilitated the ironic distance necessary for their sharp and caustic humor."[21] We should note that the prevalence of Jewish humor on comedy LPs occurred at the same historical moment when performances of overt Jewish ethnicity were disappearing from primetime network television. Television historians have described how network policies were influenced by changing audience demographics at this time, which indicated that the cultural references made by Jewish comedians such as Milton Berle lost their legibility for much of the television audience.[22] As Bruce's "Steve Allen" track indicates, comedy records by Sahl, Bruce, Shelley Berman, Mel Brooks, and Allen Sherman ran counter to these trends on network television.

That LPs presented a kind of ethnic humor not found on television is one argument for describing the public created by their circulation as a *counterpublic*: a term Warner uses to describe a dominated group that aspires to "re-create itself as a public" and in so doing comes into conflict "with the norms that constitute the dominant culture as a public."[23] Counterpublics, Warner continues, "mark themselves off unmistakably from any general or dominant public. Their members are understood to be not merely a subset of the public but constituted through a conflictual relation to the dominant public."[24] LPs by edgy nightclub comics, with their use of Yiddish slang, profanity, drug references, and verboten political sentiments, invited their listeners to consider themselves to be part of a counterpublic and so must have provided a sense of transgression and fostered a certain niche affinity among record owners. Note how Sahl often ended his act by overtly convening a counterpublic, urging listeners to "join arms and sing labor songs" and noting that "if things go well, next year we won't have to hold these meetings in secret." Elsewhere, he encouraged listeners to "break off into buzz-groups and discuss the real meaning of the material" and suggested that "those of you who have applauded have signified yourselves as group leaders. As I leave I'd like you to act as a rallying point for collective action." Such statements illustrate Kercher's claim that Sahl's comedy "reinforced a sense of solidarity and, admittedly, superiority among his well-educated, middle- and upper-middle-class liberal fans."[25] But they also suggested that the audience's presence in the club or around the hi-fi stereo constituted tacit membership in a counterpublic, despite the fact that they may not have been subalterns for any reason other than being in the club or buying the record.[26] Notably, though Sahl urges the audience to take "collective action" *after* his gig, it was only through their attention or applause that the audience could enact their membership *during* the act itself. Another emergent style of comedy performance heard on postwar LPs and originating from a space resembling the nightclub attempted to establish a more active role for the strangers who made up its audience.

CABARET

The *Oxford English Dictionary* defines *cabaret* as a "restaurant or night-club in which entertainment is provided as an accompaniment to a meal" and where that entertainment takes the form of a floorshow. As a performance space, then, the cabaret has two key attributes: the entertainment takes place on the same level as the audience, and the audience members are "active" during the show, in the sense that they eat, drink, and smoke. In her history of the European cabaret tradition, Lisa Appignanesi characterizes the form as "an intimate, small-scale, but intellectually ambitious revue" where "the relationship between performer and spectator is one at once of intimacy and hostility, the nodal points of participation and provocation."[27] European cabaret can be traced to belle epoque Paris, but Lewis Erenberg finds the origins of an American cabaret in 1911, when two vaudeville entrepreneurs, Henry B. Harris and Jesse Lasky, opened the Folies Bergère Theater in New York, modeled on a Parisian style.[28] By the late 1930s, several influential cabarets had opened in New York that combined political satire and jazz, including Barney Josephson's Café Society and Harold Jacoby's Blue Angel.[29] Economic factors helped to encourage the use of the cabaret floorshow, which did not require the extra cost of a theatrical license for stages and scenery.[30] Crucially, the floorshow meant that the audience and the performers were brought into a more intimate relationship than in the conventional theater. Appignanesi writes that in the Parisian cabaret, performers played directly to the audience, "breaking down the illusory fourth wall" of traditional theaters.[31] Erenberg describes the American floorshow along similar lines: "Performers started their acts on the platform and then stepped down onto the floor and appeared among the diners . . . the entire restaurant became the setting for performance, and customers themselves could not escape becoming involved in the action and spontaneity of the moment. In a theatre, expressiveness was limited primarily to hired performers. In the cabaret, audiences and performers were on the same level, and thus expressiveness spread to the audience as well."[32] The cabaret setting thus broke down some of the formal barriers between performer and audience by allowing them to interact to a greater degree than other forms of popular theater.

It was just this type of shared spontaneity between audience and performer that David Shepherd sought to establish on American soil in the 1950s. After studying drama at Columbia University and the Sorbonne and seeing Marcel Marceau perform in a Parisian cabaret, Shepherd decided to start his own theater.[33] He moved to Chicago and, with Paul Sills, formed the Compass Theater in 1955. Topicality helped the Compass to produce new comic material in a manner reminiscent of Mort Sahl: Compass performances featured a "Living Newspaper" segment, in which actors "attempted to weave humorous dialogue and pantomime into newspaper articles they read onstage."[34] The Compass also encouraged an interactive and spontaneous relationship between performer and audience akin to European cabaret. Shepherd had originally envisioned improvisation as a tool in the creation of a working-class theater, in which the audience provided topical scenarios. In spite of these original ideological motivations, the Compass's proximity to the University of Chicago meant that the theater attracted a progressive, well-educated, and liberal-minded middle-class audience and a similar pool of talent. New York performers like Shelley Berman and Mike Nichols further inspired a turn away from working-class drama and toward sketch comedy based on middle-class angst. In the words of one critic, the troupe moved from Shepherd's "socially conscious scenario format" to sketches based on "what the performers knew best": "What it was like to be a very bright, more-or-less neurotic denizen of the middle class." As Shephard put it, the Compass ended up addressing "the tyranny of the middle-class Jewish family."[35] The two most famous practitioners of this Compass school of improv were known to the American public in large part though LP records: Mike Nichols and Elaine May.

Nichols and May were not the first Compass graduates to find success in the record business. Shelley Berman got his start as an entertainer at the Compass, where he was often teamed up with Nichols and May. Berman set out on his own as a stand-up comedian, and his much-imitated telephone monologues were part of an act that helped to invent what is now called observational comedy, in which the performer dissects the mundane irritations, annoyances, and embarrassments of everyday life.[36] Mort Sahl convinced his record company to sign Berman, and his first release, *Inside Shelley Berman* (Verve 1959), shot to the top of the charts. As Coleman puts it, "All over the country, the 'silent generation' were retreating to their rec rooms and dormitories, listening to the 'Method Comedian' on their new hi-fi's."[37] Berman's first two LPs were released at exactly the moment in the history of the record business when unit sales of LP records were overtaking unit sales of singles.[38] As we have seen, the shift from singles to LP sales was an important turning point in the record industry, and Berman's comedy records were a significant part of that change. *Billboard* wrote in October 1960 that sales of comedy LPs were so good that record manufacturers were "laughing all the way to the bank," with comedy LPs dominating the LP charts.[39] As a sign of the times, *Billboard* introduced a new method of charting LP sales in 1960 that had two classifications: steady-selling "evergreens" that had been on the charts forty weeks or longer and newer LPs, which were "bringing to the album business some of the excitement which in the past has been associated only with single records."[40] As an indication of the importance of comedy records in this industry reassessment, the first "evergreen" to be featured on the steady-selling LP chart was *Inside Shelley Berman*. Berman's LPs, which were soon followed up the charts by the albums of Jonathan Winters and Bob Newhart, marked the beginning of the comedy LP's economic and cultural renaissance and helped to tip the industry balance toward the LP market.

Mike Nichols and Elaine May also began at the Compass and, like Berman, set out on their own in the late 1950s. An important break came when they appeared on the television show *Omnibus* in 1958, doing skits that they had developed onstage at the Compass. Though it was a television appearance that rocketed them to celebrity, the duo maintained a low profile on television even at the peak of their success, putting their creative energy instead into stage shows, radio appearances, and the release of chart-topping LPs. Their first record album, *Improvisations to*

Music (Mercury 1959), was followed by an album of their Broadway show directed by Arthur Penn, *An Evening with Mike Nichols and Elaine May* (Mercury 1960), which reached the *Billboard* top ten in 1961 and stayed on the charts for thirty-two weeks.[41] One more LP, *Nichols and May Examine Doctors* (Mercury 1962), followed, which was comprised of material recorded for the NBC radio program *Monitor.*

Not only did they concentrate on other media forms, but Nichols and May were known for a somewhat critical stance toward TV and even turned down potentially lucrative network development deals. When they appeared at the Emmy Awards show in 1959, May praised the men who, "year in, year out," were "quietly producing garbage." Nichols played the winner of the Total Mediocrity award and assured viewers that "no matter what suggestions the sponsors make, I take them."[42] The popular team was scheduled for a return performance at the 1960 Emmy Awards show, but the sponsor, Proctor and Gamble, rejected their sketch just hours before the broadcast, and Nichols and May refused to replace the censored bit with old material. The sketch was to have featured Nichols presenting May with the "David Susskind award for contributing to the maturity and dignity of television." After vigorously denying charges that television was controlled by advertisers, May was to remove a wig and make a plug for a home-permanent application. NBC and Proctor and Gamble found the bit to be "inappropriate," particularly as it was to be immediately followed by an ad for the sponsor's Lilt home permanent.[43]

Similar barbs at TV sponsorship can be found on a *Monitor* sketch called "Doing the Bard." We hear Nichols recite a soliloquy from Hamlet until he is interrupted by May, who plays the representative of a beer company sponsoring the production. She reports that the sponsor is keen to fight the idea that beer makes people overweight and so asks if he could substitute something for "this too, too solid flesh," a line that might imply fatness: "Any other kind of flesh would do," she says. "The fat angle is the thing we're against." The line "how weary, stale and flat" also needs to go, she reports, as it could be read as an implication about the beer. "I can't very well say, 'how weary, stale, with a good head on it,'" Nichols laconically replies. May laughs and says, "That's wonderful! I'm glad you have a sense of humor because *I hate this job.*" The critique of network sponsorship found here and Nichols and May's well-publicized experiences with the Emmy Awards suggest that those who listened to their act on radio and LPs may well have felt themselves to be taking a stance against mainstream network TV.

Shades of a counterpublic sensibility are one of several similarities between what I am calling the nightclub and cabaret comedy of the postwar era: both featured a prominent representation of Jewish ethnicity; the use of topical humor; and a focus on the performance of spontaneity. There are, however, some important differences between the kind of improvisation used by a performer like Sahl and players trained at the Compass. Most notably, where nightclub riffing was a solo endeavor, the Compass featured a group improvisational style modeled as much on children's play and athletics as on jazz. An important influence on the Compass style of spontaneous performance was Paul Sills's mother, Viola Spolin. Spolin had begun her career working with "ghetto children" in the 1930s, where she developed nonverbal techniques meant to "transform theater conventions into games and playing into a spontaneous act, making age, background and words irrelevant."[44] She led the Young Actors Company in Hollywood before returning to Chicago to work at the Compass. Spolin would later codify her approach to theater games in one of the most influential acting books of the postwar era: *Improvisations for the Theater* (1963).

Spolin saw her approach to improvisation as a way to combat what was a key concern of the postwar era: conformity. Spolin wrote that the spontaneity her technique generated released "personal freedom" and awakened "the total person, physically, intellectually, and intuitively."[45] Theater games, she argued, could thus "help clear the air of authoritarianism."[46] Spolin compared her theater games to athletics to emphasize a sense of teamwork and stress the importance of spontaneity: "A basketball player (the actor) is acutely conscious of everything going on around him and he's ready to react instantly. His mind is wrapped in the play of the ball . . . and his actions are determined only by the rules of the game . . . and the possibilities of his own body."[47] Elsewhere Spolin stated that "behind the bat, you can't be thinking about how you hit it last month or how you felt when you didn't hit it. You are there in the moment having to hit that ball."[48] References to athletics were part of Spolin's emphasis on "physicalization," by which she meant "the means by which material is presented to the student on a physical, non-verbal level as opposed to an intellectual or psychological approach": "Our first concern with students is to encourage freedom of physical expression, because the physical and sensory relationship with the art form opens the door for insight."[49] Spolin contrasted her notion of physicalization to a more psychological approach to acting, stating that she was not concerned with the actor's private beliefs or feelings: "We are interested only in direct physical communication. Feelings, personal to each of us, are of no use in theater . . . there is no time for 'feeling' any more than a quarterback running down the field can be concerned with his clothes or whether he is universally admired." "A player can dissect, analyze, intellectualize, or develop a valuable case history for a part," she continued, "but if one is unable to assimilate it and communicate it physically, it is useless within the theater form."[50]

Such comments reveal what M.M. Bakhtin called a discourse of "hidden polemic," where assertions are constructed in such a way as to bring a "polemical attack" against another assertion on the same topic.[51] In this case, Spolin's assertions betray a polemical attack against the Method approach of Lee Strasberg's Actors Studio. Indeed, the Chicago school of comedic improvisation has frequently been contrasted with the Method. In the Method as taught by Strasberg, improvisation involved the development of techniques that could access inner, personal emotions and affective memories, resulting in a style of performance that was often characterized by "a feeling of halting spontaneity" punctuated by emotional outbursts.[52] Paul Sills defined his technique in relation to a Method school that relied on "inner actions" or "private moments." Sills held that the Compass's improvisations, by contrast, were "public moments."[53] For Sills, improvisation was about interpersonal relations and demanded "a between-ness of at least two people." The "psychological style in theater has never interested me," he said. "It's about isolation and alienation—who needs that?"[54] For Virginia Wright Wexman, the Chicago school used improvisation "not to probe the inner depths of the actor/character's psyche in the interests of a more persuasive illusion of realism but to foreground the process of character creation itself in the interests of forging a communal bond between performer and audience."[55] Similarly, in her history of the Compass, Janet Coleman compares the Method's "one-man game" to the "extroverted material, more elliptical observations, less Sturm und Drang, [and] funnier report of things" that was the outcome of Spolin's theater games.[56] The Method emerges as a "one-man game" in its approach to improvisation, and its most iconic practitioners, such as James Dean and Marlon Brando, were adept at investing nuances of performance with emotional meaning, albeit to the detriment of the interplay between players.[57]

It is not surprising that film scholars such as Wexman have tended to focus on cinematic improvisation and on the role of the director in shaping spontaneous performances, for example, Robert Altman's assimilation of "the Second City agenda" into Hollywood filmmaking.[58]

By restricting the field of inquiry to the cinema, however, scholars have overlooked a more direct representation of Chicago school improvisational performances found on comedy LPs. Indeed, Nichols and May's LPs are perhaps the best documentation of the "between-ness" characteristic of the Compass approach. Consider "Bach to Bach," from their first LP, *Improvisations to Music,* in which a young couple tries to impress each other as they listen to a record.

> Nichols: [*Whistles along to the record*]
>
> May: You know it very well.
>
> Nichols: Better than myself in some ways.
>
> May: It's beautiful.
>
> Nichols: It has a fantastic peace.
>
> May: Yes. It's serene. It has a kind of mathematical certainty that's almost sensual to me.
>
> Nichols: Yes, yes, yes, an order, a finality finally.
>
> May: Yes, organization!
>
> Nichols: She plays it with just incredible clarity.
>
> May: Yes, she does.
>
> Nichols: Yes, yes.

The two go on to discuss "the ambivalence of the woman's role today" ("Oh, it's *incredibly* ambivalent!") as well as the work of Adler and Nietzsche: "When I read *Thus Spake Zarathustra,* a whole world opened for me," May muses, to which Nichols exclaims, "I know *exactly* what you mean!"[59] The scene gives an indication of the priorities of Compass improvisation. The humor of the scene plays on the frantic and awkward "between-ness" of the two players, and unlike the Method's "one-man game," the two are equal cocreators of the scene, subtly building on each statement made by the other.

We might say that Nichols and May make use of both the contingent and the collective nature of improvisation. Keith Sawyer claims that improvisation is both contingent, with "each moment emerging, unpredictable, from the prior flow of the performance," and collective, since individual performers influence one other from moment to moment.[60] The emergent moment changes with each performance act, becoming an "intersubjective, shared activity," with performers working together in its creation. The requirements of this cocreation constrain each performer to contributing utterances that "retain coherence with the emergent."[61] Individual creativity in such a context becomes a matter of introducing an element of novelty into the proceedings or subtly shifting the role relationships of the participants while also satisfying the "presupposing constraints of the emergent."[62] The challenge for players is thus to sustain the emergent performance moment without hogging the stage, to develop a scene while leaving sufficient openings for other players. Nichols and May's "Bach to Bach" should be heard, then, as an exercise in the balancing of individual and collective creativity, and, in that sense, it is a "public moment," whereas famous Method performances in the cinema such as Marlon Brando's "contender" speech in *On the Waterfront* (1954), James Dean's confrontation with his parents in *Rebel without a Cause* (1955), or even Jack Nicholson's tearful interaction with his unspeaking father in *Five Easy Pieces* (1970) can feel like "private moments" *despite* the presence of an interlocutor.

Film scenes such as these also reveal cinematic Method acting to be an improvisational technique for achieving the melodramatic goal of externalizing emotion.[63] Compass improvisation as enacted by Nichols and May worked in exactly the opposite way: to *avoid* externalizing the underlying emotional tenor of the situation.[64] We might say that Nichols and May specialized in antimelodrama, in the comic display not of the victory *over* repression, but the victory *of* repression. Consider a Nichols and May sketch recorded for NBC's *Monitor* entitled "About That Mustache," which begins when Nichols gently asks his companion about bleaching her facial hair.

Nichols: What's wrong with girls shaving? I never understood that. Does it come back even more bristly?

May: I don't know that . . . I don't know any girls that have the necessity to shave.

Nichols: No, I mean, if you have this little bit of mustache.

May: Mm-hmm. Well, I suppose if you have a beard and uh . . .

Nichols: No, no. [*Laughs.*]

May: But you are the only one who's ever been . . . really been that annoyed about the little bit of down I have on my upper lip.

Nichols: I mean, it's just, I mean, I, I heard people mention, you know, that there are things that can be done, otherwise I wouldn't say anything to you . . .

May: Oh, really? You've discussed it a lot I guess.

Nichols: I never said anything, no . . .

May: No, I don't care, listen . . .

Nichols: I heard Gladys say once that . . . she said, "Good grief, if I had that I would bleach it."

May: Gladys who?

Nichols: Beck.

May: The fat one?

Nichols: She isn't fat . . .

May: . . . very, fat, uh . . .

Nichols: No, she isn't fat. She has a tiny, tiny waist.

May: I know, she squeezes out from under it, you know like . . . but no, she's very attractive as a matter of fact.

Nichols: No, that's the first I knew anything could be done, you know, but . . . but I'm curious, what would happen . . .

May: When you were chatting with Gladys about it, when you two were talking about it, what did she suggest?

Nichols: Well, she just said the people that . . . the people that she knows of that have had it happen have bleached it, and see I didn't think to ask her what would happen if you shaved it.

May: No? Well the next time you and she talk about it . . .

Nichols: I . . . I wouldn't talk, I didn't talk about it . . . we were talking about mustaches.

May: What a *wonderful* subject of conversation.

Nichols: Well, you do, you grab at any subject when you're at a party.

May: What party? I was never . . . what party?

The characters here refuse to give voice to their deepest feelings: be they his apparent attraction to Gladys and unease with the appearance of his partner or her embarrassment, hurt, anger, and suspicion. Nichols and May's antimelodrama creates humor through the awkwardness of undischarged emotion. Such a comic dynamic avoids a melodramatic climax when underlying tensions are given full expression but can also be seen as the result of the contingent and collective nature of group improvisation. Though a potentially wide-ranging and unrestrained form, group improvisation must operate through a form of thematic compression. As Richard Schechner puts it, "The improvisational actor is freed from both director and drama, but s/he will therefore have to make fuller use of conventions (stock situations and characters, audience's expectations, etc.) and the physical space."[65] To maintain the collectively generated emergent moment, players must avoid abrupt moves and ruptures that would make participation difficult for other performers. In that sense it leads to the opposite of the explosive emotional outbursts so typical of the Method.[66] Indeed, a sense of thematic compression can be found in Nichols and May's performances that, despite an impressive variety of situations and themes—from the mundane (discussions of mustache bleaching) to the ridiculous (a Moose discovered in a middle-class kitchen)—feature an overall tone and pacing that remains remarkably constant. The resulting subdued, conversational tone and naturalistic pace added a sense of realism to their performances. James Naremore writes that actors who work in a mode of improvisational comedy rely on a style that is "less presentational, less clearly enunciated than any comedy in history."[67]

Charles Chaplin famously asserted that comedy was life framed in long shot, and tragedy was life framed in close-up. Nichols and May complicate this formula by performing comedy in close-up. As the close-up limits a performer's movement, so comedy in close-up avoids the melodramatic eruptions that would focus on one actor instead of the ongoing, cocreated between-ness of several. It is perhaps not surprising that the Method's solo style found an outlet in Hollywood, where film studios tended to promote individual stars and not repertory groups. The LP could certainly capture solo improv on the fly, but it was equally well suited to the Compass's conversational approach. Indeed, some Nichols and May tracks use stereo panning to place the two performers on opposite sides of the stereo picture: an audio metaphor for the democratic balance of collective, conversational improvisation.

We should also note that Nichols and May used studio editing techniques to give dramatic shape to their spontaneous dialogues. Consider a bonus track entitled "Nichols and May at Work," found on a Nichols and May compilation CD, which provides us with an unedited strip of performance in the studio. We hear the voice of an engineer or producer ask, "Should we do a doctor's spot?" Nichols suggests that May play his mother, and she begins the conversation. When Nichols informs his mother that he wants to be a registered nurse, the two flood out in spontaneous laughter. After several further attempts, May manages to deliver the line "that's my son, the nurse" before they once again crack up in laughter. We hear the producer speak over the intercom system from the control booth: "I don't know if it's in the clear or not," suggesting a production practice whereby key spoken lines will be edited away from any ensuing laughter. We can hear the results of such editing when this session was broadcast on NBC's *Monitor* show, edited down from four minutes to one and a half. Like Bing Crosby, who famously used magnetic tape recording on his radio variety show to facilitate comic ad libbing, Nichols and May used tape editing for the construction of seemingly spontaneous performances.[68] In both cases, improvisation serves as an initial stage in a regime of media production that combines improvisation with the editing capability of the recording studio.

Studio techniques such as stereo panning and editing suggest options other than a jazz aesthetic to recorded comedy. Evan Eisenberg has written that there are two ways to make a record seem "alive": live recordings, which convey a "real sense of occasion, through the spontaneity of the music-making and through accidents of ambience" and the use of "studio techniques." "Aggressive mixing and overdubbing, especially in rock," Eisenberg writes, can give a record a "sense of conscious intelligence and so of life."[69] The editing and stereo panning found on Nichols and May records suggest an incipient "rock aesthetic" that came to be fully realized with the next collection of comedy LPs I will examine.

STUDIO

Besides occasional examples of tape editing or panning, few of the nightclub or cabaret comics took much advantage of the tools of the modern recording studio. A notable exception can be found on Lenny Bruce's remarkable "The March of High Fidelity," from his debut LP, *Interviews of Our Times* (Fantasy 1958). The track begins with melodramatic piano music played in a discordant minor key. "America is in danger," Bruce announces in the exaggerated voice of a newsreel narrator, "a peril greater than any of the horrendous radioactive qualities of the hydrogen bomb tests. Every man, woman, and child, from the crisp, cool shores of Montauk Point to the great Oregon forests, live in the heinous shadow of the 'H.F.N.' The H.F.N. is a monster, and what is the H.F.N.?" We hear a sudden musical spike treated with an echo effect and then the punch line: "Hi-fi nuts!" A solemn drum-roll follows, as Bruce intones: "Years ago, there was just one unit, usually made of wood, that had a nickel-plated handle you could wind." We hear the thin strains of mechanically reproduced music, emerging presumably from such a unit. "And here he is," cries an announcer, "that silver-mouthed tenor of the airwaves: Ralph J. Gleason!" Bruce is making an inside joke here, casting the San Francisco music critic as a radio crooner. Next we hear the voices of two men, both played by Bruce, who discuss Gleason's performance. "Hey Charlie, ain't that record a riot?" says one. "Well, it's all right," answers the other. "But that loudspeaker sounds tinny."

Charlie's reaction is a symptom of the fact that he is "hooked" on hi-fi components, but we are told that, given treatment, he has kicked the habit. Sadly, just when he had practically gotten "the variable reluctance cartridge off his back," Charlie swallows some tranquilizers, thinking they are transistors. As a result, he develops "a very perplexing hum" coming from his "DAK-OK 3000 power amplifier." Over the sounds of warbling electronic tones, Charlie's voice is sped up and slowed down, lending it an unsteady, woozy quality. Now other voices appear, a chorus of men and women who describe Charlie as he goes through a bizarre transformation. "Look, his mouth is getting bigger and bigger!" someone shouts. "His arms are shrinking!" "So are his legs." "His mouth is really wide now." "You can't see him." "His eyes have disappeared, so have his legs." "There's nothing left but a mouth!" At one point, a man suggests that they get some lumber, and a box is built around Charlie's expanding mouth. Electrical static crackles as wires are placed on his teeth and his ear is switched on. The track ends as Ralph J. Gleason reprises his song through the cyborg Charlie unit.

Bruce's track parodies the kind of male hi-fi enthusiast described in chapter 3 but also depicts a surreal audio nightmare that should be read as a precursor to David Cronenberg's *Videodrome* (1982), with its depiction of a pulsating, breathing television set with an engulfing mouth and characters that morph into zombified videocassette players.[70] Bruce seems to have been something of a H.F.N. himself: note Gleason's claim that Bruce was "a true tape freak. He recorded everything—performances, phone conversations, interviews." Besides reflecting Bruce's own addictions, "The March of High Fidelity" demonstrates an early example of the tools of the postwar recording studio being used to manipulate sound and create a complex, layered sonic drama that did not simply document a live performance.

In these ways, Bruce's track is indicative of an era when popular musicians like Buddy Holly, Eddie Cochran, and Les Paul were experimenting with the possibilities of the multitrack recording studio: a third performance space to compare with the nightclub and cabaret. The *Oxford English Dictionary* defines *studio* as "the work-room of a sculptor or painter," but notably, the term was quickly adopted for areas where labor in the modern media industries took place: production spaces for photography, film, radio, television, and sound recording have all been referred to as *studios*. The moniker *studio* confers Western notions of the Romantic artist onto what was oftentimes a factory mode of production. The term also suggests a certain dynamic between performer and audience resembling Erving Goffman's category of the backstage, where a performance is prepared separate from the eyes and ears of an audience.[71] The studio implies a different temporality of circulation than the nightclub or cabaret, since large investments of time and money are required to create a finished studio performance before it is mass-produced and distributed to a widely dispersed public.[72] It is useful here to consider Warner's distinction between a "nominal addressee of rhetoric and a targeted public of circulation."[73] On live records of comedians who adopted the jazz aesthetic, the comic's nominal addressee was the copresent nightclub or cabaret audience, whereas the "public of circulation" consisted of those many more who heard the LP. For studio productions, the distinction between the nominal addressee and circulating public collapses and the loss of an authenticity rooted in the documentation of a copresent event is replaced by new strategies for forging a closer relationship with the circulating public. One comedy group in particular explored the possibilities of the studio-constructed LP record: the Firesign Theatre. Firesign's work represented a new ontology of the comedy LP in which the record itself became the central work: a rock aesthetic as opposed to the jazz aesthetic described previously. As Robert B. Ray has pointed out, recording allowed for a shift in the ontological status of music, most dramatically in genres such as rock and roll, which made the record the central work and not the written score or live performance.[74] The Firesign Theatre represented an analogous shift in recorded comedy.

The origins of the Firesign Theatre can be traced to Peter Bergman, who, after graduating from Yale in 1961, spent time in London, where he worked with Spike Milligan of the classic BBC radio comedy program *The Goon Show.* Inspired by the Goons as well as by the Beatles, Bergman conceptualized a four-man comedy group that would write and perform its own material. By 1966 he had moved to Los Angeles and was working as a radio disc jockey on Pacifica KPFK, hosting a late night show called *Radio Free Oz.* Phil Proctor, who had been at Yale with Bergman, came to Los Angeles in a touring theater troupe, and the two began working together at the radio station. Phil Austin and David Ossman were kindred spirits working at KPFK, and the four of them soon teamed up on radio broadcasts where they staged satiric call-in shows and invented wacky characters, often lampooning the LA counterculture of which they were a part. In fact, Bergman has the distinction of coining the phrase *love-in* and organized a "happening" under that name that drew 40,000 people to LA's Elysian Park. In the wake of

FIGURE 6. Firesign Theatre: pioneers in the production of studio-based multitrack comedy LPs. Photo by Film Proctor.

that event, Columbia Records approached Bergman and Proctor about making a love-in album. Columbia's interest was eventually transferred to their four-man comedy team, now dubbed the Firesign Theatre. Their first LP, *Waiting for the Electrician or Someone Like Him,* was released in 1968 and benefited from the fact that their Spoken Arts record contract stipulated unlimited studio time in exchange for a relatively low royalty rate. The resulting luxury of time in the studio helped to shape their subsequent three LPs, widely considered to be comedy classics: *How Can You Be in Two Places at Once When You're Not Anywhere at All* (1969), *Don't Crush That Dwarf, Hand Me the Pliers* (1970), and *I Think We're All Bozos on This Bus* (1971). The peak of their sales was *Don't Crush That Dwarf,* which sold approximately 325,000 copies. Their influence, however, went beyond that sales figure: these early records inspired a devoted fan following and enthusiastic critical response and effectively changed the popular notion of what a comedy record could be.

The rock press fawned over the group, in part because of their references to countercultural concerns such as the war in Vietnam, drugs, and rock music, and also because they were clearly inspired by rock acts such as the Beatles in their exploration of the expressive possibilities of the recording studio. Ossman, for example, stated that Firesign was aiming to bring rock and roll production to the comedy album.[75] Though clearly a product of the 1960s, Firesign's output had less in common with the comedy records of that decade than with an earlier generation of radio drama. Ossman said that he had laughed at Mike Nichols and Elaine May LPs but was less influenced by that duo than by golden age radio couple Fibber McGee and Molly.[76] Indeed, the group's name is a reference both to aspects of the counterculture (all the members were astrological fire signs) and to old-time radio (the Fireside chat). Proctor stated that Firesign wanted to produce records "as if radio had continued into the modern era with the full force of energy it had during its so-called golden age."[77] The title of a single released in 1969, "Forward into the Past," nicely sums up Firesign's transmedia time-warp sensibility.[78]

On that single, we hear a radio announcer ask, "Remember those good old days when your Daddy and Mommy were fighting the war that made you possible? Well, you know, they didn't do it alone. No, they did it on the radio, with millions of people watching. And this is what they heard." What follows is an audio montage of radio parodies, including "Captain Equinox": "By day Adolf Tree, a mild-mannered college professor, by night Kiki, a mini-skirted habitué of Hollywood's star-struck Sunset Strip, but twice a year he's . . . Captain Equinox!" We find here Firesign's keen ear for combining the lingo of the 1960s with radio-era pop culture. Similarly, one of their most famous sketches, "The Further Adventures of Nick Danger," found on side two of *How Can You Be in Two Places at Once,* is an elaborate send-up of 1940s radio detective shows. Many of the track's gags play on the conventions of radio drama, for example, drawing the listener's attention to the techniques used to cue subjectivity in noir-esque voice-overs. Other jokes rely on knowledge of the production of radio sound effects. "It had been snowing in Santa Barbara ever since the top of the page," Detective Nick Danger narrates, "and I had to shake the cornstarch off my mukluks." He is soon greeted by the butler, Catherwood, who says, "Come in out of the cornstarch and dry your mukluks by the fire." Later, as Danger sits by the fire to warm his mukluks (another blend of 1940s noir and 1960s hippie fashion), Catherwood tells him to pull his cues "out of the cellophane before they scorch." In these examples, Firesign reference the practices of radio sound effects: using cornstarch to simulate the crunching of feet in the snow and manipulating cellophane to mimic the sound of a crackling fire.

The golden age of radio is also indexed near the end of the track, when the Nick Danger program is interrupted by an announcement of "national importance" from the White House. We hear an imitation of President Franklin Roosevelt, who explains: "My fellow Americans, this morning at 6:25 A.M. Pacific Standard Time, combined elements of the Imperial Japanese Navy and Air Forces ruthlessly attacked our naval base at Pearl Harbor in the Hawaiian Islands." This familiar radio script is given an unexpected twist when the president declares, "We have reached our rendezvous with destiny. It is our unanimous and irrevocable decision that the United States of America *unconditionally surrender.*" We are then abruptly returned to the Nick Danger broadcast. In their play with radio style and history, Firesign did indeed place listeners in two places at once or, more accurately, in two historical moments at once, and on subsequent records they developed the theme that events of the 1940s were at the heart of ongoing social issues in the 1960s and 1970s.

Besides a debt to radio, these examples demonstrate what Jay David Bolter and Richard Grusin call "remediation," or the representation of one medium in another. The jazz aesthetic comedy LPs of the early 1960s remediated nightclub entertainment, representing a documentation of a live performance to convey a sense of *immediacy,* a term Bolter and Grusin define as an attempt to "get to the real by bravely denying the fact of mediation." For example, the liner notes to the LP *Inside Shelley Berman* instruct the reader to take the record home, put it on, "turn the lights down low, and there you are—a do-it-yourself night club, with guaranteed laughs." By contrast, Firesign LPs belong to a category of media applications that "seek the real by multiplying mediation so as to create a feeling of fullness, a satiety of experience, which can be taken as reality": what Bolter and Grusin refer to as "hypermedia."[79] The LP record was well suited to a hypermedia approach, since studio techniques could remediate not just old-time radio but also a range of other sound media as well. A 1970 *Rolling Stone* review of Firesign's LP *Don't Crush That Dwarf,* stated that the group "uses records in a way that nobody else has done. All media involving sound (movies, radio, television, stage, real life) are present here, and the overlaps between them are occasionally, and intentionally, quite blurry . . . they have synthesized all of the facets there are into an approach that is unique in entertainment history, mainly because there has never been so much entertainment history to draw from. Their use of the recording medium is light years beyond anyone else's. The very least they should get for this is an Academy Award."[80] That Firesign remediated multiple media forms can be indexed by the variety of precursors and influences mentioned by reviewers: a partial list includes Bob and Ray, Lewis Carroll, James Joyce, Clarabelle the Clown, Steve Allen, the Beatles, Ernie Kovacs, the Goon Show, Monty Hall, and Flash Gordon.[81] We find figures here from high and low culture; from comedy, science fiction, and fantasy; and from radio, television, film, the record industry, and literature; all brought together in Firesign's hypermedia mix.

Foremost among the Firesign's representation of other media forms, however, was a complex engagement with television. Proctor called Firesign an audio act in the age of video, or "blind television." Many writers described Firesign's records as a form of television criticism. Greil Marcus wrote in 1976 that Firesign's LPs were "the best TV criticism of the day" and had "caught the lunacy and the hysteria of the medium; they create the media shock we need to understand what we see every day."[82] A reviewer for the *Los Angeles Times* wrote that the pleasure of the Firesign Theatre derived from "seeing someone get back at the very nearly implacable and ceaseless banality of the tube."[83] The *New York Times* wrote in 1975 that Firesign's comedy was a "casserole of the incredible voices that bombard the citizenry every day from every radio and TV set."[84] One way to understand Firesign, then, is as part of the counterculture's ambivalence about television. Aniko Bodroghkozy writes that the counterculture "rejected the content of television, leaving it and its irrelevant programming to their elders": "For members of the student protest movement or the hippie counterculture, art films and rock music were the pre-eminent arenas of cultural consumption. Any self-respecting head or campus politico would be looked at askance were she or he to exhibit a too-hardy interest in the products of the Vast Wasteland. Hip and activist young people rejected television as a commercial, network-dominated industry hopelessly corrupted by the values of the establishment."[85] Along these lines, listeners could enjoy vicariously getting back at "the banality of the tube" through Firesign's parodies of TV game shows, soap operas, cop shows, and commercials as well as the way in which the group flaunted the LP's ability to proliferate drug references that would be censored on network television.

But Firesign's LPs reveal a more complex relationship with television than simple mockery. Though Ossman claimed that radio could alter one's consciousness "much more so than television," he added that there was one way in which television could become similarly productive: channel surfing.[86] Indeed, the audio representation of channel surfing became a key formal technique on Firesign LPs: as a 1975 *Writer's Digest* article stated, Firesign had "developed a brand new dramatic device that can be used in any audio-visual project: Switching TV channels to move the action along."[87] Consider side one of *How Can You Be in Two Places at Once*. At one point in the track, an audio representation of a film being shown on *The Late, Late Show* entitled *Babes in Khaki* is interrupted by a series of channel flips: "[*click*] . . . anointed with oil on troubled waters, oh heavenly grid, help us to bear up thy standard, our chevron flashing bright across the gulf of compromise, standing humble on the rich field of mobile American thinking, here in this shell we call life . . . [*click*]" "Angels three, devils . . . [*click*]" "Osiris, what has happened to your nose? [*click*]" ". . . you've got people jumping out of them, and you've got water dropping out of them . . . [*click*]."

The idea for this technique came from Philip Proctor, who described his experience moving to LA in the mid-1960s. Feeling isolated without a car in that sprawling city, he passed time after his theater performances by flipping through late-night television: "I would click from channel to channel, [finding] these incredible synapses, where one word would lead into the other, and you were in a Roman movie, and the next thing you were in a detective movie, but they were all the same movie! I found it to be extremely amusing."[88] In fact, the title of their album *Don't Crush That Dwarf, Hand Me the Pliers* was a reference to switching television channels. On "Forward into the Past," Ossman plays the "Strange Dr. Weird," the host of a radio horror show, and delivers the line, "Don't crush that dwarf," as a playful jumbling of the broadcasting cliché "Don't touch that dial." Ossman said that for him, the subsequent LP title had a deeper meaning: "Don't turn off the television set, use this pair of pliers, to change the channels, because you've lost the knob, you know. Having lost the clicker knob, you're going to use the pliers to change the set, rather than turn it off. Don't turn off your life, try another channel."[89] Firesign's channel-surfing aesthetic was an audio representation of television watching as do-it-yourself media collage and even a metaphor for modern life, making clear that a dialogue with television was at the heart of Firesign records: as metaphor, aesthetic, and structuring polemic.

Proctor's discovery that "synapses" between television channels could reveal something about media and popular memory was made possible in part by new regimes of television programming in the 1950s and 1960s. Derek Kompare describes how forms of television repetition were developing at this time that facilitated a new experience of both the media and the past. First, old Hollywood films became "imbued with the patina of nostalgia by virtue of their continual appearance (and reappearance)" on television.[90] Second, by the end of the 1960s, the television schedule had become filled not only with films of a previous generation but with television reruns, such that "the past had become as much a part of television as the present, if not more so. . . . As the ubiquitous semiotic capsules of the recent past, off-network reruns played a key role in the new nostalgia of the seventies, and would eventually become legitimated as part of the American cultural heritage."[91] Firesign LPs were an early exploration of the startling proximity of past and present on the nation's airwaves as well as an interrogation of television's representation of the past that went far beyond nostalgia.

For example, their most famous album, *Don't Crush That Dwarf, Hand Me the Pliers,* works through a series of overlaps and resonances between media past and present. A rough overview of the LP's labyrinthine plot might look something like the following. A young man named George Tirebiter lives in a futuristic Los Angeles that has become a militarized zone. Late at night he watches television, where he comes upon a show called *Stab from the Past,* which is celebrating the career of an old man also named George Tirebiter, who once worked in Hollywood making "all those lovable stupid Porgy and Mudhead movies." When the channel is switched, we serendipitously come upon one of his films being broadcast as the "Howl of the Wolf" movie, entitled *High School Madness.* The film follows the life of young Porgy Tirebiter, who discovers that his high school has disappeared. Channel switching brings us to a Korean War film, where echoes of characters from other channels begin to proliferate: most notably, Porgy has become Lieutenant Tirebiter. Channel switching continues, and the boundaries between all of these lines of action blur: a military trial overlaps both with Porgy's trial for high school mischief (where the judge doubles for the high school principal) and with a scene in which the old man Tirebiter faces a militaristic Hollywood executive. The album ends when the old Mr. Tirebiter answers the phone and says that he's been up all night watching himself on TV.

Besides serving as a framework for Firesign's comic wordplay, the channel-switching motif found here creates "synapses" between media forms, between historical eras, and between geographical locations to make a subtle but potent social critique. That is, multiple times and places are made to overlap and coexist: the land of Hollywood myth is a futuristic fascist state is the American high school is an East Asian battlefield. Firesign thus utilizes channel switching as the sonic equivalent of parallel editing, a kind of horizontal or melodic layering in which different themes are woven in and out of prominence until they finally merge. Firesign also adds vertical layers to the narrative in a manner analogous to musical harmony or multiple planes of cinematic superimposition.[92] Consider side one of *How Can You Be in Two Places at Once,* where a television ad featuring car dealer Ralph Spoilsport is interrupted by a potential customer. Spoilsport takes the man inside a car, which becomes, through the use of reverb, a vast, surreal space. Spoilsport points out the car's features, which include a bathroom, all-weather climate control, and a color TV located under a "wild west gun rack with the look of real wood." They turn on the television, and we hear another Ralph Spoilsport ad, this one referencing a current Beatles record: "We do it in the road here at Spoilsport Motors!" As the television audio continues, Ralph and the customer comment upon it: "Can I get a little more orange in his face?" "Look at that blue horse!" Next Ralph switches on an AM radio station on which we hear manic kazoos and a frantic DJ quoting prices. An FM station is added to the mix of mediated voices, which is broadcasting the low, refined tones of an announcer who introduces classical music by "Johann Amadeus Matetski." Yet another overlapping layer of action is added when Spoilsport turns on a shortwave radio station based in Tierra del Fuego, on which we hear a Spanish language ad for, of course, Ralph Spoilsport Motors.

What results is a trademark Firesign effect, whereby mediated voices maintain multiple overlapping lines of action. This approach to audio storytelling resembles the contemporary sound design of film director Robert Altman, who often made use of multiple "mediated sound sources" such as radios, televisions, tape players, and public address systems. Altman's "non-hierarchical multi-channel soundscape" was, for film scholar Rick Altman, "an overt attempt to break out of cinema's heretofore literary model, to fight the tendency to reduce sound to its meaning, to replace the single-channel linearity of written discourse by a three-dimensional multiplicity calling for a radically different level and type of spectator—and especially auditor—activity."[93] Much the same could be said for Firesign Theatre's LPs.

An important part of the "radically different" type of auditor activity called for by Firesign's "non-hierarchical multi-channel" sound design was the necessity of multiple hearings, since all the layers of action could not be understood in a single pass. For example, if we focus on the AM radio in the scene described previously, we will miss all the other unfolding details on the FM radio, television, or shortwave. The effect of the multichannel soundscape was thus to encourage and reward repeated listening. Ossman stated that the group wanted listeners to play their LPs "as many times as they were playing the Beatles or the Rolling Stones."[94] In that regard, Firesign had solved a long-standing problem for comedy record producers and critics. In terms of the latter, note that questions of repeated listening were a prevalent topic in the critical discussion of comedy LPs. Consider the following examples:

> You wonder why any record company would ever release a comedy album . . . the essence of good comedy is spontaneity, the unexpected; and once you've heard a record a few times, you know the jokes.[95]

> There is nothing more fleeting than the appeal of a comedy record. Millions of people who bought Bob Newhart albums in the 1960s can now hardly bear to listen to the comedian's telephone routines for the 400th time. . . . comedy records are thus the purest kind of novelty record: hysterical for the few weeks or months that they are popular, and, after the thrill is gone, a hunk of vinyl you wouldn't dream of playing.[96]

> Most comedy albums attract only a cult following because laughter tends to be a onetime thing. A routine that has you rolling on the floor one night is likely to be as dull as sawdust the next morning. The element of surprise is gone, leaving you with a vinyl keepsake—a $7.98 souvenir of yesterday's yuks.[97]

> Repeated spins tend to erode the impact of recorded comedy.[98]

Concern about the problem of repetition for comedy records begs the question: why would anyone revisit *any* prerecorded media text? To my knowledge, there has not been a similar concern about comedy video-cassettes and DVDs. Indeed, Barbara Klinger notes that the television show *Seinfeld* was "among the most requested titles for DVD release," despite its ubiquity in syndication.[99] Klinger's research indicates that comedy films are frequently replayed at home, due to the fact that view-ers enjoy "the opportunity to revisit the laughs, but also because these films fit particularly well into peer settings."[100] Critical unease about repetition and the comedy LP in the 1960s and 1970s was perhaps due to the fact that such LPs were some of the earliest nonmusical, long-form media texts available for repeat hearings to a large home audience. As such, the solutions found by the Firesign Theatre are prescient of more recent developments in other forms of media production.

Consider that Firesign's narrative complexity, multiple lines of action, overlapping dialogue, and lack of closure all encourage repeated spins, similar to how recent "puzzle films" such as *Pulp Fiction* (1998), *The*

Sixth Sense (1999), and *Memento* (2000) encourage repeat viewings and DVD sales through multilayered narratives, a dense visual style, surprise endings, and "the presence of an initially occult meaning that requires re-viewing to uncover the text's mysteries."[101] Due to the resulting depth of audience engagement as well as drug references that keyed a counter-public reading, Firesign developed a "cult" following in the early 1970s. A reviewer of a Firesign appearance at the Los Angeles Lisner Auditorium in 1974 noted, "Throughout the evening the audience chimed in with dialogue known by heart from the records."[102] Five years later, the *Los Angeles Times* wrote that there were enough aficionados of Firesign to "form a small cult" and that after a recent show, one could overhear conversations about the group's records that demonstrated "the same meticulous scrutiny that would be applied by ecclesiastical analysts to ecumenical decree. The Firesign seems to draw that kind of devotion."[103] These accounts illustrate that Firesign's live appearances typically involved the recreation of sketches found on their albums in a manner similar to a concert by a rock band. The audience participation described here was fostered by Firesign's commitment to a rock aesthetic to studio-recorded comedy, an aesthetic that required repeated listening and so regimented the temporality of its circulation. Mort Sahl and the Compass Theater had forged a public through topical riffs and sketches, but that approach necessarily had a short shelf life. As the LP market matured, recording artists and the record industry sought to develop a depth of temporal engagement with audiences, paying attention not only to maximizing the reach of the circulation of texts in space but intensifying the depth of circulation in time: in other words, creating what have come to be known as market niches or "brand tribes." Firesign's "cult" following was an indication of its success in that regard, and its production techniques merit scrutiny as predecessors to subsequent media forms in an era of branding and niche marketing.

Regardless of the extent of their influence beyond the phonograph industry, Firesign's records certainly inspired other studio-based comedy records of the 1970s. A comedy group called the Credibility Gap featured Harry Shearer, who would subsequently be featured in *This Is Spinal Tap* (1984) and would become one of the key voice actors on *The Simpsons*, produced records with a Firesign-esque "forward into the past" aesthetic. The track "Who's on First," from an LP entitled *The Bronze Age of Radio*, reworked a famous radio-era Abbott and Costello routine as a dialogue between a rock promoter and a newspaper journalist having to do with a concert by the Who, the Guess Who, and Yes:

Journalist: [*with slow, seething deliberation*] Will you please tell me the name of the third act?

Promoter: Yes.

Journalist: Fine.

Promoter: Thank you.

Journalist: You're welcome.

Promoter: OK, let me see your proof of the act Wednesday and . . .

Journalist: W-wait a minute, where are you going? I asked you to tell me the name of the third act!

Promoter: I told you the name of the third act! You want me to tell you again?

Journalist: Yes.

Promoter: That's right!

Journalist: That's right's on first!

Promoter: Who's on first, Guess Who's on second and the third act . . .

Journalist: Yes?

Both: That's right!

Besides the Credibility Gap, LPs by the National Lampoon and Cheech and Chong reveal a similar studio aesthetic, without either Firesign's depth of production values or subtle engagement with media history. Firesign's influence can also be heard on records by two stand-up comedians who found ways to combine the jazz and rock aesthetic.

On his album *A Star Is Bought* (Asylum 1975), Albert Brooks worked with the Credibility Gap's Harry Shearer, which helps to explain a resemblance to the Firesign aesthetic: on that studio-based record, one can here a Firesign-esque golden age radio parody, "The Albert Brooks Show No. 112 (August 4, 1943)." On his previous record, *Comedy Minus One* (ABC 1973), Brooks combined a live performance at the Troubador Club in Los Angeles with studio-produced bits such as a parody of a stereo demonstration and a series of staged prank telephone calls. The LP begins with Brooks's introductory framing for the nightclub material: "During the live portions of this record, no laughter has been altered in any way, shape, or form. As a matter of fact, I have with me here a notary public who will swear to this fact. You're a notary public?" A man's voice answers, "Yes." "And you swear to this fact?" Brooks asks. "Sure," the man replies uncomfortably. We are then taken to the Troubador for his live act, where Brooks explicitly addresses the record's "liveness." Brooks tells the nightclub audience, "There's mikes all around here; there's a recording truck outside; a record is being made. There's nothing you have to worry about just, you know, just have a good time. Just don't identify your laughter; a lot of people like to do, 'Ha ha ha ha, said Bill Harrison of Phoenix!'" *Comedy Minus One* thus undercuts any implicit claims of an "authentic," transparent liveness or immediacy for its nightclub segments, and in the process explores the inconsistencies between the nominal audience and the circulating public.

Another record that combined live and studio material in innovative ways was Lily Tomlin's *Modern Scream* (Polydor 1975). Tomlin plays all the characters on this underappreciated LP, which features a framing narrative in which a reporter shows up at Tomlin's "luxurious Hollywood home" to record an interview. As they sit by her pool, the switching on and off of the reporter's tape machine motivates cuts to Tomlin's stand-up performance. That Tomlin's nightclub gig emerges from multiple mediated sound sources such as the tape recorder, a television, and a car radio calls into question the status of the "liveness" of the club act. Like Brooks's *Comedy Minus One*, *Modern Scream* keyed hypermediacy, not immediacy, as its operating aesthetic and represents a hybrid of jazz and rock aesthetic that reveals the conventions of both. What both of these LPs suggest is that, after the Firesign Theatre, the simple documentation of a live comedy act was no longer thought to be sufficient as an approach to the comedy record.

Despite these indications of their influence, by the time Brooks's and Tomlin's records were released, the Firesign's star was on the wane. Peter Bergman said that the end of the Vietnam War led to a change in "the whole political landscape," and as a result, "the bottom dropped out of the whole raison d'etre of The Firesign Theatre. People stopped listening to political comedy, and started putting on white suits and pointing at the ceiling and disco-ing."[104] Besides a cohort of John Travolta wannabes, the white suit Bergman mentions could refer to another rival entertainer of the late 1970s. Note that in 1968, the *Los Angeles Times* reviewed a Firesign live appearance at the Ice House in Pasadena and called the group "the most refreshing comedy act to appear in many a moon."[105] Opening the show was "a personable young comic" with a routine of stand-up comedy and magic the *Times* called "no worse and no better than average." Though he seemed "a bit anemic" by comparison to Firesign, he did demonstrate a "keen wit" through his impromptu asides. In the end, though, the best that could be said of him was that he "didn't overstay his welcome."[106] That comic was Steve Martin. Though only an opening act for Firesign in 1968, a decade later his record sales would dwarf theirs, and he would be performing to capacity crowds in sports arenas. Martin's blockbuster comedy records did not feature the studio density of Firesign's nor the improvisational techniques of Sahl's, Bruce's, or Nichols and May's. Nonetheless, Martin made use of other approaches to mediating the intimate theater of stranger relationality, and his LPs represented spaces of performance that were almost commensurate to the imaginary space created by the circulation of media texts.

STADIUM

Besides sharing the stage at the Ice House in Pasadena, Steve Martin and the Firesign Theatre also shared a common affection for radio comedy: in Martin's autobiography he described how he was introduced to comedy by listening to Bob Hope, Abbott and Costello, Amos 'n' Andy, and Jack Benny on the car radio in the 1950s.[107] He also acknowledged the influence of comedy records by postwar comedians such as Lenny Bruce and Nichols and May: Martin stated that he listened to Nichols and May records "over and over and over" and could hear "Nichols's phrasing in his own delivery."[108] Martin even claimed to have gone to sleep at night to Nichols and May LPs, adding that they were "like a song" that one could hear "over and over."[109] Martin concluded that those albums "broke ground" and led him to the important discovery that "comedy could evolve."[110]

The outlines of Martin's early career have been sketched many times: how he worked at a magic shop in Disneyland where he sold novelty arrows-through-the-head and funny noses that would later become part of his act; his move to Knott's Berry Farm, where he did a magic act and performed in the saloon melodrama; and his entrance into television as a writer for the *Smothers Brothers Comedy Hour* in 1968. Soon after, he began a stand-up act and did time on the rock circuit, opening up concerts by the Nitty Gritty Dirt Band: an early experience with performance spaces unlike a nightclub, cabaret, or studio. It was during this time that Martin transformed his act into "a parody of comedy," remaking himself as "an entertainer who was playing an entertainer, a not so good one."[111] Martin placed this career overhaul in the context of the early 1970s: "Flower Power was waning, but no one wanted to believe it yet, because we had all invested so much of ourselves in its message. Change was imminent. I cut my hair, shaved my beard, and put on a suit. . . . Overnight, I was no longer at the tail end of an old movement but at the front end of a new one. Instead of looking like another freak with a crazy act, I now looked like a visitor from the straight world who had gone seriously awry."[112] A key aspect of Martin's makeover involved stripping his act of all "political references."[113] Martin claimed that his act was "a break from all the seriousness and strict political orientation of the '60s. It's saying the individual is what's important. You don't have to worry about what other people are doing. You don't have to be 'hip' or 'cool.' It's OK to be whatever you want to be—dress up, be mindless for a while or whatever."[114] "I am consciously atopical," he said, adding that, in a telling contrast to Mort Sahl's rolled up newspaper, the person he played onstage was "oblivious to newspapers. He's full of opinions about nothing. I think people are distrustful of government; distrustful of organizations; distrustful of everything. They just want to get back to their personal lives and let those other guys do what they want."[115] "We're kicking the '60s goodbye, and I'm enjoying that," he told the *Washington Post* in 1977. "In the late '60s, it was a very informal period. You could say dirty words and insult people and it was okay to get up and dance at a movie. All that's just fashion, not good or bad or anything . . . things are going back to formalism. I like the change."[116] Statements such as these betray an element of the radical conservative to Martin: as the novelty and excitement of political comedy in the Eisenhower era was extinguished under the weight of a million Watergate jokes, Martin's politically neutral formalism struck a chord with audiences eager to move beyond the divisiveness of the Vietnam era. We can place Martin, then, in a mid-1970s zeitgeist, which includes Hollywood films such as Francis Ford Coppola's *Godfather* (1972) and ultimately, George Lucas's *Star Wars* (1977), that managed to unify the polarized American audience after what Robert Ray calls the Left and Right cycles of American cinema.[117]

Martin's rejection of topical humor would have several implications. First, as was the case with a film such as *Star Wars,* Martin's act did not signal the convening of a counterpublic and instead was unapologetically legible to a mass audience. Further, without topical references, Martin lost a powerful means of placing strangers on common ground, which, as we have seen, was a short-term solution to the challenge of producing comedy material in the era of mass media. That short-term loss, however, could facilitate a long-term gain. The *Wall Street Journal* wrote in 1979 that "tying comedy to current events may boost sales temporarily, but it also can shorten the life span of an album. Thus, topicality may heighten a perennial problem of selling comedy albums:

that of getting people to pay for the chance to hear the same material over and over."[118] Similarly, Philip Auslander writes that topical comedy "does not circulate easily through the media complex" since its references become dated, such that "it cannot be used profitably over and over again."[119] Though topical material aided in the short-term circulation of comedy, it did not provide the depth of temporal engagement required by a media economy increasingly geared toward the possibilities of repetition.

Not only did Martin abandon topicality, but he seemed uninterested in the studio-based layering techniques of the Firesign Theatre. Indeed, compared to artists such as Firesign, Martin seemed to some critics to be releasing records that were throwbacks to a previous era and lacked the requisite studio expertise. A *Los Angeles Times* critic complained that his first LP, *Let's Get Small* (Warner Bros. 1977), was a "simple documentation of his live act, as opposed to a piece of creative recordmaking" and so was not "a compelling burst of creativity but a minor, if necessary, step in his career—like a quick, adequate term paper for a required class. Were Martin truly interested in the recorded medium, he certainly could learn to handle the studio and develop a workable unifying concept." The reviewer concluded that, like other comedy recordings, "it will be hard put to withstand repeated listening."[120] The critical assessment here is clearly shaped by the ontology of Firesign's rock aesthetic: a "compelling" record required a unifying concept and techniques fitting for the recorded medium, that is, studio multitracking. Despite lacking these key ingredients of the midseventies comedy album, Martin's first two LPs were certified platinum in 1978, and *Wild and Crazy Guy* reached number two on the *Billboard* album charts. Though Martin rejected topical references and a multichannel sound design, in their place he had developed a winning technique for dealing with the challenges of repetition that had roots in radio comedy: the catchphrase.

Recall that radio comics faced a crisis of material that led to the creation of the situation comedy format. Part of the sitcom solution was the repeated use of a distinctively delivered catchphrase. Writing in 1935, the *Los Angeles Times* credited the *Amos 'n' Andy* show with originating catchphrases: "Their fans probably will recall the distressed wail, 'Awha Awha!' and 'Ain't that sompthin.'"[121] Radio comedian Ken Murray claimed that "repetition of phrases is sure fire, as you can see by the reaction we get from 'That man's here' and 'Oh, yeah.' We've got the listeners with us right off the bat when we can dispense with long-winded, laudatory introductions of our players."[122] In 1946 critic Jack

Gould wrote, "A catchy phrase or line uttered by a secondary character can become a momentary part of the nation's vocabulary and whisk a sponsor and a stooge overnight into the higher income backers," and pointed to Bert Gordon's characterization of the "Mad Russian," on *The Eddie Cantor Show,* whose "familiar trademark" was "How do you doooo."[123] The catchphrase was an outgrowth of the imperatives of radio serials but can also be seen as a particularly modern performance in that it takes advantage of the microphone's ability to capture nuances of vocal timbre and inflection.

As opposed to comedy based on jokes, puns, or witty repartee, the catchphrase is pitched to the pleasures of pure vocal delivery, to what Roland Barthes calls the "grain of the voice." In that sense, it illustrates the power of phonogeny, what Michel Chion describes as "the rather mysterious propensity of certain voices to sound good when recorded and played over loudspeakers, to inscribe themselves in the record groove better than other voices, in short to make up for the absence of the sound's real source by means of another kind of presence specific to the medium."[124] Raw phonogeny plays a large part in the singing of much recorded popular music (think: "A wop bop a loo bop a wop bam boo," or "Hey! Ho! Let's go!" or "Yeah, Yeah, Yeah!"). Notably, musical recordings such as these, like the catchphrase, are quite amenable to repetition. Unlike a punch line, which loses its shock or surprise value, a catchphrase gains with repetition due to its basis in vocal timbre. As stated in chapter 1, Theodore Gracyk has argued that, not only does the pleasure of much recorded music depend on the experience of timbre, but also, since particular timbres are difficult to retain in our memory, complexity at the level of timbre spurs the desire to listen to the same records again and again.[125] Just as we might listen to a rock record many times despite its simple lyrics, basic chord structure, and repetitive rhythm, so the Mad Russian provides reliable entertainment with each repetition of his blunt but unmistakable, "How do you doooo."

With this in mind, note that thrown away transitions and brief asides are often the funniest and most memorable parts of Martin's LPs, due in large part to his distinctive inflection and delivery: "Hey, this guy's good!"; "I'm not into that *kind* of entertainment—hey!"; "OK, we're moving now!"; "OK, enough *comedy jokes!*"; "Yes, *this* is comedy." In one bit, Martin asks the audience to imagine how stupid they would feel if they died and found themselves to be angels in heaven. He riffs on this idea, imagining himself confronted with the exact number of times he has taken the Lord's name in vain: "*Million* six? Jesus Chrit . . ."

The joke itself is unspectacular, but Martin delivers the line "*million six*" with such extravagant smarm as to transcend the material. Perhaps his most famous catchphrase was the climax of a bit in which he earnestly asked for "mood lighting" onstage and didn't get it: a simulated performance malfunction along the lines of some of Andy Kaufman's most famous work. Martin seems to break the performance frame when he complains about the club's backstage crew, suggesting that they are ex-hippies who care more about taking drugs than putting on a good show: a nice example of Martin playing the role of a "visitor from the straight world." As Martin's self-righteous outrage intensifies, however, it becomes clear that this is all part of the act, and he performs his final line, "Well, *excuuuuuse* me!" with manic, over-the-top theatrical zeal. In the immediate wake of this furious outburst, Martin quickly strikes up an impossibly cheerful tune on his banjo, providing one last abrupt change in register. Note that, since we are never really asked to believe that Martin has broken out of performance mode, the pleasure of the bit is largely a matter of reveling in the extravagant delivery of what became one of Martin's signature catchphrases.

"Excuse me" delighted audiences but troubled some critics, who made it the focal point of their discussion of Martin's catchphrases. "Martin's act is now our act and we think we're funny. He has so successfully imbedded himself in the national consciousness that everybody does a Steve Martin routine," wrote the *Washington Post* in 1979. "After you've heard 'Excuuuuuse me!' for the 800th time . . . the lines lose their spark. We laugh all right, but we also laugh when Uncle Harry says he is 'looking for the foxes' or when someone at the office party screams 'Well, excuse me!' That laughter should not be confused with the yuks that come from true ability."[126] *Chicago Times* critic Larry Kart published a lengthy analysis of the popularity of Martin's catchphrases, which he claimed was "firmly based on their usefulness in daily communication": "As anyone who has been on the receiving of a 'Well, excuse me' knows, that phrase proclaimed that the speaker was going to behave quite selfishly but wished that no one would take offense or hold him responsible for what he was about to do. The problem, of course, was that Martin's line was a joke about irresponsibility and selfishness, not a way to behave irresponsibly without causing pain. But within his audience there were so many people who needed such an emotional tool that they tried to make 'Well, ex-cuse me' function as a foolproof, self-protective code."[127] Though I am impressed by the fact that these reviewers comment on the social function of Martin's comedy, I disagree with their conclusions. For one thing, Martin's joke doesn't seem to me to be about" anything besides a kind of formal play for the sake of existential humor. Further, both reviewers struggle with the way in which the catchphrase was open to audience appropriation and so seemed to lack clear authorship, ownership, or artistry. In short, if Uncle Harry can get laughs with it, it must not have any artistic or social value. We can hear in such a view echoes of Theodor Adorno and Max Horkheimer's famous essay on the "culture industry," in which the authors linked the rapid spread of commercial language to Nazi radio propaganda:

> When the German Fascists decide one day to launch a word—say, "intolerable"—over the loudspeakers the next day the whole nation is saying "intolerable." . . . The general repetition of names for measures to be taken by the authorities makes them, so to speak, familiar, just as the brand name on everybody's lips increased sales in the era of the free market. The blind and rapidly spreading repetition of words with special designations links advertising with the totalitarian watchword. The layer of experience which created the words for their speakers has been removed; in this swift appropriation language acquires the coldness which until now it had only on billboards and in the advertisement columns of newspapers. Innumerable people use words and expressions which they have either ceased to understand or employ because they trigger off conditioned reflexes.[128]

For Adorno and Horkheimer, Uncle Harry's use of Martin's catchphrases would be a troubling indication of how postwar consumers are being homogenized along the lines of "the model served up by the culture industry" in the inflection they use in even "the most intimate situation" and in their "choice of words in conversation."[129] The critics cited previously stop short of any overt connections between Martin's act and totalitarianism, but they are certainly ambivalent about catchphrases because of how they seem to involve an inauthentic overinvestment on the part of the audience and a cheap substitute for quality material on the part of the performer.

There are other, more productive ways, however, to understand the social life of a catchphrase. Note that for Warner, the catchphrase is an important component of public discourse that aims to *circulate* instead of just be "emitted in one direction": "Even mass media, which because of their heavy capitalization are conspicuously asymmetrical, take care to fake a reciprocity that they must overcome in order to succeed." Warner claims that media texts like advertisements achieve this sense of reciprocity by lacing their message with catchphrases that then suture it to informal speech and so help to create "the impression of a vital feedback loop despite the immense asymmetry of production and reception that defines mass culture."[130] Warner offers the example of the series of Budweiser television ads that used the expression, "Whassup?" Besides constructing a "feedback loop" between commercial and everyday discourse, the catchphrase adds to the degree of temporal engagement with the message by stimulating its repetition in daily interaction. Steve Martin seems to have known as well as Budweiser that vernacular catchphrases could add temporal depth to the circulation of comedy material to a public of strangers.

Warner's analysis opens up the possibility of recognizing forms of audience engagement with catchphrases that go beyond a neurotic "emotional tool" or "self-protective code" dished up by a coercive media industry. Warner asserts that audiences do not "mechanically repeat signature catchphrases" but perform through them a specific "social placement": "Different social styles can be created through different levels of reflexivity in this performance. Too obvious parroting of catchphrases . . . can mark you in some contexts as square, unhip, a passive relay in the circulation. In other contexts, it could certify you as one of the gang, showing that you, too, were watching the show with everyone else."[131] Similarly, Klinger has demonstrated that the quoting of film dialogue can serve multiple social functions, such as marking a social group, displaying "mastery and proficiency" within that group, and even rehearsing types of masculinity.[132] Klinger's research concerns the rewatching of films on VCRs and DVD players, but as we have seen throughout this book, the LP provided repeatable home entertainment before the VCR, and catchphrases on comedy LPs like Martin's were certainly mobilized to perform a similar range of stances and functions. In other words, the young men who rehearsed Martin's catchphrases were precursors to a similar demographic who would memorize and repeat lines from Adam Sandler and Quentin Tarantino movies.

Martin's catchphrases spoke to, and were spoken by, a younger cohort of LP buyers than those of the era of Sahl, Bruce, or even the Firesign Theatre. In an article on how Steve Martin was helping to revitalize the comedy album market, a record executive described a new youth audience for comedy albums: "To be cool, kids have to memorize all the latest jokes the way they used to learn Led Zeppelin guitar chords."[133] The comparison between Martin and Led Zeppelin is suggestive in several ways. First, that band functioned for many Americans as what Roland Barthes has called "musica practica": music meant to be played as much as listened to, and so that is experienced through the body, through musical practice.[134] Led Zeppelin's records provided an encyclopedia of guitar riffs that were "musica practica" in dorm rooms across the country, just as Martin's catchphrases functioned as a similar form of "comedia practica." Second, Led Zeppelin was associated with new contexts of stadium performance that often featured guitar riff–driven rock acts of the early 1970s.

The *Oxford English Dictionary* defines *stadium* as "an enclosed area for sporting events equipped with tiers of seats for spectators." The early 1970s saw the emergence of *stadium rock,* which the OED helpfully defines as "a type of rock music perceived as sounding grandiose, anthemic, or bombastic, and characteristically performed at lavish stage shows in sports stadiums before huge audiences." The era of stadium rock was presaged by the Beatles' August 15, 1965, appearance at New York's Shea Stadium in front of 55,600 fans. At their American concert performances, the Beatles had contended with notoriously bad sound systems, and as a result the band could rarely hear themselves over the screams of the crowd. By the early 1970s, rock performance in stadiums had become professionalized, and a range of rock bands was appearing in sports stadiums and civic centers: Grand Funk Railroad played in front of 55,000 at Shea Stadium on July 9, 1971; David Cassidy sold out the Houston Astrodome on March 5, 1972; and more than 30,000 attended an Osmond Brothers concert at Anaheim Stadium on September 8, 1972.[135] Stadium concert tours became firmly established over the course of the 1970s, and acts such as Kiss, Alice Cooper, and Pink Floyd brought a sense of overt theatricality to rock as a stadium spectacle. In a review of Pink Floyd's pompous *The Wall* tour in 1979, a *New York Times* writer stressed the historical importance of developments in sound amplification to "fill large spaces with sound as well as sights": electronic amplification and music that made use of that potential had given birth to multimedia events that appealed to "the thousands or even the hundreds of thousands."[136] Stadium rock can also be seen as the culmination of modern developments in acoustics. Emily Thompson describes the growing belief among sound engineers beginning in the 1920s that the reverberation-free outdoors provided the best acoustic environment for listening. The interest in outdoor acoustics led to the creation of venues such as the Hollywood Bowl, where the Beatles performed in 1964 and 1965.[137]

How would the development of such huge, outdoor performance spaces affect live comedy? If Nichols and May presented comedy in close-up, what might comedy in extreme long shot look and sound like? Note that, for Marc, the directness of communication between the artist and audience is a "definitive feature" of stand-up comedy: a view that clearly owes something to the cabaret tradition discussed above.[138] Huge stadium audiences could thus appear to go against the grain of certain core stand-up values. During the live nightclub performance heard on his album *Comedy Minus One*, Albert Brooks talked about his experiences opening up shows for Neil Diamond (where he faced stadium audiences yelling for "Kentucky Woman") and for Ritchie Havens (where he was greeted by hostile chants of "Ritchie! Ritchie! Ritchie!"). "Concert halls are getting too big," he complained, and riffing on the idea, suggested that soon a band like Three Dog Night would no longer play in buildings at all: "They get onto a jet plane in New York and fly to Los Angeles and play in the plane, let the military promote the concert, and have everyone in the country pay a dollar." Brooks's routine reveals the practical and conceptual problems that stadium crowds posed for stand-up comics: they worked by a different logic than a nightclub audience and were so large as to almost seem tantamount to the national audience itself.

As we have seen, comics had faced challenges of overexposure and repetition since the dawn of the mass media, but perhaps none to quite the degree that Steve Martin did in the late 1970s. As the attendance at his shows reached the thousands, Martin began wearing his trademark white suit: "I worried about being seen at such distances—this was a small comedy act. For visibility, I bought a white suit to wear onstage."[139] Martin's second LP, *Wild and Crazy Guy* (Warner Bros. 1978), nicely brackets the transition between two comedy performance spaces: side one is a recording of a show at the Boarding House nightclub in San Francisco, and side two is a stadium appearance at Colorado's Red Rocks Amphitheater. In the fairly intimate nightclub setting of the Boarding House, we hear several moments of apparently spontaneous ad libbing: Martin is thrown off his stride by a baby in the audience, and later, he returns a withering comeback to a loudmouthed patron at the club. ("Yeah, I remember my first beer.") That zinger was probably a tried-and-true technique for silencing hecklers and so was as much a part of Martin's repertoire as anything else, and yet it was singled out by critics for its sense of liveness and tangible interaction with the audience. For critics, those were exactly the qualities that the stadium appearance on side two lacked: "Martin's one-on-one, nightclub approach gives way to massive crowd contact, and the intimacy disappears under a style of broad burlesque."[140] The transition between nightclub and stadium on *Wild and Crazy Guy* is stunning to hear. Martin tells the Boarding House audience that he is required to make a financial disclosure, explaining, for example, how the development of new material merits .0000001 percent of his earnings. He then lays out his concert income for a three thousand–seat hall at $3 per ticket: a gross of $9000. "Just for fun," he adds, he has worked out that a three thousand–seat hall at $800 a ticket would gross $2,400,000. "This is what I'm shooting for," he concludes, "one show, *goodbye*." An abrupt cut brings us the sound of the Red Rocks audience as Martin takes the stage: over sixty seconds of deafening cheers, whoops, and whistles. When confronted with the audio spectacle of the stadium audience, critics often noted the absence of anything that they could define as laughter:

> Much of the time his fans don't laugh at all. Instead, they cheer, hailing the arrival of familiar routines the way a pop music audience greets a rock star's "greatest hits.". . . I'm left with the feeling that I've been eavesdropping on a revival meeting or a political rally rather than a comedy concert.[141]

> Audiences came not so much to laugh as cheer their favorite Martin routines (his greatest hits), not waiting for punch lines, bursting into applause at the first hint of an attack of "happy feet."[142]

> They scream Martin's name as though he were the sexiest of rock stars; they greet with cheers his by now familiar lines . . . in fact they do just about everything but laugh.[143]

For these critics, the frame of reference for such an event was either stadium rock, where live performances involved the enactment of popular records ("greatest hits") to an adoring crowd, or the irrational mass spectacle of a political rally or religious meeting: both at odds with the spontaneity, interaction, and risk required of "authentic" stand-up performance.[144]

The sound of the stadium audience could also inspire unease because of the way in which it laid bare the troubling dimensions of the media public. The dispersed national audience that was implicit behind the intimate nightclub ambiance of "live" albums or represented on network broadcasting through proxies such as the laugh track or carefully stage-managed studio audiences were here given voice, with the scale of the media public and its relation to the performer made shockingly manifest. The asymmetry of that relationship did not favor the manipulative media industry but the audience, which, in the rhetoric of some critics, could literally consume the performer: Martin's "sharklike fans" had begun to eat him alive, Kart wrote, and were "devouring the comic with approval."[145] Side two of *Wild and Crazy Guy* presents a sonic picture of the sheer enormity of the public created by the media and so destroys the pretense of immediacy and intimacy on "live" records as well as on television chat shows, where comics and celebrities are encountered in what resembles face-to-face interaction: what Naremore refers to as parasocial interaction.[146] Like the LPs of Albert Brooks and Lily Tomlin, *Wild and Crazy Guy* revealed the inherent dissonances between the nominal addressees of comedy and its circulating public, and Martin's stadium act exposed as convention the typical gestures that managed those dissonances: "How many people have cats?" Martin asked the massive crowd at one point, and then made a half-baked attempt to count the innumerable hands: "1, 2, 3, 4 . . . OK, 10!" In this sense, *Wild and Crazy Guy* was as much a form of "blind television" as the records of the Firesign Theatre, since it presented an audio picture of what network television did not show: the massive scale of its own audience.

COMEDY CENTRALIZED

Martin's phenomenal success was of course closely linked to his appearances on NBC's *Saturday Night Live (SNL)*, which debuted in 1975.[147] If the LP served as a comedy alternative to network television during the 1960s and 1970s, *SNL* certainly represented a turning point, when some kinds of peripheral comedy were allowed access to the national stage. I've been arguing that the comedy LP remediated television, but I will end this chapter by pointing out some ways in which both *SNL* and cable television remediated types of comedy that had been experienced in large part on LP records. First, *SNL*'s cast, the Not Ready for Primetime Players, was modeled after and drew on talent from Chicago's Second City, the improvisational comedy cabaret opened by Paul Sills after the demise of the Compass Theater. As we have seen, a key medium for the Chicago school of comedy before *SNL* had been the LP. Due in no small part to *SNL*'s success, Viola Spolin's group improvisation became, via Second City, as influential to television comedy as the Actors Studio was to film drama, and press coverage of Second City typically invoked a litany of its superstar alumni: Peter Boyle, Alan Arkin, Valerie Harper, Joan Rivers, John Belushi, Dan Aykroyd, Gilda Radner, Martin Short, Bill Murray, Shelley Long, Amy Sedaris, Robert Klein, Harold Ramis, Alan Alda, Jerry Stiller, Linda Lavin, and Paul Mazursky. But this emphasis on stars makes clear the conflicts and contradictions inherent in the

Chicago school of improvisational comedy: what was more important, group dynamics or the creation of stars? Was improvisation meant to produce therapeutic spontaneity or create and stockpile new material? Did improvisational theater empower the audience or simply provide an efficient technique for developing material with which to entertain them? For Coleman, David Shepherd's initial intention for the Compass to be an "inexpensive vehicle for throwing light on and into the lives of common people" was, in the form of Second City, "transmogrified into a show-business boot camp, a rung on the short, steep ladder of the funny business."[148] Second City became, in the words of another critic, a corporation whose business was the creation and distribution of comedy, which included three touring groups that served as a "farm team for the franchise" and a "corporate division" that sent actors to firms as business consultants, "teaching levity as a management tool."[149] Though initially defined in opposition to Method acting, the Chicago school arguably shared a similar fate as the Actors Studio, which, as Naremore writes, was a system of training that aimed to "transcend mere playacting" but that came to depend on a star system.[150]

In addition to a cabaret-style revue format, *SNL* also repackaged the nightclub comedian tradition of Lenny Bruce and Mort Sahl in the form of guest comics such as George Carlin. Besides appearing on *SNL,* comics such as Carlin also found an important outlet on cable television. Home Box Office (HBO) began broadcasting via satellite in 1975 and was soon reaching a large national audience. HBO sought out niche programming not found on the networks, such as boxing, exclusive movies, and, notably, comedy specials: HBO's *On Location* series of comedy concerts was launched in 1975 with Robert Klein.[151] George Carlin's first HBO special in April 1977 contained his famous routine about the "seven dirty words" that could not be broadcast, an indication of how cable would provide a new kind of platform for stand-up comics.[152] Auslander describes the importance of cable television for comics of this era: "Broadcast television had traditionally offered stand-up comics very few opportunities to ply their trade," he writes, but cable stations "were willing and able to offer stand-up comics places in programs that duplicate the conditions under which they perform in clubs."[153] What becomes clear is that the postwar "liberal satire" that had been distributed to a national public on comedy records prefigured and eventually became a key element of cable programming, allowing cable stations to supplant the comedy LP as the home medium for edgy adult humor. Phil Proctor of the Firesign Theatre stated that cable "changed everything" for the comedy record market because it allowed comedians to "do their outrageous material for the camera," and from then on, "people wanted to *see* their comedians, and records were just edited versions of the live performance."[154]

The hypermedia TV criticism of Proctor's comedy group was also remediated on television in the late 1970s in the form of *SNL*'s parodies of television ads. As a telling indication of where the comedy market was headed in the mid-1970s, note that during the same year as the debut of both *SNL* and HBO, Firesign was dropped by Columbia Records who, by one account, had decided that "comedy was no longer practical" in the record marketplace.[155] Besides influencing the production of studio-based comedy albums, Firesign also spawned a subgenre of comedy sketch films that took television as their subject, such as *Groove Tube* (1974), which featured future *SNL* star Chevy Chase; *Kentucky Fried Movie* (1977), with Chase again; *Tunnel Vision* (1976), with *SNL* cast member Lorraine Newman and SCTV's John Candy; and *Americathon* (1979). *Tunnel Vision* presented a future world in which cable television provided an outlet for countercultural satire. The Firesign's Phil Proctor plays the role of Christian A. Broder, the owner of a cable television station being investigated by Congress for corrupting the nation's youth. The jury is shown a selection of content supposedly taken from a broadcast day on Broder's station, beginning with a psychedelic station identification. The film's dubious sense of humor in the sketch comedy bits that follow becomes evident quickly: the first sketch is a parody ad for a correspondence course in proctology. Nevertheless, the film is notable for its faith in cable TV as an avenue for cutting edge, even countercultural content. Proctor and Bergman had made similarly optimistic predictions about cable on their LP *TV or Not TV* (Columbia 1973), an album that suggested that cable television would provide an outlet for amateur, underground broadcasts. Proctor and Bergman would eventually find a cable niche for their "forward into the past" studio aesthetic on the USA Network's *Night Flight* programming, which put their *J-Men Forever!* (1979)—a satirical reworking of Hollywood serials—in regular rotation.

We can see then how the nightclub, cabaret, and studio comedy heard on postwar comedy LPs found a new outlet on the television of the late 1970s, most notably on HBO. HBO also became the U.S. home of perhaps the most brilliant comic of recent years: Ricky Gervais, the cocreator and star of BBC's *The Office* (2001–2003) and *Extras* (2005–2006). Gervais's work was strongly influenced by the Chicago improvisational school of "comedy in close-up" via several routes: HBO's *Curb Your Enthusiasm,* which featured Compass alumnus Shelley Berman as Larry David's father as well as a mode of production based on group improvisation; the film *Spinal Tap* (1984), which was directed by Rob Reiner, a vocal proponent of Viola Spolin's theater games; and the "mockumentaries" of Christopher Guest, whose improvisational approach Gervais often sites as his most important influence. Approaches to television comedy performance became one of the key themes of the second season of *Extras,* which tracked the compromises made by Andy Millman (Gervais) in his pursuit of a successful career in television. The most galling of those compromises is the requirement to use a catchphrase: as the ultimate sign of his sellout, Millman stars in a sitcom called *When the Whistle Blows* on which he must don a funny wig and glasses and utter the catchphrase, "Are you having a laugh?" Judging by the logic of the show, the catchphrase is still widely considered to be on the bottom of a hierarchy of comedy performance.[156]

An even more stunning indication of the current status of both the catchphrase and stadium comedy took place when Gervais appeared at the Concert for Diana at Wembley Stadium on July 1, 2007. A truly global media event, the concert was broadcast to 140 countries and had an estimated television audience of 500 million. There were 63,000 people in Wembley Stadium when Gervais took the stage and performed the song "Freelove Freeway" from *The Office* with costar Mackenzie Crook. At the end of his prepared bit, Gervais was taken off guard when he was asked to stay onstage and fill time during a delay in readying the next act. Not wanting to use jokes from his current stand-up tour in front of such a huge television audience, Gervais awkwardly groped for a way to entertain the crowd: a condensed enactment of the perpetual problem of comic material in the era of broadcasting. As he hesitated, the audience began calling for him to perform what had become one of the signature moments from *The Office*: the humiliating impromptu dance done by Gervais's seedy boss character, David Brent. After a tense, cringe-inducing few minutes, Gervais finally broke down and danced for the crowd.

It was hard to know exactly what to make of this strange and uncomfortable spectacle: a television star working in a tradition of comedy in close-up struggling to reframe his persona in extreme long shot; a fiercely independent and original writer and performer with contempt for catchphrase comedy made to enact a dance that was the visual equivalent of a well-known catchphrase by the chanting crowd.

In the press coverage that followed, many critics interpreted the incident as a shameful loss of artistic credibility: Gervais had been "eaten alive" by the stadium audience. I hope, however, that my examination of comedy in the era of the LP record might facilitate a more nuanced reading of the event. For one thing, the audience had it right: reenacting the dance from *The Office* was an entirely appropriate response to the scale of stadium comedy. Further, Gervais's dance, like one of Martin's catchphrases, represented a tangible if limited dialogue between the star performer and the copresent embodiment of a public that knew him from television. That critics and even Gervais himself—one of the most exceptional and successful comedic performers of our time—are so reluctant and uncertain about that dialogue suggests that we have all yet to fully understand the intimate comic theater of stranger relationality in the era of modern media.

Conclusion

Perhaps the single most celebrated episode of *Saturday Night Live* was broadcast on April 22, 1978, and featured Steve Martin as guest host. The show included the debut of Martin's new novelty song "King Tut"; a mock-Hollywood musical dance sequence featuring Martin and Gilda Radner; an appearance by the two "wild and crazy" Festrunk brothers as played by Martin and Dan Aykroyd; and musical performances by the Blues Brothers. Near the end of the episode, Martin, Aykroyd, and Jane Curtain appeared as a panel of psychics on a mock–current events discussion show entitled "Next Week in Review." At one point, Martin predicted that the cover of the following week's *Time* magazine would feature a four-word message from an extraterrestrial civilization that had encountered NASA's Voyager spacecraft. You might recall from the introduction to this book that each Voyager carried a golden record containing a massive compilation of speeches, sound effects, and a cross-section of music from around the world, including works by J.S. Bach, compositions for the Javanese gamelan, and Chuck Berry's "Johnny B. Goode." The psychic pundit played by Steve Martin announced that the alien race that had heard the golden records had been moved to communicate to the people of Earth: the first "positive proof that other intelligent beings inhabit the Universe." Martin held up a copy of the soon-to-be published *Time* cover to reveal the message from the stars: "Send more Chuck Berry." This joke nicely punctures the pomposity of the rhetoric surrounding the Voyager mission but also provides me with a convenient catchphrase to organize some concluding remarks about the preceding chapters.

One way to interpret the line "Send more Chuck Berry" is to say that Martin and the writers of the sketch had projected onto the aliens a preference for media products like rock and roll records that were marketed to a niche demographic. The case studies in this book have shown that the record industry took part in a process by which market segmentation became the "operational matrix" for American marketing and media production during the decades after World War II. Media scholars have accounted for the emergence of market segmentation and niche marketing in numerous ways, pointing to such things as magazine specialization, innovations in market research, the cultural division of the 1960s, and new media platforms. In the case of American television, the 1970s saw a turn toward "narrowcasting," most notably in cable programming and the network pursuit of a "quality" demographic.[1] The spoken word records described in this book reveal the record industry to have been adept at narrowcasting in the 1950s and 1960s, a time often described as the "broadcasting era."

Bringing the record industry into the discussion of postwar trends in media marketing provides a new vantage point on the gradual and uneven shift in the cultural industries toward market segmentation, which has accelerated in recent years, such that many marketers and critics now see media audiences as "brand tribes" bound together "more by affinity and shared interests than by default broadcast schedules."[2] Opinions differ about the social consequences of that shift. Some agree with Dwight MacDonald that the more the "mass audience" is divided, the better, as this results in higher-quality media texts and more audience agency. Others feel that segmentation has caused a "profound sense of division in American society," such that media audiences now inhabit "the electronic equivalents of gated communities."[3] I agree with Joseph Turow that the ideal scenario is a balance between "segment-making media" that encourage "small slices of society to talk to themselves" and "society-making media" that allow various groups to "move out of their parochial scenes to talk with, argue against, and entertain one another." For Turow, the proper balance of the two results in "a rich and diverse sense of overarching connectedness: what a vibrant society is all about."[4] During the postwar era, phonograph records frequently provided a "segment-making" home media alternative to the dominant "society-making" media of network broadcasting. This helps to explain the affective charge provided by records containing risqué content or

humor that could not be presented on television, parodies of broadcasting genres and personalities, or "educational" content marginalized
in network programming. Records convened audiences around shared
interests that were often underrepresented in the broadcast media, making them a powerful vehicle for the formation of group identity during
the postwar decades. "Send more Chuck Berry" stands, then, as an indication of a generational preference for the narrowcast over the broadcast and thus as a portent of trends in media production and marketing
in the decades that followed.

Besides its suggestion of a general turn toward market segmentation, Martin's joke champions one market niche in particular: the youth
demographic served by rock records. The aliens' disregard for Voyager's
collection of sound effects, speeches, and classical and world music in
their zeal for a single rock track resembles the boomer historiography
that came to see the record industry only in terms of popular music, in
particular rock and roll. Despite the undeniable cultural influence of
rock music, a single-minded focus on youth records limits our view of
the phonograph industry and the functions of recorded sound in the
home. Along these lines, Richard Dyer has warned against taking at face
value claims that postwar icons of youth rebellion such as James Dean
or Marlon Brando represented real challenges to the dominant ideology.
"Youth," Dyer writes, is in fact the "ideal material term on which to
displace social discontent": young people, after all, always "grow up."[5]
One of my goals has been to think about the postwar record industry
beyond the youth market and the genres of music with which it is associated. A richer, more complex and contested history emerges when we
hear Bozo records alongside the Beach Boys; Caedmon's Dylan Thomas
records alongside Bob Dylan; Rusty Warren alongside Janis Joplin; the
Kopykat impressionists alongside the anticomics of the 1970s; Dooto's
African American comedy records alongside Stax and Motown; Nichols
and May alongside Hollywood Method actors such as Dean and Brando
and the white rockers that they inspired. In short, the youth market was
only part of the story of the postwar record industry, and spoken word
genres allow us to account for a more diverse cross-section of the performers and audiences associated with phonograph records.

Perhaps I've been misreading the motivations behind the alien communication: maybe the plea "Send more Chuck Berry" was an indication
that extraterrestrial listeners had worn out the Voyager golden discs from
repeated spins, just as young children in the 1940s had done with their
Bozo records and teenagers had done in the 1950s with their 45 rpm rock

singles. After all, rock and roll became the dominant genre in the record industry not only because of the whims of teenagers and savvy industry marketing, but also because artists and producers working in that genre developed performance styles and studio techniques that encouraged and rewarded repeated listening. Artists and producers working in spoken word genres were also exploring an aesthetics of repetition: recall the arresting soundscapes heard on Capitol's kidisks; the Firesign Theatre's dense, multitrack narratives; and the dynamics of imitation and performance found on many comedy records. The development of recorded performances made to withstand multiple hearings merits additional study in a contemporary mediascape in which repetition has become the norm, not just for records, but for films and television programs on videocassette and DVD.[6] Indeed, the market for adult party records and kidisks prepared the ground for two of the key genres in the video marketplace: hardcore pornography and family entertainment. Also consider that one of the first breakthrough hits of the videotape market was *Jane Fonda's Workout* (1982), which signaled new uses for repeatable video content in the American home. The record industry had been releasing exercise records since the 1920s, and Bonnie Prudden's 1960s exercise LPs prefigured Fonda's videotape by two decades. Spoken word records pioneered the market for home entertainment that was unmoored from network scheduling, a topic that media scholars have discussed under the rubric of the VCR's ability to allow viewers to tape shows and watch them later. Further research remains to be done on how records such as Kermit Schaefer's collections of broadcast "bloopers" and recorded compilations of radio history like Columbia's *I Can Hear It Now* records reveal how the phonograph was put in the service of a long-standing public desire to freeze the flow of broadcasting. I hope that the studies in this book will encourage future scholarly work, not only on the record industry, but on the links between adjacent and interdependent media forms, what we might call the *media ecology* of the home.

Since we are on the subject of repetition, I hope you will permit me a final iteration of the catchphrase "Send more Chuck Berry." Might this suggest the aliens' preference for a long-playing Berry album over the single track? Rick Altman's "crisis historiography" of new media technologies has shaped my understanding of how spoken word records can be seen within the process whereby the LP became the dominant medium for recorded sound. Spoken word genres played an important role in establishing a popular market for the LP and demonstrated that the long-playing record could be defined in a variety of ways. When the economic and cultural ascendancy of rock music coincided with the emergence of new media platforms that usurped some of the LP's functions in the home, spoken word genres were pushed to the peripheries of the industry. Nonetheless, one of the lessons of the work of scholars like Altman and Lisa Gitelman is that the study of "unsuccessful" and "short-lived" media technologies and practices are as potentially illuminating as those that become established.[7] Spoken word records may not have become the dominant form of recorded sound, but they still have much to tell us about postwar media culture and provide a more complete compass of the experience of the phonograph in American homes. Orson Welles once referred to radio as an "abandoned mine," whose aesthetic potential, like silent cinema's, had been prematurely foreclosed upon due to American culture's "technological restlessness." In the digital era, when an ever-increasing number of music consumers carry entire record collections in their hip pockets, the time is right for the rediscovery of the abandoned mine of spoken word recordings, a rich but largely forgotten part of the heritage of American recorded sound.

The period of the LP's most profound cultural resonance was coming to an end when Steve Martin made his appearance on the 1978 broadcast of *Saturday Night Live*. That year, as Martin delivered his punch line about Voyager's golden records, the record industry was handing out more of its own gold and platinum record awards for album sales than ever before.[8] After twenty-five years of uninterrupted growth, the record business reached its zenith in 1977 and early 1978, buoyed not only by Martin's bestselling comedy LPs but by the disco craze, a wave of nostalgia purchases set off by the death of Elvis Presley, and a cohort of blockbuster albums by the likes of Peter Frampton, the Eagles, Boston, and Fleetwood Mac.[9] A key factor in this explosive growth in record sales was the "after-teen" market. Industry market research indicated that 77 percent of all record buyers were eighteen or older and accounted for 82 percent of all record purchases.[10] In March 1978 Elektra/Asylum ran an advertisement in *Billboard* featuring ad copy that fused the terminology for phonograph "rotations per minute" with the aging of the baby boom generation: "It's '78," the ad declared, "and all those born in '45 are about to be 33⅓." The generation "born in '45" had bought records all their life, and now, "33⅓ odd years later," these "war babies" were continuing to drive the industry. What is more, the baby boomers had passed their "fanaticism" to a "new generation" of album "nuts," and so were responsible for a record industry "expanding happily in a multibillion dollar marketplace." Both the trade and popular press reported that, thanks to the aging boomers and their children, records were out-grossing the cinema box office, despite the success of films such as *Star Wars* (1977), and that record operations in media conglomerates were, in some cases, accounting for more than half of total corporate profits.[11] There was little cause for those in the record industry to worry that the sales boom might come to an end any time soon. Joe Smith, the chairman of Elektra/Asylum Records, stated that he could see "nothing but blue skies ahead." "We've already gone through the roof," said another record executive. "Now we're going for the sky."[12]

As an indication of the central place of the record business in the media industries of this time, consider that just three months after Steve Martin sang "King Tut" on *Saturday Night Live,* he made his debut on American cinema screens with a cameo in a film meant to ride the coat-tails of the booming record business. At the center of the 1977–78 block-buster year was the Robert Stigwood Organization's (RSO) soundtracks to *Saturday Night Fever* (1977) and *Grease* (1978), with the former becoming the top-grossing album of all time. Stigwood planned to follow up his phenomenally successful soundtrack-driven hits with a new franchise, one that, according to the president of Stigwood's record label, could make the *Saturday Night Fever* soundtrack look like "a test run for the main event."[13] The success of the new project seemed certain: it was based on perhaps the most celebrated LP of them all; featured an all-star cast, including Steve Martin in the role of a psychotic doctor and two of the most successful musicians of the boom year, Peter Frampton and the Bee Gees; and contained the classic hits of the postwar era's most beloved songwriters. It was not a surprise, then, when Stigwood's RSO Records announced that the double-album soundtrack to the upcoming film *Sgt. Pepper's Lonely Hearts Club Band* (1978) had "gone platinum" by shipping over four million copies before it went on sale and that meeting the expected demand for the soundtrack had become the "greatest manufacturing task ever undertaken."[14] The soundtrack made history all right, but not in the way that Stigwood had hoped. The *Sgt. Pepper* film was a commercial and critical flop, and of the four million copies of the soundtrack shipped to record stores before the film's release, two million were returned unsold to the record company, making it the first album in history to go platinum on the return trip.[15]

The *Sgt. Pepper* soundtrack was the canary in the coalmine, heralding the onset of what became a prolonged record industry slump. Sales fell from 521.3 million units in 1978 to 502.2 million units in 1979, and corporate losses amounted to more than $200 million. Earnings at CBS Records alone fell from \$93.8 million in 1978 to \$51 million in 1979.[16] There was much discussion in the popular press about the causes of the slump, with pundits pointing to increases in album prices, consumer nervousness about a downturn in the U.S. economy, rising gasoline prices that pushed up the production cost of records and cut into teenage spending, overpaid pop superstars releasing fewer records, the growing threat of home taping on compact cassettes, and competition from cable television and the first wave of home video games.[17] The record industry recovered after a few years, and profits resumed their upward climb in 1983, but it was a very different record industry that emerged after the slump, one built around a new business model, with music videos and MTV as its center of gravity. Not only did the post-slump record business feature a new configuration of record and television industry synergy, but recorded sound was now consumed primarily on cassettes and CDs rather than LPs.[18] The 1979 slump and the *Sgt. Pepper* debacle thus provide a signpost for the end of the LP era that has been the focus of this book.

It is fitting to end with reference to the Beatles' album *Sgt. Pepper's Lonely Hearts Club Band* (1967), since mid-1960s rock albums have served as a kind of structuring absence to the foregoing discussion. Like the "new generation" of "album nuts" who acquired a fanaticism for records from their "war baby" parents, I grew up with my own stack of Bill Cosby, *Sesame Street,* and *Star Trek* LPs but was particularly transfixed by used copies of Beatles albums that my mother brought home from garage sales. I vividly remember listening to *Sgt. Pepper* as a child and gazing at the assemblage of celebrity cutouts that surround the Beatles on the famous pop art cover designed by Peter Blake. Often regarded as the peak of "summer of love" optimism and 1960s pop modernism, I now see that cover as a statement about the LP's remarkable flexibility as a postwar medium. When seen in the context of the richness and diversity found on the case studies in the foregoing chapters, many of the faces that can be found on the *Sgt. Pepper* cover index not just the band's eclectic influences, but the LP's ability to repackage a multitude of sound entertainments for home consumption: we have poetry in the person of Dylan Thomas; children's entertainment in Lewis Carroll; modes of improvised film acting in Marlon Brando; standup comedy in Lenny Bruce; and burlesque in Mae West. The presence of these diverse personalities surrounding the Fab Four represents a quiet acknowledgment of a larger history of recorded sound in postwar American culture, a history still largely untold.

Notes

INTRODUCTION

1. Lynn Spigel and Jan Olsson, eds., *Television after TV* (Durham, NC: Duke University Press, 2004), p. 21.

2. Jack Gould, "Soon You'll Collect TV Reels, Like LP's," *New York Times*, September 3, 1967, p. 69.

3. Keir Keightley, "Long Play: Adult-Oriented Popular Music and the Temporal Logics of the Post-war Sound Recording Industry in the USA," *Media, Culture & Society* 26, no. 3 (2004): 386–87.

4. Ibid., p. 376.

5. Tim J. Anderson, *Making Easy Listening* (Minneapolis: University of Minnesota Press, 2006), p. xxxiii.

6. Patrick Feaster, *The Following Record: Making Sense of Phonographic Performance, 1877–1908* (PhD diss., Indiana University, Bloomington, 2006), pp. 672–74.

7. Rick Altman, *Silent Film Sound* (New York: Columbia University Press, 2004), pp. 22–23.

8. Ibid., pp. 19–21.

9. Susan A. Glenn, "'Give an Imitation of Me': Vaudeville Mimics and the Play of the Self," *American Quarterly* 50, no. 1 (1998): 48.

10. Quoted in Emily Thompson, *The Soundscape of Modernity* (Cambridge: MIT Press, 2002), p. 131.

CHAPTER I. TURNTABLE JR.

1. See Wendy Cole, "The Last Pratfall," *Time,* June 25, 2001, p. 6; and Phil Rosenthal, "There Ought to Be Bozo, but Try Telling Tribune," *Electronic Media* 20, no. 25 (June 18, 2001).

2. *Billboard* wrote that *Bozo at the Circus* passed the 2.3 million sales mark in 1952, making it "a current and probably all-time high in the disk biz" ("Cap Kid Fave Sells 2,300,000 Records," *Billboard,* November 15, 1952, p. 20). Local Bozos were said to be appearing at parent-teacher associations, theaters, and schools: "Capitol has a complete operating procedure laid down for anyone who plays Bozo, and no man is permitted to wear the uniform unless he is both conscientious and sober" (Bob Rolontz, "$2,000,000 on Capitol's Bozo," *Billboard,* January 14, 1953, p. 1).

3. Juliet B. Schor, *Born to Buy* (New York: Scribner, 2005), p. 9. See also Schor, 17, and Stephen Kline, *Out of the Garden* (London: Verso, 1993), p. 165.

4. Lisa Jacobson, *Raising Consumers* (New York: Columbia University Press, 2004), p. 17.

5. The Bubble Books were inducted into the Library of Congress National Recording Registry in 2003 on the grounds of being the first book and record hybrid. See http://www.loc.gov/exhibits/treasures/trr150.html.

6. See, for example, Amanda Bruce, "Children's Media Consumption and Struggles for Cultural Authority in the Nineteenth and Twentieth Centuries," in *Children and Consumer Culture in American Society,* ed. Lisa Jacobson (Westport, CT: Praeger, 2008).

7. Norma Odom Pecora, *The Business of Children's Entertainment* (New York: Guilford Press, 1998), p. 118.

8. See, for example, Thomas A. Edison (1878), "The Phonograph and Its Future," *North American Review* 126, no. 262 (May/June 1878): 527.

9. Gaby Wood, *Edison's Eve* (New York: Alfred A. Knopf, 2002), p. 161.

10. This advertisement is part of the RCA-Victor holdings at the Camden County Historical Society library, Camden, New Jersey.

11. *McClure's Magazine,* November 1907, p. 39.

12. This cylinder can be heard on the Internet: http://www.tinfoil.com/archive.htm.

13. "New Victor Booklet," *Voice of the Victor,* January 1907, p. 9.

14. An earlier series of 5½-inch records called Little Wonder records were an important part of the industrial backstory to the Bubble Books, but since they did not primarily feature material intended for children, I have not included them in the discussion here. For more information, the best source is http://www.littlewonderrecords.com/little-wonder-history.html.

15. R.M. Rhodes, "New Fields Opened by Appealing to Children," *Printers' Ink Monthly,* June 1921, p. 23.

16. Ibid.

17. Ibid., p. 25.

18. Viewed at http://www.littlewonderrecords.com/Advertisement%20BB%20Harpers%20Mag%20Adv%206-20.jpg.

19. For a complete discography of the Bubble Books, see http://www.little wonderrecords.com/bubble-book-discography.html. For children's records from the period between the 1930s and 1950s, see http://kiddierecords.com/ and Peter Muldavin's http://www.kiddierekordking.com/.

20. On the rise of the American toy and game industry, see Gary Cross, *Kids' Stuff* (Cambridge, MA: Harvard University Press, 1997), pp. 29–30; and William Leach, *Land of Desire* (New York: Vintage Books, 1993), p. 85.

21. Daniel Thomas Cook, *The Commodification of Childhood* (Durham, NC: Duke University Press, 2004), pp. 18–19.

22. Rhodes, "New Fields Opened," p. 25.

23. *Talking Machine World*, August 15, 1923, p. 57.

24. "Victor Bubble Books Open New Market," *Voice of the Victor*, September 1924, p. 13.

25. Schor, *Born to Buy*, 61–62; see also Jacobson, *Raising Consumers*, 31.

26. *Talking Machine World*, May 15, 1921, p. 63.

27. E. Gruber Garvey, *The Adman in the Parlor* (New York: Oxford University Press, 1996), p. 49.

28. Rhodes, "New Fields Opened," p. 25.

29. *Talking Machine World*, May 15, 1922, p. 134.

30. "There's a School in Every Town," *Voice of the Victor*, October 1924, p. 6.

31. *Talking Machine World*, June 15, 1919, p. 153.

32. Terry Staples, *All Pals Together* (Edinburgh: Edinburgh University Press, 1997), p. 8.

33. *Talking Machine World*, September 15, 1920, p. 14.

34. "Books for Children," *Bookseller, Newsdealer and Stationer*, November 15, 1920, p. 477.

35. Lisa Jacobson, "Advertising, Mass Merchandising, and the Creation of Children's Consumer Culture," in *Children and Consumer Culture in American Society*, ed. Lisa Jacobson (Westport, CT: Praeger, 2008).

36. Ellen Seiter, *Sold Separately* (New Brunswick, NJ: Rutgers University Press, 1995), p. 20.

37. Ellen Seiter, "Children's Desires/Mothers' Dilemmas," in *The Children's Culture Reader*, ed. Henry Jenkins (New York: New York University Press, 1998), p. 301.

38. Cook, *Commodification of Childhood*, p. 53.

39. Roland Marchand, *Advertising the American Dream* (Berkeley: University of California Press, 1985), p. 229.

40. *Talking Machine World*, April 15, 1924, p. 19.

41. Nicholas Sammond, *Babes in Tomorrowland* (Durham, NC: Duke University Press, 2005), p. 111.

42. *Ladies' Home Journal*, November 1919, p. 105.

43. Advertisements found online at http://www.littlewonderrecords.com/ cutout-bubble-book.html.

44. Schor, *Born to Buy*, p. 63.

45. *Ladies' Home Journal*, November 1919, p. 105.

46. Ibid.

47. *Atlantic Monthly,* October 1920, p. 24.

48. Seiter, *Sold Separately,* p. 67.

49. Ibid., p. 68.

50. "Can You Reach and Hold Your School Market?" *Voice of the Victor,* February 1924, p. 29.

51. "Somebody Is Getting This School Business," *Voice of the Victor,* October 1924, p. 9.

52. "Music Memory Contests," *Voice of the Victor,* March 1922, p. 49.

53. Garvey, *Adman in the Parlor,* p. 58.

54. Jacobson, "Advertising," p. 11.

55. Rhodes, "New Fields Opened," p. 25.

56. *St. Nicholas,* December 1920, viewed at http://www.littlewonderrecords .com/advertisements.html.

57. *Ladies' Home Journal,* November 1918, p. 48.

58. "Children's Records for Home and School," *Voice of the Victor,* March 1920, p. 49.

59. Cook, *Commodification of Childhood,* p. 73.

60. Ibid., p. 64.

61. Marchand, *Advertising the American Dream,* pp. 223–24.

62. *Talking Machine World,* viewed at http://www.littlewonderrecords.com/ advertisements.html.

63. *Talking Machine World,* April 15, 1923, viewed at http://www.littlewonder records.com/advertisements.html.

64. *Talking Machine World,* May 15, 1923, p. 157.

65. "Today's Radio Program," *New York Times,* April 2, 1922, p. 32; and "Events Tonight," *Christian Science Monitor,* July 28, 1923, p. 2.

66. Rhodes, "New Fields Opened," p. 25.

67. *Appleton [WI] Post-Crescent,* November 7, 1921, p. 12.

68. Leach, *Land of Desire,* p. 87.

69. Ibid., p. 330.

70. M. Formanek-Brunell, *Made to Play House* (Baltimore: Johns Hopkins University Press, 1993), p. 178.

71. Richard deCordova, "The Mickey in Macy's Window," in *Disney Discourse,* ed. Eric Smoodin (New York: Routledge, 1994), pp. 204–205.

72. Staples, *All Pals Together,* p. 51.

73. Sammond, *Babes in Tomorrowland,* pp. 73–74.

74. Jacobson, *Raising Consumers,* p. 23.

75. Amanda Bruce, "Children's Media Consumption and Struggles for Cultural Authority in the Nineteenth and Twentieth Centuries," in *Children and Consumer Culture in American Society,* ed. Lisa Jacobson (Westport, CT: Praeger, 2008), p. 29.

76. See Lynn Spigel, *Make Room for TV* (Chicago: University of Chicago Press, 1992), p. 25.

77. Richard deCordova, "Ethnography and Exhibition: The Child Audience, the Hays Office and Saturday Matinees," *Camera Obscura* 23 (May 1990): 95.

78. Ibid., p. 96. See also Roberta Pearson and William Uricchio, "'The Formative and Impressionable Stage': Discursive Constructions of the Nickelodeon's Child Audience," in *American Movie Audiences: From the Turn of the Century to the Early Sound Era*, ed. R. Maltby and M. Stokes (London: BFI, 1999).

79. Spigel, *Make Room for TV*, p. 55.

80. See, for example, ibid., p. 50.

81. Jacobson, *Raising Consumers*, p. 55.

82. See Rolontz, "$2,000,000 on Capitol's Bozo, p. 1; and Keith Monroe, "He Tickles the Tykes," *Saturday Evening Post*, June 4, 1955, p. 20. Bozo tie-ins ranged from a "$10 Bozo doll to a 25-cent package of balloons," and Capitol was said to be "continually promoting the Bozo series thru Bozo parties and exploitation appearances in record stores and theaters" ("Cap Kid Fave," p. 20). Bozo products in 1952 "racked up sales of close to $2,000,000 on the retail level" (Rolontz, "$2,000,000 on Capitol's Bozo," p. 1).

83. Herbert Mitgang, "Children's Stories and Songs on Disks," *New York Times*, October 14, 1956, p. X13.

84. Andre Millard, *America on Record* (New York: Cambridge University Press, 2005), pp. 164–66.

85. Monroe, "He Tickles the Tykes," p. 21.

86. See Millard, *America on Record*, p. 183. Jeff Smith describes how the growth of the record industry continued throughout the 1950s, fueled by the massive popularity of rhythm and blues and rock and roll with teenagers. "The total sales of all types of records increased dramatically between 1946, during which eight million disks were sold, and 1951, during which some 180 million disks were sold" (Jeff Smith, *The Sounds of Commerce* [New York: Columbia University Press, 1998], p. 32).

87. Howard Taubman, "Blank Disks by Millions," *New York Times*, January 18, 1942, p. SM11. Another incentive for record companies to diversify their product, and one that deserves further research, was the American Federation of Musician recording strikes in 1942 and 1948: "The exuberant outpouring of records for children during the last few years and the recent frantic efforts to fill the reservoir before Mr. Petrillo's new ban goes into effect leave no doubt of the widespread awareness that the entertainment and education of children is an exceedingly profitable enterprise" (Maria Cimino, "Watering Down on Wax," *Saturday Review of Literature*, December 27, 1947, p. 38).

88. "Moppet Disks in Big Mop-Up; Top Pix-Radio Names Boom Wax Works," *Variety*, October 9, 1946, p. 1.

89. Ibid., p. 72.

90. Jack Sher and John Keating, "Children's Records," *Los Angeles Times*, July 28, 1946, p. E8.

91. Philip Eisenberg and Hecky Krasno, "What Sells Children's Records?" *Saturday Review of Literature*, November 27, 1948, p. 47. Hecky Krasno of Columbia Records' children's division stated that "it has been estimated that between 20,000,000 and 30,000,000 kiddie disks were sold last year—or 1,500 per cent more than in 1939" ("Platters for Junior," *Newsweek*, December 15, 1947, p. 84).

92. "$15,000,000 Kidisk Sales in '51," *Variety,* December 26, 1951, p. 37.

93. M. Harper, "After Hours," *Harper's Magazine,* March 1951, p. 99.

94. "Kidisks' Grow to $50,000,000," *Variety,* February 24, 1960, p. 89.

95. Film industry statistics from Joel W. Finler, *The Hollywood Story* (London: Octopus, 1988), pp. 286–87.

96. "$15,000,000 Kidisk Sales in '51," p. 37. New retail outlets for records played an important role in the kidisk boom, as many records were sold in supermarkets, drugstores, and discount outlets: "The kids go to into the grocery store with momma and force her to buy the records they want" (Robert E. Dallos, "Record Makers Enjoy Sales Rise by Amusing, Educating Children," *Wall Street Journal,* November 23, 1962, p. 1); "Little Golden Records generally are the first acquired by parents for their youngsters' record players because they are inexpensive and in drugstores" (Mitgang, "Children's Stories," p. X13). *Printer's Ink* wrote in 1921 that "the Bubble Books have gone into many classes of stores which never before sold either books or phonograph records, and in some cases the result has been that lines of regular phonograph records have been taken on" (Rhodes, "New Fields Opened," p. 25).

97. "Coast Department Stores in All-Out Kidisk Xmas Drives; Supply Plentiful," *Billboard,* November 23, 1946, p. 18. Kidisks also increased the sales of phonograph players: "Tot platters have been paying off in kid phono machine sales. As one record department head puts it, sell a parent enough kid records and he'll be back for a record platter the first time Junior jams up the good machine" ("Coast Department Stores," p. 18).

98. See "Circulating Records," *New York Times,* September 14, 1941, p. SM27; and "Recordings Given to Library to Bring Classics into Homes," *Washington Post,* January 11, 1940, p. 7.

99. Jack Sher and John Keating, "Children's Records," *Los Angeles Times,* July 28, 1946, p. E8.

100. "Moppet Disks in Big Mop-Up," p. 72.

101. Beatrice Freeman and Ira Freeman, "Hi-Fi in the Public School System," *New York Times,* March 21, 1954, p. XX5.

102. Sammond, *Babes in Tomorrowland,* p. 361.

103. Dallos, "Record Makers Enjoy Sales Rise," p. 1.

104. Aniko Bodroghkozy, *Groove Tube* (Durham, NC: Duke University Press, 2001), p. 23.

105. Spigel, *Make Room for TV,* p. 190.

106. Herbert Mitgang, "Kiddies' 'Pops,'" *New York Times,* April 8, 1956, p. X18. This contrast with television was still being expressed in 1962, when the *Wall Street Journal* quoted the president of a record label that produced children's records: "Lots of parents are worried because they think their children watch too much television . . . they feel they're better off spending the time listening to records that are wholesome and educational" (Dallos, "Record Makers Enjoy Sales Rise," p. 1).

107. Beatrice Landeck, "New Records for Children," *New York Times,* November 20, 1955, p. XX9. A 1952 issue of *High Fidelity* magazine explained, "Youngsters learn most eagerly when they can choose and experiment most freely and actively. This makes phonograph records an excellent medium of

learning . . . give children a supply of good disks, plus access to the family record shelves and perhaps to the lending facilities of their local library, and the results can be impressive. Here are experiences that they can 'turn on' when they wish and go about the business of extending their musical and literary horizons at their own pace, in their own way, and without age level ceilings to stop them" (Emma Dickson Sheehy, "From Mother Goose to Captain Hook," *High Fidelity*, November–December 1952, pp. 62–63). As early as the 1920s, phonograph dealers reported that "people who have phonographs in their living rooms come in and buy a smaller machine for their nurseries so that their children may play the Bubble Book records themselves" (Rhodes, "New Fields Opened," p. 25).

108. "Kidisks' Grow To $50,000,000," p. 89.

109. Herbert Mitgang, "The Child's Record Player," *New York Times*, March 16, 1958, p. XX15.

110. Harper, "After Hours," p. 100.

111. Herbert Mitgang, "First, Let the Child Have Fun," *New York Times*, November 17, 1957, p. XX7.

112. Thomas I. Lucci, "Raise Your Own Audiophiles," *High Fidelity*, June 1954, p. 31.

113. Cross, *Kids' Stuff*, p. 60.

114. Mitgang, "First, Let the Child Have Fun," p. XX7.

115. Freeman and Freeman, "Hi-Fi in the Public School System," p. XX5.

116. Mark Katz, *Capturing Sound* (Berkeley: University of California Press, 2004), pp. 61–66.

117. "Mrs. Clark Addresses National Conference," *Voice of the Victor*, June 1924, p. 108.

118. Note, for example, that President Roosevelt included the Federal Music Project in the Works Progress Administration (WPA) between 1935 and 1939, a program that provided musical instruction in symphonic music and regular concerts at schools (Kenneth J. Bindas, *All of This Music Belongs to the Nation* [Knoxville: University of Tennessee Press, 1995], p. 16).

119. Frank Biocca, "Media and Perceptual Shifts: Early Radio and the Clash of Musical Cultures," *Journal of Popular Culture* 24, no. 2 (Fall 1990): 7. The *Washington Post* described in December 1936 how the audience for the NBC *Music Appreciation Hour* had "expanded to the amazing total of 7,000,000": "Countless schools throughout the country designate the Friday afternoon music appreciation hour officially as part of the regular course of studies. Teachers provided with manuals supplied at printing and handling cost by the National Broadcasting Co., in many cases, give brief lectures to their pupils in advance of the weekly broadcasts, and many follow the broadcasts proper with reviews and even tests" ("Music Appreciation Hour of Mr. Damrosch Prized in Many Schoolrooms throughout U.S.," *Washington Post*, December 6, 1936, p. TC5).

120. See Biocca, "Media and Perceptual Shifts," 9; and Michele Hilmes, *Radio Voices* (Minneapolis, University of Minnesota Press, 1997), p. 17.

121. Edward Moore, "Music Powwow Leaves Topics for Discussion," *Chicago Daily Tribune*, April 6, 1930, p. G1.

122. Theodor W. Adorno's essay "Analytical Study of the NBC *Music Appreciation Hour*" is better remembered today than the show itself. Written between

1938 and 1941, while Adorno was working at the Princeton Radio Research Project, Adorno's essay argues that the program was "insufficient musically and pedagogically" and led to a "fictitious musical world ruled by names of personalities, stylistic labels, and pre-digested values" (Theodor W. Adorno, "Analytical Study of the NBC *Music Appreciation Hour*," *Musical Quarterly* 78, no. 2 [Summer 1994]: 326).

· 123. Harper, "After Hours," p. 99.

124. Christopher Small, *Music, Society, Education* (Hanover, NH: Wesleyan University Press, 1977), p. 195.

125. Glenn Gould, "The Prospects of Recording," in *The Glenn Gould Reader*, ed. Tim Page (New York: Vintage, 1984), p. 340. Critiques of music appreciation sometimes appeared in the press: "Nowadays a great deal of time and ingenuity is devoted to making music study, especially in the early stages, as palatable as possible; to get the beginner over the hump of sheer mechanical drudgery which must be gotten through before he can derive even moderate enjoyment from his playing . . . opposed to the Appreciation method is the armchair, or phooey-on-the-experts method in which one simply plays music for the children to listen to. If they ask what instrument is playing the second theme at the beginning of the recapitulation section, one tells them. Otherwise, one does not worry about it. To heretics of this sort, Music Appreciationism . . . is a little like saying that one must be a chemist in order to enjoy a highball" (John Briggs, "Education on Disks," *New York Times*, October 17, 1954, p. X11).

126. Henry Jenkins, "'No Matter How Small': The Democratic Imagination of Dr. Seuss," in *Hop on Pop*, ed. Henry Jenkins, Tara McPherson, and Jane Shattuc (Durham, NC: Duke University Press, 2002), p. 189. Henry Jenkins describes how the cold war context made postwar permissive childrearing "politically meaningful, a patriotic responsibility, a way to strike a blow for freedom, and thus helped to reconcile them to domestic containment" (p. 196).

127. Henry Jenkins, "The Sensuous Child: Benjamin Spock and the Sexual Revolution," in *The Children's Culture Reader*, ed. Henry Jenkins (New York: New York University Press, 1998), p. 212.

128. I refer to Raymond Williams's famous distinction between dominant, emergent and residual culture in *Marxism and Literature* (Oxford: Oxford University Press, 1977), pp. 122–23. For a useful discussion, see Charles R. Acland, ed., *Residual Media* (Minneapolis: University of Minnesota Press, 2007).

129. Small, *Music, Society, Education*, p. 195.

130. Christopher Small, *Musicking* (Hanover, NH: Wesleyan University Press, 1998), p. 73.

131. Robert L. Garretson, *Music in Childhood Education* (New York: Appleton-Century-Crofts, 1966), pp. 67, 73. The use of recordings in music pedagogy would, of course, move to a whole new level of cultural prominence with the Suzuki method. For a discussion of Suzuki and the use of records, see Robert Fink, *Repeating Ourselves* (Berkeley: University of California Press, 2005), pp. 213–35.

132. Dr. Seuss's interest in sound technology is also demonstrated by the striking use of sound effects in the UPA animated short *Gerald McBoingBoing* (1950).

133. Monroe, "He Tickles the Tykes," p. 21.

134. "Sonovox," *Time*, July 24, 1939, p. 46. For more on the Sonovox, see my essay "Tearing Speech to Pieces: Voice Technologies of the 1940s," *Music, Sound, and the Moving Image* 2, no. 2 (Autumn 2008): 183–206.

135. "Robby's First Records," *House Beautiful* 93 (August 1951): 52–53.

136. Theodore Gracyk, *Rhythm and Noise: An Aesthetics of Rock* (Durham, NC: Duke University Press, 1996), pp. 59–60.

137. Jenkins makes a connection between postwar permissive child-rearing and the 1960s counterculture: "One can't help but ask whether a mode of child-rearing which empowered children to challenge adult institutions had an impact on how the postwar generation thought about themselves and about their place in the world" (Jenkins, "'No Matter How Small,'" p. 203).

138. Note that *Genie the Magic Record* features a sonic collage of bells, chimes, and alarms that resembles Pink Floyd's *Dark Side of the Moon* (1973).

139. "$15,000,000 Kidisk Sales in '51," p. 37.

140. Harper, "After Hours," p. 101. Alan Livingston stated in 1955 that "today music is as free as the air, and there's nearly as much of it—radio, home phonographs, TV and jukeboxes. This abundance is bound to have effects. A generation ago, kids heard only a fraction of the music they hear today. If music has any power to make kids happier and finer, then we'll see the results in the next generation" (Monroe, "He Tickles the Tykes," p. 117).

2. HI-FI MIDCULT

1. Paul Ferris claims that the women used their initials to ensure that Thomas would not mistake their intentions (*Dylan Thomas: The Biography* [London: J. M. Dent, 1977], p. 285). Barbara Holdridge stated that they "had no idea that Dylan had a reputation as a womanizer when we signed our first initials and last names to that note" but did so in order that "he would take our business proposal seriously" (personal correspondence, April 2008). Likewise, Mantell stated that they signed their initials "so he wouldn't know we were unbusiness-like females" ("Closing the Poetry Gap," *Time*, November 7, 1960, p. 88).

2. Samuel Grafton, "They've Sold a Million Dollars' Worth of Other People's Poetry," *Good Housekeeping*, February 1956, p. 71.

3. Ferris, *Dylan Thomas*, p. 285.

4. "Caedmon Inks Drama Stars for Big New Sales Pitch," *Billboard*, April 14, 1956, p. 31.

5. John M. Conly, "Literature on LPs," *Atlantic Monthly*, May 1954, p. 90.

6. "Closing the Poetry Gap," p. 88.

7. See Ferris, *Dylan Thomas*, p. 329.

8. Joanne Meyerowitz, "Beyond the Feminine Mystique: A Reassessment of Postwar Mass Culture, 1946–1958," in *Not June Cleaver: Women and Gender in Postwar America, 1945–1960*, ed. Joanne Meyerowitz (Philadelphia: Temple University Press, 1994), p. 237.

9. William Howland Kenney, *Recorded Music in American Life* (New York: Oxford University Press, 1999), pp. 89–96.

10. Patrick R. Parsons, "The Changing Role of Women Executives in the Recording Industry," *Popular Music and Society* 12, no. 4 (1988): 34. Writing in

1984, Sue Steward and Sheryl Garratt claimed that the rock business was "still a boy's game": "Even now, very few women get into positions of *real* power where they have direct influence on the look or the sound of the finished product" (*Signed, Sealed and Delivered: True Life Stories of Women in Pop* [London: Pluto Press, 1984], p. 63).

11. Richard D. Barnet and Larry L. Burriss, *Controversies of the Music Industry* (Westport, CT: Greenwood, 2001), pp. 107–108.

12. Steward and Garratt, *Signed, Sealed and Delivered*, pp. 68–69.

13. Holdridge, personal correspondence.

14. Ibid.

15. John Crosby, "The Spoken Word Is Paying Off Now, Too," *Washington Post*, February 5, 1961, p. G15.

16. "Closing the Poetry Gap," p. 88.

17. The year after Edison invented the phonograph, he described the possibility of "phonographic books" read by professional readers: "The advantages of such books over those printed are too readily seen to need mention" (Thomas A. Edison, "The Phonograph and Its Future," *North American Review* 126, no. 262 [May/June 1878]: 534). In 1888, when he was unveiling his "perfected" phonograph, he described the possibility of *Nicholas Nickleby* in "phonogram form": "Authors . . . can . . . publish their novels or essays exclusively in phonogram form, so as to talk to their readers personally" (Thomas A. Edison, "The Perfected Phonograph," *North American Review* 146, no. 379 [June 1888]: 647).

18. Jason Camlot, "Early Talking Books: Spoken Recordings and Recitation Anthologies, 1880–1920," *Book History* 6 (2003): 148.

19. Jed Rasula, "Understanding the Sound of Not Understanding," in *Close Listening*, ed. Charles Bernstein (New York: Oxford University Press, 1998), p. 234; and Camlot, "Early Talking Books," p. 159.

20. Michael Anderegg, *Orson Welles, Shakespeare and Popular Culture* (New York: Columbia University Press, 1999), pp. 39, 55.

21. Dan Lewis, "Poetry, Plays Forte of New Disk Firm," *Pasadena Independent Star-News*, July 23, 1967, p. 33.

22. Susan M. Hartmann, "Women's Employment and the Domestic Ideal in the Early Cold War Years," in *Not June Cleaver: Women and Gender in Postwar America, 1945–1960*, ed. Joanne Meyerowitz (Philadelphia: Temple University Press, 1994), pp. 85, 97–98.

23. Meyerowitz, "Beyond the Feminine Mystique," pp. 250–51.

24. Ibid., p. 231.

25. Ibid., pp. 232–33.

26. Lewis, "Poetry, Plays," p. 33.

27. John Larson, "Job Dissatisfaction Starts Young Girls on Long Career," *Times Recorder* (Zanesville, OH), October 4, 1965, p. 14.

28. Olga Curtis, "Literary Snobbery Makes Money for Young, but Smart, Brunettes," *Haywood (CA) Daily Review*, May 13, 1954, p. 4.

29. Meyerowitz, "Beyond the Feminine Mystique," p. 237.

30. Grafton, "They've Sold a Million Dollars' Worth of Poetry," p. 211.

31. "Thriving Business Built on Shoestring, Chivalry," *Hartford Courant,* June 9, 1959, p. 5B.

32. Curtis, "Literary Snobbery Makes Money," p. 4; Grafton, "They've Sold a Million Dollars' Worth of Poetry," p. 70.

33. Grafton, "They've Sold a Million Dollars' Worth of Poetry," p. 71.

34. Meyerowitz, "Beyond the Feminine Mystique," p. 237.

35. Holdridge, personal correspondence.

36. Lloyd Frankenberg, "Poetry Read by Poets—a Rediscovery," *New York Times,* November 26, 1950, p. SM9.

37. Ibid. The *Times* suggested several causes for the resurgence of interest in poetry, including curiosity about poets as "personalities," increasing attention to poetry in schools and colleges," and a "real desire on the part of more and more Americans for literate entertainment" (Frankenberg, p. SM9).

38. J. Donald Adams, "Speaking of Books," *New York Times,* January 16, 1955, p. BR2. For more on postwar enthusiasm for the arts, see Lynn Spigel, *TV by Design* (Chicago: University of Chicago Press, 2008).

39. Jack Gould, "Radio and Television," *New York Times,* January 12, 1953, p. 36.

40. Conly, "Literature on LPs," p. 92.

41. "The Happy Ham," *Time,* March 31, 1952, p. 62.

42. "The Dickens You Say," *Christian Science Monitor,* March 4, 1952, p. B12.

43. "Hearing a Good Book," *New York Times,* March 2, 1952, p. E8.

44. "Charles Laughton Says: Try Family Reading," *Los Angeles Times,* July 17, 1955, p. G18.

45. Grady Johnson, "When Laughton Reads the Bible," *Coronet,* August 1952, pp. 92–95.

46. Laramee Haynes, "Well-Read Yarns That Knit Families," *Los Angeles Times,* December 16, 1962, p. A18.

47. Camlot, "Early Talking Books," p. 164.

48. Mark Morrisson, "Performing the Pure Voice: Elocution, Verse Recitation, and Modernist Poetry in Prewar London," *Modernism/Modernity* 3, no. 3 (1996): 25. Charles Berstein has argued that the essence of the poetry reading is "its lack of spectacle, drama, and dynamic range," which he refers to as its "anti-performative mode": "In an age of spectacle and high drama, the anti-expressivist poetry reading stands out as an oasis of low technology that is among the least spectaclized events in our public culture. Explicit value is placed almost exclusively on the acoustic production of a single unaccompanied speaking voice, with all other theatrical elements being placed, in most cases, out of frame" (introduction to *Close Listening,* ed. Charles Bernstein [New York: Oxford University Press, 1998], p. 10).

49. Alison Byerly, "From Schoolroom to Stage: Reading Aloud and the Domestication of Victorian Theater," in *Culture and Education in Victorian England,* ed. Patrick Scott and Pauline Fletcher [London: Bucknell University Press, 1990], pp. 125–26. There was a culture of English working-class readings as well, part of middle-class efforts to educate the working classes via "rational

recreation" (Byerly, p. 130). For more on "penny readings" in late-nineteenth-century England, see Evelyn M. Sivier, "Penny Readings: Popular Elocution in Late Nineteenth-Century England," in *Performance of Literature in Historical Perspectives,* ed. David W. Thompson (Lanham, NY: University Press of America, 1983). Also see Cecelia Tichi's discussion of "a widely and repeatedly expressed conviction on the split existing between two worlds," one of books, and the other of television. In *Electronic Hearth* (New York: Oxford University Press, 1991), pp. 174–75.

50. Byerly, "From Schoolroom to Stage," p. 134.

51. "For TV Listeners," *Time,* January 12, 1953, p. 68. *This Is Charles Laughton* ran from January to July 1953 and was shown in the evening on WPIX New York and on WTOP-CBS in Washington, D.C.

52. "Reading by Laughton Is Stimulating, Restful," *Christian Science Monitor,* January 30, 1953, p. 10.

53. Gould, "Radio and Television," p. 36. Gould added, "Somewhere between the stage and the home screen much of the magic was lost": "The intangible sense of spontaneity and audience communion common to 'live' television is exactly what is needed for reading aloud" (p. 36).

54. "For TV Listeners," p. 68.

55. Johnson, "When Laughton Reads the Bible," p. 92.

56. Erik Barnouw, *The Golden Web* (New York: Oxford University Press, 1986), p. 27. Barnouw writes, "Educators had been among the most avid broadcasting pioneers; in the early 1920s, scores of colleges and universities had launched stations. Financial pressures, unfavorable channel assignments, interference from other stations, and disgust over the increasing commercialization of the air had been factors edging educators out of the broadcasting spectrum" (p. 23). The Wagner-Hatfield amendment, which proposed to set aside one-fourth of all channels for noncommercial use, was defeated in 1934, and the subsequent Communications Act of 1934 was "an almost total victory for the status quo" (pp. 24–26).

57. Susan L. Brinson, "Frieda Hennock: FCC Activist and the Campaign for Educational Television, 1948–1951," *Historical Journal of Film, Radio and Television* 18, no. 3 (1998): pp. 411–12.

58. Susan L. Brinson, "Missed Opportunities: FCC Commissioner Frieda Hennock and the UHF Debacle," *Journal of Broadcasting and Electronic Media* 44, no. 2 (2000): 257.

59. Brinson, "Frieda Hennock," p. 422.

60. See Ralph Steetle, "The Changing Status of Educational Television," *Journal of Educational Sociology* 32, no. 9 (May 1959): 427–33.

61. Anna McCarthy, "Television, Culture, and Citizenship at the Ford Foundation" (working paper no. 13, International Center for Advanced Studies, New York University, November 2003), p. 24.

62. Marsha F. Cassidy, *What Women Watched* (Austin: University of Texas Press, 2005), p. 137. See also Spigel, *TV by Design,* p. 27.

63. Cassidy, *What Women Watched,* p. 155.

64. McCarthy, "Television, Culture, and Citizenship," p. 51. In terms of production, spoken word LPs like those of Caedmon were sometimes referred

to almost as an antidote to the excesses of hi-fi culture: "In the tumble and hurly-burly of stereophonic excitement, and the problems that derive from it . . . there is an oasis of tranquility and quiet, marked 'Spoken Word.'" These records' appeal had "nothing to do with the quality of the sound" (Thomas Lask, "Monophonic Oasis," *New York Times*, November 23, 1958, p. X19).

65. Daniel Belgrad, *The Culture of Spontaneity* (Chicago: University of Chicago Press, 1998), p. 233.

66. Barbara Wilinsky, *Sure Seaters* (Minneapolis: University of Minnesota Press, 2001), p. 82.

67. Marianne Conroy, "Acting Out: Method Acting, the National Culture, and the Middlebrow Disposition in Cold War America," *Criticism* 35, no. 2 (Spring 1993): 241.

68. Janice A. Radway, *A Feeling for Books* (Chapel Hill: University of North Carolina Press, 1997), p. 222. Radway writes that "such middlebrow culture and the particular configuration of taste it cultivated developed as a kind of social pedagogy for a growing class fraction of professionals, managers, and information and culture workers as well as for those who aspired to the status of this class, to its work routines, and to its privileges" (p. 15).

69. Dwight MacDonald, *Against the American Grain* (New York: A Da Capo Press, 1962), p. 37. Radway states, "The space of the middlebrow was occupied by products that supposedly hid the same machine-tooled uniformity behind the self-consciously worked mask of culture" (*A Feeling for Books*, p. 222).

70. MacDonald, *Against the American Grain*, pp. 38–39.

71. Thomas Lask, "Disk Material Still Unspoken," *New York Times*, November 29, 1959, p. X20.

72. Melvin Maddocks, "The Caedmon Story," *Christian Science Monitor*, June 6, 1962, p. 10.

73. Wilinsky, *Sure Seaters*, p. 24.

74. MacDonald, *Against the American Grain*, pp. 73–74.

75. Quoted in Bess Furman, "Poetry Rates Hi with Expert's Fi: LP's Will Boom in Library Room," *New York Times*, September 6, 1956, p. 27.

76. Inez Robb, "Two Eggheads Get Rich by Recording Modern Poetry," *El Paso Herald-Post*, November 10, 1953, p. 3.

77. Note as well that Caedmon operated two mail-order clubs similar to the Book-of-the-Month Club: Theater Records and Shakespeare Records (Lewis, "Poetry, Plays," p. 33).

78. Crosby, "The Spoken Word Is Paying Off," p. G15.

79. In 1956 a critic predicted that Caedmon's records would "alter the course of future scholarship": "A hundred years from now, no Ph.D. candidate will dare to be without his hi-fi set, and critics of the future . . . will have a high time pondering slurred words, dropped lines, and changed rhymes" (Thomas Lask, "Poetry on Records," *New York Times*, January 24, 1956, p. X8).

80. W. T. Lhamon Jr, *Deliberate Speed* (Cambridge, MA: Harvard University Press, 1990), p. 99.

81. In the *New York Times*, February 2, 1969, p. BR41.

82. Holdridge, personal correspondence.

83. Patrick Feaster, "The Following Record: Making Sense of Phonographic Performance, 1877–1908" (PhD diss., Indiana University, Bloomington, 2006), p. 369.

84. Eric Schaefer, *Bold! Daring! Shocking! True!* (Durham, NC: Duke University Press, 1999), p. 331.

85. John Malcolm Brinnin, *Dylan Thomas in America* (London: J.M. Dent & Sons, 1956), p. 61.

86. "Undying Voice," *Newsweek*, January 27, 1964, p. 40.

87. Janet Coleman, *The Compass* (New York: Alfred A. Knopf, 1990), p. 142. The Chicago Compass Theater, described in chapter 5, put on a send up of Thomas's *Under Milk Wood* entitled *Under Deadwood*, which made use of Nichols's imitation of Thomas (Coleman, *The Compass*, p. 142).

88. Brinnin, *Dylan Thomas*, pp. 181–82.

89. Lhamon, *Deliberate Speed*, pp. 99–100.

90. We might note Thomas biographer George Tremlett's assertion that the poet was "the first rock star" (George Tremlett, *Dylan Thomas: In the Mercy of His Means* [London: Constable, 1991], p. 158). Tremlett argues that Thomas died "just as the world of verbal imagery was changing": "For centuries writers had expressed themselves through the printed word, but in his lifetime radio, cinema and television had brought a new technology to the communication of words and ideas. Since his death, the process has further advanced so that now writers who convey their thoughts through recorded sound—the Bob Dylans, Van Morrisons and John Lennons, who are the poets of the new technology—can reach an audience of millions of people through one creative act: the making of a sound" (p. 179).

91. Bob Dylan, *Chronicle* (New York: Simon & Schuster, 2004), p. 78.

92. Thomas Willis, "Bob Dylan: Artist of Songs of Protest," *Chicago Tribune*, December 28, 1963, p. 12.

93. Keir Keightley, "Long Play: Adult-Oriented Popular Music and the Temporal Logics of the Post-war Sound Recording Industry in the USA," *Media, Culture & Society* 26, no. 3 (2004): 386.

94. William D. Laffler, "Dylan Thomas Disc Put 'Em in Business," *Washington Post*, September 3, 1961, p. G4.

95. Gaile Dugas, "Record Business in Culture," *Blytheville (AR) Courier News*, April 17, 1962, p. 3.

96. Robb, "Two Eggheads Get Rich," p. 3.

97. Grafton, "They've Sold a Million Dollars' Worth of Poetry," p. 70.

98. Larson, "Job Dissatisfaction," p. 14. In 1961 the *Saturday Review* wrote that no one was certain about who was listening to spoken word LPs: "There are reports of businessmen and other culture seekers who take doses of recordings as they do adult education courses, and of busy housewives who listen as they work, operating on a higher level than the conventional busy housewife with her radio and television. Others buy talking books and other spoken-word records for the pleasure of hearing professional readings, a nineteenth-century amusement which has been having a revival in the theatre with actors who read from Dickens, Twain, Sandburg and others" (John Tebbel, "Rise of the Talking Book," *Saturday Review*, August 5, 1961, p. 43).

99. See Keightley, "Long Play," p. 383. A 1961 *Billboard* article attributed the growth and stability of the spoken word market to the fact that "educational institutions and libraries [had] begun to use these albums to a greater degree for classroom use and drama studies, as well as for pure entertainment." As a result, many college students had developed an interest in "this type of material and continue to purchase them after college." Another important factor was "the quantity and quality of portable phonographs available has increased greatly in the past five years. Many students now have inexpensive portables that they can easily move from home to campus" (Niki Kalish, "Spoken Word LP's Garner Steady Coin," *Billboard,* November 20, 1961, p. 13).

100. Kenney, *Recorded Music,* p. 90.

101. Pamela Robertson Wojcik, "The Girl and the Phonograph, or The Vamp and the Machine Revisited," in *Soundtrack Available,* ed. Pamela Robertson Wojcik and Arthur Knight (Durham, NC: Duke University Press, 2001), p. 440.

102. M. Harper, "After Hours," *Harper's Magazine,* March 1951, p. 101.

103. Ann Gray, *Video Playtime* (London: Routledge, 1992), p. 98.

104. Epsie Kinard, "Intrigue Your Mind while Your Hands Work," *House Beautiful,* September 1963, p. 102.

105. It is ironic that, given the importance of the musical quality of the voice on their records, Caedmon was named after an English monk who had such a terrible singing voice that "he refused to sing with other monks in the monastery, and finally started reciting. He became England's first poet" (Lewis, "Poetry, Plays," p. 33).

106. Brinnin, *Dylan Thomas,* p. 18.

107. Thomas Lask, "Record Makers—the Friends of Contemporary Poets," *New York Times,* February 9, 1964, p. X18.

108. Clifton Fadiman, "Party of One," *Holiday,* April 1953, p. 6.

109. Edward Tatnall Canby, "The Spoken Word on Records," *Harper's Magazine,* October 1954, p. 112.

110. Rasula, "Understanding the Sound," p. 236.

111. Reuven Tsur, *What Makes Sound Patterns Expressive?* (Durham, NC: Duke University Press, 1992), p. 12.

112. Peter Quartermain argues that Thomas was "enormously influential" as a reader and set a standard for "mellifluous expressiveness that could famously lull the hearer along on the wings of poesy" ("Sound Reading," in *Close Listening,* ed. Charles Bernstein [New York: Oxford University Press, 1998], p. 219).

113. Thomas Lask, "Spoken Word," *New York Times,* March 16, 1958, p. XX20. See also the comment in the *Atlantic Monthly:* "Thomas already is being called the Caruso of the spoken word, probably with justification" (Conly, "Literature on LPs," p. 94).

114. Quoted in Furman, "Poetry Rates Hi," p. 27.

115. John Gordon, "Being Sylvia Being Ted Being Dylan: Plath's 'The Snowman on the Moor,'" *Journal of Modern Literature* 27, nos. 1/2 (Fall 2003): 190.

116. "Undying Voice," p. 40.

117. "Secrets of Charm: Voice Training Helped by Listening to Others," *Los Angeles Times,* April 6, 1952, p. D13.

118. Helen Roach, *Spoken Records* (New York: Scarecrow Press, 1963), p. 13.

119. Tebbel, "Rise of the Talking Book," p. 42.

120. Kinard, "Intrigue Your Mind," p. 102.

121. Ibid., p. 103. The article continues: "I can give an example from my own experience. With a big chest of drawers to refinish and my favourite fantasy, *The Time Machine* (H.G. Wells) to listen to, word for word, on a talking book, I decided to do those two things together to kill the tedium of the world's most boring task. It worked. With my mind up in the clouds, journeying with the Time Traveler 800,000 years hence into the world of the future which Wells describes with words that flame like a torch, I scraped, sand-papered, rubbed, and painted for four uncomplaining hours" (p. 103).

122. Holdridge, personal correspondence.

123. Lizabeth Cohen, *A Consumers' Republic* (New York: Knopf, 2003), p. 140.

124. Elaine Tyler May, *Homeward Bound* (New York: Basic Books, 1988), pp. 78–79.

125. Ibid., p. 84.

126. Kinard, "Intrigue Your Mind," p. 115. In 1955 *Los Angeles Times* wrote that adult learning was "rapidly becoming a national craze": "35,000,000 adults are taking some kind of organized course of study in their spare time." The article quoted Malcolm Knowles, the administrative coordinator of the Adult Education Association, as saying that "it is becoming accepted in our culture that it is normal—and essential—for adults to keep on learning as it is for children to go to school." Notably, the article ended with this sentence: "Junior! Turn that TV set lower! How can Mommy concentrate on her homework?" (David Lester, "35,000,000 Grownups Are Back in School," *Los Angeles Times*, September 11, 1955, p. J38).

127. "Television," *Time*, August 9, 1963, p. 2.

128. Kinard, "Intrigue Your Mind," p. 114.

129. Quoted in ibid.

130. Epsie Kinard, "How to Have Conversations in Your Living Room," *House Beautiful*, February 1962, p. 115.

131. Lynn Spigel and Jan Olsson, eds. *Television after TV* (Durham, NC: Duke University Press, 2004), p. 31.

132. Kathy Peiss, *Hope in a Jar* (New York: Metropolitan Books, 1998), p. 73.

133. Conroy, "Acting Out," p. 241.

134. Richard Rutter, "Education in U.S. Big and Growing," *New York Times*, September 5, 1965, p. F1.

135. Lewis, "Poetry, Plays," p. 33.

136. Holdridge, personal correspondence. *Billboard* wrote in 1956 that Cademon's market was broken down as follows: "50 percent sold through regular record stores; 30 percent through book stores, including university book shops; 20 percent sold directly by Caedmon to schools and libraries" ("Caedmon Inks Drama Stars for Big New Sales Pitch," p. 31).

137. Daniel Marcus, "Public Television and Public Access in the US," in *The Television History Book*, ed. Michele Hilmes (London: BFI, 2003), p. 56.

138. Stefan Kanfer, "Heard Any Good Books Lately?" *Time,* July 21, 1986, p. 71.

139. Sarah Kozloff, "Audio Books in a Visual Culture," *Journal of American Culture* 18, no. 4 (Winter 1995): p. 89.

140. Ibid., p. 89.

141. Kanfer, "Heard Any Good Books Lately?" p. 71.

142. Frederick Wasser, *Veni, Vidi, Video* (Austin: University of Texas Press, 2001), pp. 77–80.

143. Holdridge, personal correspondence.

144. Barnet and Burriss, *Controversies of the Music Industry,* pp. 105–13. On allegations of sexual harassment in the record industry during the 1990s, see Chuck Philips's series of articles for the *Los Angeles Times* as well as Barnet and Burriss. For references to female record executives such as Warner Music Group's Sylvia Rhone, see those same sources as well as Steward and Garratt on Carol Wilson at InterDisc, Sylvia Robinson at Sugarhill Records, and the "women's music" industry.

145. Ferris, *Dylan Thomas,* p. 306.

146. Joseph A. Barry, "The Theater in the Living Room," *House Beautiful,* March 1955, pp. 110–11.

147. Bernstein, *Close Listening,* pp. 9–10.

3. 33⅓ SEXUAL REVOLUTIONS PER MINUTE

1. Moore's *Eat Out More Often* (1970) peaked at number twenty-four on the *Billboard* soul chart in the week of August 29, 1970.

2. Robert C. Allen, "From Exhibition to Reception: Reflections on the Audience in Film History," in *Screen Histories,* ed. Annette Kuhn and Jackie Stacey (Oxford: Clarendon Press, 1998), p. 17.

3. Karin Barber, "Preliminary Notes on Audiences in Africa," *Africa* 67, no. 3 (1997): 353–54.

4. "Fights Obscene Recordings," *New York Times,* November 1, 1942, p. 49.

5. "Obscene Records Cause of Arrest," *Lincoln Journal,* October 1, 1948, p. 13.

6. In earlier eras, law enforcement targeted artists such as Russell Hunting, who recorded small batches of "blue cylinders." See the CD *Actionable Offenses* (Archeophone 2007), which contains examples of risqué recordings from this era as well as insightful liner notes by phonograph scholar Patrick Feaster.

7. "'Indecent' Records Eligible for Mails," *Berkshire (MA) Evening Eagle,* June 2, 1949, p. 19.

8. "Obscene Record Ruling," *New York Times,* June 1, 1949, p. 42.

9. "Bill on Obscene Records Signed," *New York Times,* May 28, 1950, p. 46.

10. "Three Indicted in Shipment of Pornographic Disks," *Variety,* May 3, 1950, p. 41.

11. "N.Y. Police Seize Obscene Records," *Syracuse (NY) Herald-Journal,* April 2, 1958, p. 21.

12. Keir Keightley, "'Turn It Down!' She Shrieked: Gender, Domestic Space, and High Fidelity, 1948–1959," *Popular Music* 15, no. 2 (1996): 155–56.

13. Ibid., p. 157.

14. See my essay "Filling the Embarrassment of Silence: Erotic Performance on Recorded 'Blue Discs,'" *Film Quarterly* 58, no. 2 (Winter 2004–2005): 26–35, and chapter 2 of *Vocal Tracks* (Berkeley: University of California Press, 2008).

15. This advertising copy was offered as evidence in a 1961 post office investigation of Fax Records.

16. Hal Boyle, "Pilots Parody Ovations Given Returning Heroes," *Salamanca (NY) Republican-Press,* May 19, 1945, p. 10.

17. See Keightley, "'Turn It Down!'" p. 150.

18. The bachelor pad typically contained gadgets such as the hi-fi stereo, which Bill Osgerby has described as "phallic accessories that could shore up a sense of masculine power" (*Playboys in Paradise* [Oxford: Berg, 2001], p. 133).

19. Steven Cohan, *Masked Men* (Bloomington: Indiana University Press, 1997), p. 265.

20. See ibid., p. 266; and Osgerby, *Playboys in Paradise,* p. 134.

21. Rich Cante and Angelo Restivo, "The Voice of Pornography," in *Keyframes,* ed. Matthew Tinkcom and Amy Villarejo (New York: Routledge, 2001), p. 221.

22. United States Postal Service, P.O.D. docket no. 1/160, accessed at http://www.usps.com/judicial/1960deci/1–160.htm.

23. The record's apparent failure to register as hard-core sex is also illustrated by popular press accounts that frequently compared the Davis case to that of William and Dorothy Redmond. The Redmonds took nude pictures of each other and sent the undeveloped film through the mail. For this offense, William was sentenced to nine months in jail and Dorothy, six months. Unlike the Davis case, the Supreme Court threw out the Redmond's conviction, arguing that while the photos were indeed obscene, they had showed no intent to appeal to the public's prurient interest. The Davis case was the inverse: while the LPs themselves were frequently not considered obscene, by advertising and selling it as a titillating product, Davis had displayed prurient intent. Conservative columnist James J. Kilpatrick compared the two cases and argued that, while the records Davis sold were not obscene, his conduct had "made them so" ("Court Takes Sensible View in Latest Obscenity Cases," *Los Angeles Times,* May 31, 1966, p. A5).

24. Linda Williams, *Hard Core* (Berkeley: University of California Press, 1989), p. 126.

25. Eric Schaefer writes, "In 1961 there were 377 convictions on charges of using the mail to carry obscenity. By 1965 the number of convictions reached 874. The number of 'suppressions'—an inspector notifying a sender that what he or she was mailing was considered illegal—jumped nearly ten-fold, from just over 1,000 in 1961 to just under 10,000 in 1965" ("Plain Brown Wrapper: Adult Films for the Home Market, 1930–1969," in *Looking Past the Screen,* ed. Jon Lewis and Eric Smoodin [Durham, NC: Duke University Press, 2007], pp. 215–16).

26. Pamela Roberston Wojcik found that young women were "routinely being hailed as phonograph users" in popular magazines between 1944 and

1960 and concludes that "the phonograph is something of a free-floating signifier: it is, alternately, a toy, a decorative item, a serious technology, a party
machine, and a key to access a world of music. Thus coincident with a masculine discourse about hi-fi technology, we find a flexible and positive feminine
discourse about phonography" ("The Girl and the Phonograph, or The Vamp
and the Machine Revisited," in *Soundtrack Available,* ed. Pamela Roberston
Wojcik and Arthur Knight [Durham, NC: Duke University Press, 2001], pp.
439–40).

27. V. Vale and Andrea Juno, *Re/Search: Incredibly Strange Music* (San Francisco: Re/Search Publications, 1994), 2:56.

28. "*Knockers Up* Fans, Attention," *San Mateo (CA) Times,* March 15, 1963,
p. 23.

29. Warren noted that her fans would come to her appearances "on big buses
that were chartered from fifty-sixty miles away, because I had written and told
them I was going to be performing nearby, and they would make plans to come
in with their friends, stay the weekend—it was party time!" (Vale and Juno, *Re/
Search,* 2:58).

30. "Barnyard Girl," *Time,* January 11, 1963, pp. 58–59.

31. Vale and Juno, *Re/Search,* 2:58.

32. Robert C. Allen, *Horrible Prettiness* (Chapel Hill: University of North
Carolina, 1991), p. 243.

33. A writer for the *Washington Post* found in 1905 that "the voices of
American women are becoming too shrill and harsh": "Some one has taken the
trouble to contrast feminine tones in this country with those of other nations,
and the verdict is said to be against us. Our attention is called to the rich and
musical voices of the women in England, to the soft and sibilant utterances of
our sisters in France, to the low and pleasing whispers of the quaint little girls in
Japan. Nowhere, except in the United States, says the indictment, is there such
a strident tone or voice so coarse and loud" ("The Voices of American Women,"
Washington Post, January 9, 1905, p. 6). The voice emerged in that context as
a tool of social distinction, used to divine social status when visual cues could
increasingly be bought. Consider an article in the *Chicago Tribune* from 1932:
"The voice tells more of truth about a person in a brief contact than clothes,
complexion, coiffure, shoes, carriage, anything and everything, in fact. . . . It is
the voice . . . that distinguishes the 'golden' from the 'gilded'" (Antoinette Don-
nelly, "Woman's Voice Reveals Charm or Lack of It," *Chicago Daily Tribune,*
September 16, 1932, p. 21).

34. Michael Bronski, "Funny Girls Talk Dirty," *Boston Phoenix,* issue date
August 15, 2003, archived at: http://www.thebostonphoenix.com/boston/news_
features/other_stories/documents/03090915.asp.

35. David Allyn, *Make Love, Not War* (Boston: Little, Brown, 2000), p. 11.

36. Barbara Ehrenreich, Elizabeth Hess, and Gloria Jacobs, *Re-making Love*
(New York: Anchor Books, 1986), pp. 57–59. Susan J. Douglas warns against
the view that Gurley Brown was "some paragon of feminism, since the bottom
line of her message has always been the absolute importance of pleasing men,"
but goes on to assert that her book represented "some stirrings of female liberation . . . by throwing the [sexual] double standard out the window" (*Where*

the Girls Are [New York: Times Books, 1994], p. 68). For Osgerby, *Sex and the Single Girl* was "undoubtedly groundbreaking, both in its candid affirmation of women's sexual desire and its enthusiasm for the pleasures of personal consumption" (*Playboys in Paradise*, p. 169).

37. Gurley Brown also released a series of LPs of her own in 1963 on Crescendo Records.

38. Quoted in Vale and Juno, *Re/Search*, 2:58.

39. Accessed at http://www.knockers-up.org/about.php.

40. Ehrenreich, Hess, and Jacobs, *Re-making Love*, p. 97.

41. We should note that Warren's records were marketed to both men and women. One approach to promoting her records to men was through offering "certificates" for the Playboy-esque Knockers Up Club. Warren stated in an email interview that her record company "thought up the 'Knockers Up Club' stuff. The guys bought the certificate, the gals marched around the backyard, and the party was on."

42. Vale and Juno, *Re/Search*, 2:56.

43. Janice M. Irvine, *Disorders of Desire* (Philadelphia: Temple University Press, 1990), pp. 72–73.

44. Ibid., p. 188.

45. Ibid., pp. 189, 192.

46. Barbara Lewis, "The Sensuous Author," *Chicago Tribune*, August 9, 1970, p. J58.

47. Ehrenreich, Hess, and Jacobs, *Re-making Love*, p. 83.

48. "*Sensuous Woman LP,*" *Screw*, November 29, 1971, p. 12.

49. Linda Lee Landis, "The Sensuous Record," *Chicago Tribune*, September 8, 1974, p. D5.

50. See also Vern L. Bullough, *Science in the Bedroom* (New York: Basic-Books, 1994), p. 203.

51. Don Sloan, "The Dual Therapy Approach to the Treatment of Sexual Dysfunction," in *Gynecology and Obstetrics*, ed. John J. Sciarra (Philadelphia: Harper and Row, 1983), p. 10.

52. Ibid., p. 11. Sloan's program closely resembles that devised by Masters and Johnson, who worked with couples, stressed that "the 'relationship' is considered to be the patient," and included a "sensate focus" involving "a series of massage-like exercises implemented by the couple in their hotel room." See Irvine, *Disorders of Desire*, pp. 193–94.

53. Sloan, "The Dual Therapy Approach," pp. 6–7.

54. Angela Carter, *The Sadeian Woman and the Ideology of Pornography* (New York: Harper and Row, 1978), p. 14.

55. Kermit Mehlinger, "The Sexual Revolution," in *Sexual Revolution*, ed. Jeffery Escoffier (New York: Thunder's Mouth Press, 2003), p. 45.

56. Eric Schaefer notes that the "sexual revolution" of the 1960s was primarily a matter of an increasingly "sexualized media": "I think that it is instructive to reframe what we have called 'the sexual revolution' of the late 1960s as a media revolution in which the distinctions between the private and the public became seriously destabilized . . . it was not that vast numbers of people were suddenly leaving their bedrooms and backseats to have sex in the streets. It was

that the mass media was becoming a vehicle for sex to move from the private realm to one that was public" (Schaefer, "Plain Brown Wrapper").

57. Many records with bawdy content made before the 1960s were released anonymously and so are difficult to date. For the sake of clarity, I will use the term *blue discs* to refer to 78 rpm singles that were in circulation before the 1950s, and *party albums* to indicate 33⅓ rpm long-playing records that were made after the 1950s.

58. Bambi Haggins's *Laughing Mad* (New Brunswick, NJ: Rutgers University Press, 2007) has recently blazed a scholarly trail through this important cultural material.

59. Philip H. Ennis, *The Seventh Stream: The Emergence of Rock 'n' Roll* (Hanover, NH: Wesleyan University Press, 1992), p. 135.

60. Ibid., p. 136. See also Richard A. Peterson, "Why 1955? Explaining the Advent of Rock Music," *Popular Music* 9, no. 1 (January 1990): 105.

61. See Kathy M. Newman, "The Forgotten Fifteen Million: Black Radio, Radicalism, and the Construction of the 'Negro Market,'" in *Communities of the Air*, ed. Susan Merrill Squier (Durham, NC: Duke University Press, 2003), p. 111.

62. Ibid., p. 115. Radio industry surveys indicated that "over 90 percent of the black households in urban centers had at least one radio receiver, while in the rural areas, the figure was near 70 percent" (William Barlow, *Voice Over: The Making of Black Radio* [Philadelphia: Temple University Press, 1999], p. 125).

63. Barlow, *Voice Over*, pp. 125–27.

64. Ibid., p. 97. Barlow writes that African Americans were an important market for the phonograph industry since the 1910s, and especially after blues records of the 1920s alerted the industry to "the existence of a large new market among African Americans" (p. 18). In the mid 1920s, Barlow estimates that African Americans were purchasing "6 million discs annually" (p. 19).

65. Andre Millard, *America on Record* (New York: Cambridge University Press, 2005), pp. 226–28; see also Ennis, *The Seventh Stream*, p. 176, and Peterson, "Why 1955?" p. 105.

66. Millard, *America on Record*, p. 229.

67. "New Ideas, Talent Key to Disc Firm Success, Williams Says," *Chicago Defender*, May 23, 1963, p. 29.

68. A.S. "Doc" Young, "Dootsie Does It Again," *Los Angeles Sentinel*, January 12, 1967, p. A7.

69. A.S. "Doc" Young, "Dooto Records Celebrates Its 15th Anniversary," *Los Angeles Sentinel*, July 6, 1961, p. C1.

70. "Dooto Sets New Sales Records," *Los Angeles Sentinel*, October 22, 1959, p. C3.

71. "How Dooto Brought Comic Disc into the Spotlight," *Chicago Defender*, July 22, 1961, p. 10.

72. "What Next in Those Comic Records?" *Chicago Defender*, September 6, 1962, p. 15. Williams was reportedly attending summer sessions on film and television writing and production at UCLA and "envisioned a ready commercial market for short subjects, comedies, documentary films dealing with Negro

America. In the near future, he plans to produce an entertainment short in color built around a night club show, with pretty chorines, singers, feature acts" ("Dooto Disc Head Opens Film Mart," *Chicago Defender,* July 29, 1958, p. 18).

73. "Dooto Music Center: A Community Asset," *Los Angeles Sentinel,* March 21, 1963, p. C2.

74. Donald Bogle, *Primetime Blues* (New York: Farrar, Straus and Giroux, 2001), p. 57.

75. Ibid., p. 171.

76. Mel Watkins, *On the Real Side* (Chicago: Lawrence Hill, 1999), p. 360.

77. "Rudy Ray Moore Hits Big as 'Dolemite,'" *Los Angeles Sentinel,* October 9, 1975, p. B7.

78. See Bruce Jackson, *Get Your Ass in the Water and Swim Like Me* (Cambridge, MA: Harvard University Press, 1974), p. 5.

79. For a useful discussion of the temporal effects of recording technology, see Mark Katz, *Capturing Sound* (Berkeley: University of California Press, 2004), pp. 74–77.

80. Moore's performance is also an instance of marking. For further discussion, see chapter 5. Note that marking is often used to expose "contextually inappropriate" instances of "impression management," such as affectations to "talking proper," through mocking quoted speech in a high, falsetto voice, with the words "enunciated carefully so as to avoid loss of sounds and elision characteristic of fluid speech" ("Signifying and Marking: Two Afro-American Speech Acts," in *Directions in Sociolinguistics,* ed. John J. Gumperz and Dell Hymes [New York: Holt, Rinehart and Winston, 1972], pp. 176–77). We should note that this is precisely the approach taken by Moore in his performance of Clotia.

81. See John D'Emilio and Estelle B. Freedman, *Intimate Matters: A History of Sexuality in America,* 2nd ed. (Chicago: University of Chicago Press, 1997), pp. 261–65; and Robert E. Staples, "The Mystique of Black Sexuality," *Liberator* 7, no. 3 (March 1967): 8.

82. Eugene D. Genovese, *Roll, Jordan, Roll* (New York: Vintage Books, 1976), pp. 465–66.

83. Staples, "The Mystique of Black Sexuality," p. 10.

84. Samuel A. Floyd Jr., "Ring Shout! Literary Studies, Historical Studies, and Black Music Inquiry," *Black Music Research Journal* 11, no. 2 (Autumn 1991): 271.

85. Moore and Reed's dialogue reflects a tendency found in some segments of the black community to view sex primarily as a social rather than a moral issue: "Unlike the Victorian code of sexual behavior so endemic to whites," Staples writes, "Africans saw sex as a matter between individuals and not determined by God" ("The Mystique of Black Sexuality," p. 8).

86. This representation of black male sexuality might be compared to Jacquie Jones's description of the depiction of black male characters in mainstream American films: "By depriving the Black on-screen male of a connection to society through any type of humanizing relationship, mainstream motion pictures offer only models of violence and other forms of antisocial behavior" ("The Construction of Black Sexuality," in *Black American Cinema,* ed. Manthia Diawara [New York: Routledge, 1993], p. 250).

87. D'Emilio and Freedman, *Intimate Matters,* p. 273. D'Emilio and Freedman define *sexual liberalism* as "an overlapping set of beliefs that detached sexual activity from the instrumental goal of procreation, affirmed heterosexual pleasure as a value in itself, defined sexual satisfaction as a critical component of personal happiness and successful marriage, and weakened the connections between sexual expression and marriage by providing youth with room for some experimentation as preparation for adult status" (p. 241).

88. Williams, *Hard Core,* p. 123.

89. See Smith, *Vocal Tracks,* p. 68.

90. Lawrence W. Levine, *Black Culture and Black Consciousness* (New York: Oxford University Press, 1977), p. 338. Myths and stereotypes about black sexuality could have been understood in a more positive light during the era of the sexual revolution. Alvin Poussaint wrote in *Ebony* in 1971 that "many Caucasians" had been anxious to grant that blacks were "sexually superior," and now that sex had been "elevated to the status of something good and desirable," blacks could expect that "some whites, true-to-form, will be clamoring for the title of sexual superiority" (Alvin Francis Poussaint, "Blacks and the Sexual Revolution," *Ebony,* October 1971, p. 113). Similarly, in a 1971 essay on Melvin Van Peebles's *Sweet Sweetback's Baadasssss Song* (1971), Lerone Bennett wrote that "some black men" found white stereotypes about black sexuality to be "very serviceable" and so were hesitant to "destroy all the myths" (Lerone Bennett Jr., "The Emancipation Orgasm: Sweetback in Wonderland," *Ebony,* September 1971, p. 116).

91. Jackson, *Get Your Ass in the Water,* p. 17.

92. For example, passages about masturbation from the book are followed by a verbal description of orgasm, performed by Connie Z. in a breathy whisper. Other extended sections of breathy, ecstatic whispering can be found during discussions of anal intercourse and pointers on orgy etiquette.

93. Poussaint, "Blacks and the Sexual Revolution," pp. 114–16.

94. Ehrenreich, Hess, and Jacobs, *Re-making Love,* p. 83.

95. Joan Garrity (a.k.a. "J"), *The Sensuous Woman* (New York: Lyle Stuart Inc., 1969), pp. 10–11. Press accounts frequently mentioned Garrity's physical unattractiveness: "Joan is as starched, pressed and as modestly made up as one of the Nixon daughters . . . a sex goddess she isn't" (Lewis, "The Sensuous Author," p. J58).

96. Mark Jancovich, "Naked Ambition: Pornography, Taste and the Problem of the Middlebrow," *Scope: An Online Journal of Film Studies,* June 2001, http://www.scope.nottingham.ac.uk/article.php?issue=jun2001&id=274& section=article. D'Emilio and Freedman make a similar argument concerning class: "Class differences also played an important role in the maintenance of the double standard. By pursuing sex with working-class girls, middle-class males could expect chastity from their peers without relinquishing access to intercourse themselves" (*Intimate Matters,* p. 263).

97. We might compare the multiple meanings for the "naturalness" of black sexuality to Richard Dyer's discussion of Paul Robeson, who, Dyer argues, was "taken to embody a set of specifically black qualities . . . that were equally valued and similarly evoked, but for different reasons, by whites and blacks":

"Black and white discourse on blackness seems to be valuing the same things—spontaneity, emotion, naturalness—yet giving them a different implication. Black discourses see them as contributing to the development of society, white as enviable qualities only blacks have" (*Heavenly Bodies* [London: BFI, 1986], pp. 70, 74).

98. Garrity, *The Sensuous Woman*, pp. 33–34.

99. Ehrenreich, Hess, and Jacobs write: "J's practical attitude toward sex and her everyday language turned her predecessors into dinosaurs by comparison . . . [and] was also extremely phallocentric. She assumed that women were typically nonorgasmic, and that this condition could be lived with—for better or worse" (*Re-making Love*, p. 84).

100. Garrity, *The Sensuous Woman*, p. 41.

101. Ibid., p. 97.

102. Michel Foucault, *The History of Sexuality* (New York: Vintage Books, 1990), 1:24.

103. Williams, *Hard Core*, p. 149; Foucault, *History of Sexuality*, 1:63.

104. Michael Warner, *Publics and Counterpublics* (New York: Zone Books, 2002), pp. 192–93.

105. Ibid., p. 193.

106. Mark Jason Murray writes, "Moore's comedy albums were always recorded at his home instead of in a club. He would invite his friends over, serve drinks, with an engineer there to record the proceedings" ("Rudy Ray Moore: Biography," at http://www.shockingimages.com/dolemite/biography.php, accessed November 7, 2006).

107. Floyd, "Ring Shout!" p. 277.

108. Carter, *Sadeian Woman*, p. 13.

109. Ibid., p. 17.

110. See also D'Emilio and Freedman's discussion of sexual liberalism in *Intimate Matters*, p. 241.

111. Hilary Radner, introduction to *Swinging Single: Representing Sexuality in the 1960s*, ed. Hilary Radner and Moya Luckett (Minneapolis: University of Minnesota Press, 1999), pp. 4, 2.

112. Irvine, *Disorders of Desire*, p. 199.

113. Andre Millard writes in his history of the recording industry that "the availability of low-cost stereo equipment played a crucial part in the commercial success of progressive rock in the 1960s" (*America on Record*, pp. 302–303). Similarly, Simon Frith describes how "rock forms of production and consumption" characterized by "rich and elaborate sounds" made for "expensive stereos and FM radio and campus concerts" were perfected between 1967 and 1971 (*Sound Effects* [New York: Pantheon, 1981], p. 213).

114. See Roland Gelatt, *The Fabulous Phonograph* (London: Cassell, 1977), pp. 319, 327.

115. Wasser argues that erotica was "the first big genre for prerecorded cassettes": "Many pornographers anticipated that the VCR made possible a new use of pornography for intimate viewing by married couples . . . through the end of the 1970s 'X-rated' cassettes accounted for half of all prerecorded sales" (Frederick Wasser, *Veni, Vidi, Video* [Austin: University of Texas Press, 2001], p. 94).

116. Michel Chion, *The Voice in Cinema* (New York: Columbia, 1999), pp. 49–51.

4. MIMETIC MOMENTS

1. See *"The First Family,"* *Time*, November 30, 1962, p. 20.

2. Richard Bauman, *Verbal Art as Performance* (Prospect Heights, IL: Waveland Press, 1977), pp. 10–11.

3. Michael Taussig, *Mimesis and Alternity* (New York: Routledge, 1993). Lee Grieveson notes, "Mimetic relations at the movies became the central issue animating a sense of urgency about studying cinema" ("Cinema Studies and the Conduct of Conduct," in *Inventing Film Studies*, ed. Lee Grieveson and Haidee Wasson [Durham, NC: Duke University Press, 2008], p. 11).

4. Susan A. Glenn, "'Give an Imitation of Me': Vaudeville Mimics and the Play of the Self," *American Quarterly* 50, no. 1 (1998): 48.

5. Ibid., p. 57.

6. Leo Braudy, *The Frenzy of Renown* (New York: Oxford University Press, 1986), p. 4.

7. Peter M. Robinson describes the outcry caused when Will Rogers imitated President Calvin Coolidge on the radio in 1928. Rogers announced, "I want to introduce a friend of mine who is here and wishes to speak to you": "Tightening his lips and affecting Calvin Coolidge's high-pitched nasal tone—that a majority of Americans had only rarely, if ever, heard—he impersonated a president for the first time in front of a mass audience." According to Robinson, the uproar was "loud and immediate," and "millions of people" thought the impersonation was really Coolidge. Though he apologized, Rogers struggled to "validate impersonation as a legitimate tool in the political comic's repertoire" ("The Dance of the Comedians: The People, the President, and the Performance of Political Standup Comedy in America" [PhD diss., Miami University, Oxford, OH, 2006], pp. 72–75).

8. Daniel Boorstin called FDR the first "modern master" at exploiting the press (Daniel J. Boorstin, *The Image: A Guide to Pseudo-events in America* [1961; reprint, New York: Vintage Books, 1992], p. 20), and Thomas Doherty characterizes him as not just a familiar radio voice, but as a "vibrant cinematic personality," featured in newsreels, biopics, and studio short-subjects to support the New Deal (*Pre-code Hollywood* [New York: Columbia University Press, 1999], p. 77).

9. "Roosevelt Mimic Is Cut Off the Air," *New York Times*, April 11, 1937, p. 52.

10. Ibid.

11. Art Carney's first job was said to be on a program called *Report to the Nation*, in which he imitated the voices of Roosevelt and Winston Churchill (Gilbert Millstein, "TV's No. 1 Second Comedian," *New York Times*, April 18, 1954, p. SM19).

12. Michael Maury, "Dean Murphy Used to Make Banana Splits. Now . . . ," *Los Angeles Times*, December 12, 1943, p. E15.

13. Harvey Sacks, *Lectures on Conversation* (Oxford: Blackwell, 1992), 1:479.

14. Ibid., 1:480.

15. Warren I. Susman, *Culture as History* (New York: Pantheon, 1984), p. 277.

16. Ibid., p. 280.

17. Erving Goffman, *Frame Analysis* (Boston: Northeastern University Press, 1986), pp. 537–39.

18. Glenn, "'Give an Imitation of Me,'" pp. 51–62.

19. Kathleen Rowe has described exceptional examples of "unruly" female comedic performers. In contrast to the cultural ideal that women be composed and introspective, the "unruly woman" used her body and speech to create "a disruptive spectacle of herself" (*The Unruly Woman* [Austin: University of Texas Press, 1995], p. 31).

20. See Elaine Tyler May, *Homeward Bound* (New York: Basic Books, 1988), pp. 20–22.

21. "In Hollywood," *Gazette and Bulletin [Williamsport, PA],* June 14, 1946, p. 4.

22. "Mimic Finds Himself Back in Spotlight," *Oakland Tribune,* May 20, 1948, p. 55.

23. Gene Handsaker, "Film Stars Don't Mind Being Imitated, Declares Impersonator Arthur Blake," *Kingsport (TN) Times,* November 7, 1949, p. 11.

24. In an email interview, Will Jordan claimed that Dean Murphy was gay.

25. "Night Club Reviews," *Variety,* April 17, 1946, p. 62.

26. Aaron Bates, "Arthur Blake: A Pearl in a Rotten Oyster," in *Gay,* December 1971.

27. Same-sex imitation could certainly reveal elements of gender masquerade. Consider Steven Cohan's insightful discussion of Tony Curtis's imitation of Cary Grant in *Some Like It Hot* (1959), which represented his "celebrated persona as a performance, specifically designed as a masquerade, constructing 'masculinity' out of voice, clothes, bearing" (*Masked Men* [Bloomington: Indiana University Press, 1997], p. 29).

28. Christian Williams, "Rich Little: Trying for a Lasting Impression," *Washington Post,* January 20, 1981, p. A1. In the 1950s and 1960s, the Truman Capote routine might be read as second-order "swish" stereotype—a way to do gay stereotype characters in the context of the "comedy of personality."

29. Jackie Stacey has written that audiences prize movie stars for being different, for "taking them into a world in which their desires could potentially be fulfilled," but also value them for their similarity, which enables the recognition of qualities they already have ("Feminine Fascinations: A Question of Identification?" in *The Celebrity Culture Reader,* ed. P. David Marshall [New York: Routledge, 2006], p. 253). We might note Michael Taussig's suggestion that the "magic of mimesis" is always "pulling you this way and that, mimesis plays this trick of dancing between the very same and the very different . . . mimesis registers both sameness and difference, of being like, and of being Other" (*Mimesis and Alterity,* p. 129).

30. Robinson, "The Dance of the Comedians," p. 104.

31. Lawrence Laurent, "Will Jordan's 'Shew' Has Gone Over B-I-G," *Washington Post,* July 25, 1958, p. D10.

32. Gerald Nachman, *Seriously Funny* (New York: Backstage Books, 2004), p. 519.

33. Ibid., p. 518.

34. Laurent, "Will Jordan's 'Shew,'" p. D10. Nachman paints a picture of Jordan as a man haunted by issues of ownership, since he was convinced that other comics were mercilessly ripping off his routines (in *Seriously Funny*, p. 522).

35. Goffman, *Frame Analysis*, pp. 534–35.

36. Rosemary Coombe, "Author(iz)ing the Celebrity," in *The Celebrity Culture Reader*, ed. P. David Marshall (New York: Routledge, 2006), p. 723.

37. Ibid., p. 754.

38. Quoted in Nachman, *Seriously Funny*, p. 514.

39. Consider Jane M. Gaines's insightful discussion of the 1984 legal debate over the appearance of a Jacqueline Kennedy Onassis look-alike in a Christian Dior advertisement. The court ruled that the look-alike's body counted as a use of Onassis's "portrait or picture" without her permission. Dior might have had avoided this suit if it had taken a lesson from Will Jordan. Gaines writes that if she had "performed a parodic interpretation of Onassis, U.S. copyright law would have protected that expression" (*Contested Culture* [Chapel Hill: University of North Carolina Press, 1991], p. 97). Indeed, press coverage often noted that impressionists such as Jordan and later David Frye did not physically resemble the figures they animated.

40. Coombe, "Author(iz)ing the Celebrity," pp. 723, 727.

41. Robert Dallek, *John F. Kennedy: An Unfinished Life, 1917–1963* (London: Penguin Books, 2003), p. 558.

42. Nicholas J. Cull, "No Laughing Matter: Vaughn Meader, the Kennedy Administration, and Presidential Impersonations on Radio," *Historical Journal of Film, Radio and Television* 17, no. 3 (1997): 384–85.

43. Merriman Smith, "Spoofing Kennedys on Air Causes Stir," *Los Angeles Times*, December 2, 1962, p. 13. One article described how Robert Kennedy ran into difficulty trying to make a business call on the telephone: "'Yes, this is the Attorney General,' Mr. Kennedy said. 'Yes, yes, I tell you I AM the Attorney General.' After a pause, the Attorney General said, 'Very Well,' and hung up. 'That guy thinks I'm Vaughn Meader,' he said. 'He's going to call me back just to make sure'" ("Random Notes from All Over: 'This is the Attorney General,'" *New York Times*, June 24, 1963, p. 14).

44. Behind the scenes, Arthur Schlesinger Jr., special assistant to the president, expressed serious concern about Meader's LP confusing the listening audience, calling the danger "acute" (Cull, "No Laughing Matter," pp. 386–89).

45. Art Seidenbaum, "Spectator, '63: Mimics, Arise!" *Los Angeles Times*, August 22, 1963, p. C2. Meader's act was also encouraged by Kennedy's famous wit, which biographer Robert Dallek argues endeared him to "those reporters who had soldiered through the Eisenhower years with a president who often left the press puzzling over what he had actually said or meant to say" (*John F. Kennedy*, p. 478). Some writers suggested that Kennedy's wit encouraged comedians by making them feel that he was "sharp and witty enough to appreciate what they were doing and big enough to laugh at it himself. His presence seemed to

call out the best efforts of writers and producers" (Thomas Lask, "Now They Kid the Politicos," *New York Times*, April 2, 1967, p. 122). When asked about the *First Family* LP at a December 12 press conference, Kennedy stated that he'd heard the record but that he thought it sounded more like his brother Teddy than it did him (Cull, "No Laughing Matter," p. 389).

46. Dallek, *John F. Kennedy*, p. 478.

47. Michael Curtin, *Redeeming the Wasteland* (New Brunswick, NJ: Rutgers University Press, 1995), p. 86.

48. Seymour Hersh, *The Dark Side of Camelot* (London: HarperCollins, 1998), p. 224.

49. Braudy, *The Frenzy of Renown*, p. 568.

50. The record played on public fascination with the young couple in the highest office in the land. Anthropologist Margaret Mead told *Life* magazine in 1962 that this was "the first time we've had a young couple in the White House. It's certainly hard to imagine people going out and copying the suits of other recent first ladies" (Peter Bunzel, "A Kennedy Spoof Full of 'Vigah,'" *Life*, December 14, 1962, pp. 83–84).

51. Tony Hendra argues that Meader's LPs "came as close to Kennedy propaganda as to anything else" (*Going Too Far* [New York: Doubleday, 1987], p. 151).

52. Cull, "No Laughing Matter," p. 394. Bob Booker stated that the comic Henny Youngman was in the habit of declaring to him that "Vaughn Meader shot Lee Harvey Oswald" (Cull, p. 398).

53. Val Adams, "News of TV and Radio: Good Taste," *New York Times*, December 1, 1963, p. 203.

54. "Meader Is Dropping Kennedy Imitation," *New York Times*, November 30, 1963, p. 17.

55. Note Cull's claim that "Meader's place in the record books for the fastest selling album of all time fell to a compilation of old Kennedy speeches" ("No Laughing Matter," p. 394).

56. Carlton Brown, "The Kennedy Memorial Albums," *Redbook*, July 1964, p. 30.

57. Nachman, *Seriously Funny*, p. 510.

58. Burt Prelutsky, "Ape Act," *Los Angeles Times*, May 28, 1972, p. W4.

59. Nachman, *Seriously Funny*, p. 521.

60. Hedda Hopper, "Actor Gorshin Has to Get the Attitude," *Los Angeles Times*, June 9, 1964, p. C8.

61. Frank Gorshin, "Who Am I? Musings of an Impressionist: Alter-Egotism," *Variety*, January 5, 1977, p. 138.

62. James Naremore, *Acting in the Cinema* (Berkeley: University of California Press, 1988), p. 23.

63. Richard Schechner, *Between Theater and Anthropology* (Philadelphia: University of Pennsylvania Press, 1985), p. 36. Schechner writes that "restored behavior is living behavior treated as a film director treats a strip of film" and that "restored behavior is the main characteristic of performance" (p. 35).

64. Victor Turner, *From Ritual to Theatre* (Baltimore: PAJ Publications, 1982), p. 105.

65. Jane Gaines cites Barry King, to the effect that, to secure a monopoly on "his or her carefully developed persona," the actor "types himself in real life according to his image on screen" (*Contested Culture*, p. 33).

66. Barry King, "Articulating Stardom," *Screen* 26, no. 5 (1985): 30.

67. Ibid., pp. 46–47.

68. Thanks to Dale Lawrence for pointing this out to me.

69. Braudy, *The Frenzy of Renown*, pp. 405–406.

70. *Variety* wrote in its review of the LP that it ranked as "a standout item for the comedy-on-disk market" ("Album Reviews," *Variety*, September 23, 1959, p. 80).

71. Hal Holbrook, *Mark Twain Tonight!* (New York: Pyramid Books, 1959), p. 15.

72. Ibid., p. 64.

73. Ibid., p. 71.

74. Cecil Smith, "Anniversary Sees Mark Twain Revival," *Los Angeles Times*, May 8, 1960, p. O3. The year 1967 was the fiftieth anniversary of Twain's death, and the country was said to be on "a Twain kick. Particularly, via television" (Smith, p. O3).

75. Holbrook, *Mark Twain Tonight!* p. 43.

76. "Mark Twain Given High Viewer Score," *New York Times*, March 9, 1967, p. 79.

77. Hal Humphrey, "Holbrook's 'Twain' Poetic Portraiture," *Los Angeles Times*, March 7, 1967, p. D16.

78. Mac Benoff, "Actor Puts Essence of Twain on Paper," *Los Angeles Times*, January 3, 1960, p. E7.

79. Joe Finnigan, "Holbrook's Twain above Commercials," *Washington Post*, January 3, 1960, p. H10.

80. Holbrook also was said to have turned down "over one million dollars worth of offers" to do commercials as Twain, stating that "they were things I didn't feel should be done with Twain" (Finnigan, "Holbrook's Twain above Commercials," p. H10).

81. Clay Gowran, "Word to Wise: Watch Holbrook as Twain," *Chicago Tribune*, January 31, 1967, p. A6.

82. Seymour Raven, "Holbrook 'Mark Twain'—Cure for Sick Humor," *Chicago Tribune*, October 24, 1959, p. 16.

83. Gilbert Millstein, "One as Twain," *New York Times*, April 19, 1959, p. SM24.

84. "Holbrook Does Real Research for 'Mark Twain,'" *Los Angeles Times*, December 10, 1959, p. C12.

85. Richard L. Coe, "Abe Lincoln Ably Revived," *Washington Post*, January 31, 1963, p. B9. What was sometimes thought to be an early recording of Twain was really the voice of William Gillette, "the famous actor who was a friend and Connecticut neighbor of Twain" (Richard L. Coe, "Hal Holbrook Makes His Mark Playing Twain," *Washington Post*, October 25, 1959, p. H3).

86. "A Restoration Comedy," *New Yorker*, April 18, 1959, p. 78.

87. Schechner, *Between Theater and Anthropology*, p. 38.

88. Ibid., p. 43.

89. "A Restoration Comedy," p. 79.

90. King, "Articulating Stardom," p. 47.

91. Holbrook, *Mark Twain Tonight!* p. 73. Holbrook stated that "occasionally a happy thing happens. An actor finds a role in which the memories of his own experiences rush out to join those of the character he is creating. It is much the same as if you made the acquaintance of someone at a party and found that you shared common interests, experiences, convictions—and you talked all night. My relationship with Mark Twain has been something like that. I find in him reflections of myself" (Holbrook, p. 74).

92. Ibid., p. 20.

93. Holbrook also described his first ride on a Mississippi ferryboat: "That's how I found my walk for Mark Twain" (ibid., p. 26).

94. Unlike virtually all of the people who saw his show, Holbrook had in fact seen the real Mark Twain in motion, via a rare Thomas Edison film of the author that, crucially, did not have sound. Holbrook wrote about his anxiety at first seeing the film: "I had worked many years to create the character, mainly by intuition and research, and now I was to receive a verdict. The film flickered into action; I saw him before me and experienced a jolt of delightful recognition. There was no sound, just the jaunty pantomime of this old friend passing in review, but I laughed and laughed until I felt good all over" (ibid., p. 85).

95. Walter Kerr, "Holbrook Possesses Talent to Be Twain," *Los Angeles Times,* March 30, 1966, p. C14.

96. Critics sometimes compared Holbrook's act to the "sick" comics of the era: "The pleasantest thought is that here stands before us an example of what individualism could be like before it died and had to return to life disguised as 'off beat' in order to wiggle back to the audience. . . . Back in the days when you could meet an author without trying to balance a martini at the same time, when lecturing was a form of entertainment, and humor was healthy, healthy, healthy" (Raven, "Holbrook 'Mark Twain,'" p. 16).

97. Richard Schickel, *"Hal Holbrook Tonight!" Holiday,* August 1966, p. 104.

98. Ibid., p. 106.

99. Holbrook, *Mark Twain Tonight!* p. 40.

100. Shelley Fisher Fishkin, *Was Huck Black?* (New York: Oxford University Press, 1993), p. 4.

101. Eric Lott, "All the King's Men: Elvis Impersonators and White Working-Class Masculinity," in *Race and the Subject of Masculinities,* ed. Harry Stecopoulos and Michael Uebel (Durham, NC: Duke University Press, 1997), pp. 203–204. We might note the prevalence of Al Jolson and Brando in postwar impressionists' repertoire. Frank Gorshin often told the press that he had gotten his start as a mimic after working as an usher in a movie theater, when he began imitating Jolson after seeing repeated screenings of *The Jolson Story* (1946)—a film that itself featured an elaborate act of imitative performance by Larry Parks. "I was about 16 when I first saw *The Jolson Story,*" Gorshin said. "When I came out of the movie theater, I discovered I could sing like Jolson. For a long time, I didn't even try doing anyone else. Just doing

Jolson, I started winning a lot of talent contests in Pittsburgh" (Prelutsky, "Ape Act," p. W4).

102. Sacks, *Lectures on Conversation,* 1:479–80.

103. Homi Bhabha, "Of Mimicry and Man: The Ambivalence of Colonial Discourse," *October* 28 (Spring 1984): 126–30.

104. Lynn Abbott, "Play That Barber Shop Chord," *American Music* 10, no. 3 (Autumn 1992): 303.

105. Claudia Mitchell-Kernan, "Signifying and Marking: Two Afro-American Speech Acts," in *Directions in Sociolinguistics,* ed. John J. Gumperz and Dell Hymes (New York: Holt, Rinehart and Winston, 1972), p. 176.

106. "Home-Grown George Kirby to Star in Giant Regal Stage Show Tomorrow," *Chicago Defender,* July 26, 1962, p. 16.

107. "Mimic, Musician, Comedian: Kirby," *Chicago Defender,* October 19, 1974, p. A12.

108. "George Kirby Will Be the First Negro Comedian at NY's Copa," *Pittsburgh Courier,* January 20, 1962, p. A18.

109. Clarence Petersen, "George Kirby: A Favorable Impression," *Chicago Tribune,* August 17, 1972, p. B25. Donald Bogle asserts that Sammy Davis Jr. represented the "first time in pop culture history" that "white audiences saw a Black man openly (but gently) mock a white one" (*Primetime Blues* [New York: Farrar, Straus and Giroux, 2001], p. 85). Note that Kirby had been appearing since the late 1940s, several years before Davis's rise to fame.

110. Robert Toll, *Blacking Up* (New York: Oxford University Press, 1974), p. 36.

111. "Mimic, Musician, Comedian: Kirby," p. A12.

112. Arthur Gelb, "Comedian Makes a Surprise Comeback at 35," *New York Times,* May 17, 1961, p. 43.

113. Clarence Petersen, "George Kirby? Superb," *Chicago Tribune,* March 10, 1972, p. B3.

114. John S. Wilson, "Throng Hears Bible According to Cosby," *New York Times,* January 29, 1968, p. 27.

115. Will Leonard, "A Delightful Storm of Sound—Cosby," *Chicago Tribune,* August 27, 1967, p. A4.

116. "Kirby Joins Star Cast on Mimicry," *Chicago Defender,* January 20, 1971, p. 15.

117. Clarence Petersen, "Somewhere There Is a Mimic Who Does a Great Paul Newman," *Chicago Tribune,* February 10, 1972, p. W13.

118. Tony Hendra, *Going Too Far* (New York: Doubleday, 1987), p. 437.

119. Hendra writes at length about John Belushi's impersonation of Joe Cocker while Cocker was a guest on *Saturday Night Live:* "Nothing brought home how far he'd come (or sunk) than the spectacle of Belushi imitating Cocker's pained contortions with the singer himself alongside, gazing in hurt puzzlement. When Belushi had done exactly the same thing in *Lemmings,* he was appearing in the context of an over-riding premise, in a cocky Off-Broadway revue that attacked the very foundations of rock celebrity. Now here he was—a celebrity himself—certainly as 'big' as his target. So what did this mean? How

was it satirical? It certainly wasn't a compliment—it just looked absurd in itself, a sadistic video game" (ibid., p. 443). And yet on the same page, Hendra describes Dan Akroyd as "the ultimate nonstar, pure satirist, a man who became his targets so thoroughly that his own personality was irrelevant to the process. A craftsman so accurate, so reliable, you could practically see the satirical tools hanging off his workbelt. And no one, therefore, who needed television less."

120. Ibid., p. 444. Notably, NBC's *Saturday Night Live* did not maintain Chase's and Kaufman's early critique of celebrity impressions. Hendra discusses *SNL*'s fall from satirical grace largely in terms of imitative performance. Hendra points out that Joe Piscopo, one of the most successful members of subsequent *SNL* casts, was "first and foremost an impressionist" who animated Frank Sinatra, Ed McMahon, Tom Snyder, and David Letterman with the help of "costume, makeup, hair styling, and even prosthetics." "Whatever this was," Hendra muses, "it wasn't satire, dissent, or even parody" (p. 444).

121. Philip Auslander, *Presence and Resistance* (Ann Arbor: University of Michigan Press, 1992), p. 137.

122. Florian Keller, *Andy Kaufman* (Minneapolis: University of Minnesota Press, 2005), p. 33.

123. Ibid., p. 143.

124. Auslander compares Kaufman's act to 1970s punk rock: his "audacity" was in "refusing simultaneously to fulfill the demands of the stand-up comedy context and to insist that he was redefining that context, he put his own authority as a performer (to say nothing of his career) at risk by allowing his work to be read as merely incompetent. Arguably, the appearance of incompetence (which is actually the mask of a different kind of mastery) is an appropriate strategy of resistance in the context of a mediatized culture dominated by the glossy surface of 'professionalism'" (*Presence and Resistance*, p. 142).

125. Keller, *Andy Kaufman*, p. 83.

126. Ibid.

127. J. L. Austin, *Philosophical Papers* (Oxford: Oxford University Press, 1961), p. 268.

128. Kaufman did not make comedy records, but records were a big part of his act. One of Foreign Man's other signature bits was miming to the *Mighty Mouse* theme song.

129. Furthermore, there was a new wave of stand-up comics such as Sam Kinison, Jerry Seinfeld, Jay Leno, and Steven Wright appearing in middle-class comedy clubs whose acts did not feature celebrity impressions.

130. "The New First Family, 1968," advertisement, *Billboard*, January 21, 1967, p. MGM46. In the ad, Booker stated that he had been inspired by the rise of film actor and president of the Screen Actors Guild George Murphy, who became a California senator in 1964, and then Ronald Reagan, who became the governor of California in 1967.

131. Hugh Brogan, *Kennedy* (Harlow, England: Longman, 1996), p. 216.

132. Cull, "No Laughing Matter," p. 393.

133. Naremore, *Acting in the Cinema*, pp. 69–70.

134. Vera Servi, "Frank Gorshin's Rise Was No Riddle," *Chicago Tribune*, November 7, 1971, p. N14.

135. Earl Calloway, "George Kirby: Impressionist Extraorinaire!" *Pittsburgh Courier*, December 3, 1977, p. 17.

5. BLIND TELEVISION

1. Richard Zoglin, *Comedy at the Edge* (New York: Bloomsbury, 2008), p. 2.

2. See Stephen E. Kercher, *Revel with a Cause: Liberal Satire in Postwar America* (Chicago: University of Chicago Press, 2006); Tony Hendra, *Going Too Far* (New York: Doubleday, 1987); Janet Coleman, *The Compass* (New York: Alfred A. Knopf, 1990); Gerald Nachman, *Seriously Funny* (New York: Backstage Books, 2004).

3. Michael Warner, *Publics and Counterpublics* (New York: Zone Books, 2002), pp. 66–67.

4. Ibid., p. 108.

5. Ibid., p. 76.

6. W.T. Lhamon Jr. states that "improvisation became a linchpin in North American art" during the 1950s (*Deliberate Speed* [Cambridge, MA: Harvard University Press, 1990], p. 179). Daniel Belgrad argues, "A will to explore and record the spontaneous creative act characterized the most significant developments in American art and literature after World War II" (*The Culture of Spontaneity* [Chicago: University of Chicago Press, 1998], p. 1).

7. Lewis A. Erenberg, "From New York to Middletown: Repeal and the Legitimization of Nightlife in the Great Depression," *American Quarterly* 38, no. 5 (Winter 1986): 774.

8. Abel Green, "World War II Spending Responsible for Creating the Nightclub Habit," *Variety*, January 9, 1946, p. 271.

9. Vivian Sobchack writes, "The intimacy and security of home and the integrity and solidity of the home front are lost to wartime and postwar America and to those films we associate at both the core and periphery of that cinematic grouping we circumscribe as noir" ("Lounge Time: Postwar Crises and the Chronotope of Film Noir," in *Refiguring American Film Genres: History and Theory*, ed. Nick Browne [Berkeley: University of California Press, 1998], p. 146).

10. In 1960 comic Alan King told *Variety*, "The current unprecedented click of comedy records owes to television's default." "There isn't enough of the sharp, raucous humor on TV anymore," he said. "TV has plenty of situation comedy but not enough of that personal kind that people go to nightclubs for" ("TV Default Opens Way to Comic LPs: Alan King," *Variety*, June 22, 1960, p. 45).

11. David Marc, *Comic Visions* (Boston: Unwin Hyman, 1989), pp. 44–45.

12. Bruce Weber, "Industrial-Strength Comedy," *New York Times*, December 21, 1999, p. E1.

13. "Be the Underdog, Says Cantor," *Washington Post*, October 25, 1936, p. AA4. In *New York Times* critic Jack Gould's words, it was "radio's inexhaustible demand for material" that was "the real problem for the comedian" ("How Comic Is Radio Comedy?" November 21, 1948, p. SM22).

14. John K. Hutchens, "Serious Business, This Radio Humor," *New York Times*, March 15, 1942, p. SM16.

15. Warner, *Publics and Counterpublics*, pp. 94–95.

16. Belgrad, *Culture of Spontaneity*, p. 119.

17. Hendra, *Going Too Far*, pp. 31–34; see also Kercher, *Revel with a Cause*, pp. 205–206.

18. See Michael Jarrett, *Sound Tracks* (Philadelphia: Temple University Press, 1998), p. 53; Mark Katz, *Capturing Sound* (Berkeley: University of California Press, 2004), pp. 77–79.

19. As a telling comparison between a jazz and rock aesthetic, note that one of the only "live" albums released by a 1950s rock performer captured a very different performance space: Ritchie Valens's *In Concert at Pacoima Jr. High* (Del-Fi 1960). Thanks to Dale Lawrence for pointing this out.

20. See Scott DeVeaux, *The Birth of Bebop* (Berkeley: University of California Press, 1997), p. 214; Belgrad, *Culture of Spontaneity*, p. 180.

21. Kercher, *Revel with a Cause*, p. 2.

22. Susan Murray, *Hitch Your Antenna to the Stars* (New York: Routledge, 2005), p. 91.

23. Warner, *Publics and Counterpublics*, p. 112.

24. Ibid., p. 118.

25. Kercher, *Revel with a Cause*, p. 211.

26. See Warner, *Publics and Counterpublics*, p. 121.

27. Lisa Appignanesi, *The Cabaret* (New York: Macmillan, 1975), pp. 9, 12.

28. Lewis A. Erenberg, *Steppin' Out* (Chicago: University of Chicago Press, 1981), p. 115.

29. See Michael Denning, *The Cultural Front* (London: Verso, 1996), pp. 325–26.

30. Erenberg, *Steppin' Out*, p. 122.

31. Appignanesi, *The Cabaret*, p. 12.

32. Erenberg, *Steppin' Out*, p. 124.

33. Coleman, *The Compass*, p. 47; Kercher, *Revel with a Cause*, p. 121.

34. Kercher, *Revel with a Cause*, p. 125. For at least some critics, this element of audience activity was understood as "an antidote to the perceived poison of television," which had dehumanized drama "by erecting a panoply of technology between performer and audience and cramming the result into a piece of furniture in the living room" (Hendra, *Going Too Far*, p. 53).

35. Larry Kart, "25 Years of Second City," *Chicago Tribune*, December 9, 1984, p. K15.

36. Coleman, *The Compass*, p. 245.

37. Ibid., p. 248.

38. Bob Rolontz, "LP's Top Singles in Unit Sales for First Time," *Billboard*, February 15, 1960, p. 1.

39. June Bundy, "Record Business Develops a New Ticklish Funnybone," *Billboard*, October 3, 1960, p. 1.

40. Sam Chase, "The *Billboard* Intros New LP Sales Charts," *Billboard*, January 4, 1960, p. 3.

41. Coleman, *The Compass*, p. 270.

42. John O'Connor, "Ever Wicked and Witty on the Wing," *New York Times*, May 22, 1996, p. C13.

43. Val Adams, "Sponsor Dropped Emmy TV Sketch," *New York Times,* June 22, 1960, p. 71.

44. Barry Hyams, "Spolin Game Plan for Improvisational Theater," *Los Angeles Times,* May 26, 1974, p. L34.

45. Viola Spolin, *Improvisation for the Theater,* 3rd ed. (Evanston, IL: Northwestern University Press, 1999), p. 6.

46. Ibid., p. 9.

47. Hyams, "Spolin Game Plan," p. L34.

48. Coleman, *The Compass,* p. 32.

49. John Corbett makes a comparison between jazz improvisation and sports, stating, "Sports and games provide a fine metaphor for the constant transgression and reestablishment of codes in the process of improvising" ("Ephemera Underscored: Writing around Free Improvisation," in *Jazz among the Discourses,* ed. Krin Gabbard [Durham, NC: Duke University Press, 1995], p. 233).

50. Spolin, *Improvisation for the Theater,* pp. 16–17.

51. Mikhail Bakhtin, "Discourse Typology in Prose," in *Readings in Russian Poetics,* ed. Ladislav Matejka and Krystyna Pomorska (Ann Arbor: University of Michigan Press, 1978), p. 187.

52. James Naremore, *Acting in the Cinema* (Berkeley: University of California Press, 1988), p. 202.

53. "Saving the Evening," *Time,* March 1, 1971, p. 60.

54. Robert Koehler, "Sills Always Trying to Improve on Improv," *Los Angeles Times,* April 24, 1985, p. E1.

55. Virginia Wright Wexman, *Creating the Couple* (Princeton, NJ: Princeton University Press, 1993), p. 184.

56. Coleman, *The Compass,* p. 28. I follow Marianne Conroy in her gloss of the Method as a reference to "three related contexts": "The studiously naturalistic style of performance popularized in mid-century American theater and film, in which actors produce the effect of emotional intensity through 'ordinary' voice and everyday gesture; the theory of preparation for performance that supports that style through its emphasis on the actor's emotional identification with characters; and the institution that formally introduced both the style and the preparation technique to America: the Actors Studio" ("Acting Out: Method Acting, the National Culture, and the Middlebrow Disposition in Cold War America," *Criticism* 35, no. 2 [Spring 1993]: 242).

57. Wexman writes that, under Strasberg, "Method acting became more confessional than communal. Such an emphasis on the actor in isolation undermined the ensemble-oriented aspect of Stanislavsky's system, producing actors like James Dean, whose on-screen aura of alienation from those around him was enhanced by a solipsistic acting technique that could lead him to step on the speeches of his fellow performers with line readings of his own that were often inaudible. At the Actors Studio Stanislavsky's conception of improvisation as a way to develop a sense of community among actors was replaced by an approach to improvisation that largely celebrated the neurosis of the individual performer" (*Creating the Couple,* p. 166).

58. Ibid., p. 189.

59. It is apt to examine a seduction scene as an example of Nichols and May's "between-ness," since Nichols stated in an interview that one of May's watchwords was "when in doubt . . . seduce" (Deirdre Carmody, "Mike Nichols Reflects on Movies—and Life," *New York Times,* April 20, 1985, p. 9).

60. R. Keith Sawyer, "The Semiotics of Improvisation: The Pragmatics of Musical and Verbal Performance," *Semiotica* 108, nos. 3–4 (1996): 270.

61. Ibid., p. 279. See also Richard Bauman's discussion of "the emergent quality of performance," which he states "resides in the interplay between communicative resources, individual competence, and the goals of the participants, within the context of particular situations" (*Verbal Art as Performance* [Prospect Heights, IL: Waveland Press, 1977], p. 38).

62. Sawyer, "The Semiotics of Improvisation," p. 280.

63. Peter Brooks has characterized melodrama as involving "a victory over repression, a climactic moment at which the characters are able to confront one another with full expressivity" and so "give voice to their deepest feelings, dramatize through their heightened and polarized words and gestures the whole lesson of their relationship." Brooks describes how characters in the melodramatic mode assume "primary psychic roles, father, mother, child, and express basic psychic conditions" (*The Melodramatic Imagination* [New York: Columbia University Press, 1985], p. 4; see also Ben Singer, *Melodrama and Modernity* [New York: Columbia University Press, 2001], p. 45). Brooks's formulation of melodrama clearly applies to the taxicab scene in *On the Waterfront,* where brothers relate as brothers, making underlying family dynamics explicit by saying things that they have long felt but never admitted.

64. As Wexman puts it, "Whereas the intense audience identification fostered by Method performances is best achieved in the context of complex, melodramatic, realistically drawn plots involving close romantic and familial conflicts that gradually reveal the interior conflicts of one central character," Chicago school performance styles are "best suited to short, satirical skits in which the spectators enjoy recognizing social foibles that a group of actors show them by caricaturing recognizable social types. Where a Method performance seeks emotional 'truth,' the Second City performance aims for acute social observation" (*Creating the Couple,* p. 187).

65. Richard Schechner, *Performance Theory* (London: Routledge, 2005), p. 18.

66. Virginia Wright Wexman argues that "films that employ a great deal of improvisation are more dependent on a clearly defined narrative structure than are more traditional productions; for the lifelike sense of the unexpected that titillates audiences during moments of improvisation must be tempered by an awareness of predictability, a sense of intelligible form that underlies the vagaries of spontaneity" ("The Rhetoric of Cinematic Improvisation," *Cinema Journal* 20, no. 1 [Autumn 1980]: 34–35).

67. Naremore, *Acting in the Cinema,* p. 282.

68. See my discussion of tape editing in Jacob Smith, *Vocal Tracks* (Berkeley: University of California Press, 2008), p. 175.

69. Evan Eisenberg, *The Recording Angel* (New York: Penguin, 1987), p. 113.

70. See Scott Bukatman, *Terminal Identity* (Durham, NC: Duke University Press, 1993), pp. 89–90.

71. Erving Goffman, *The Presentation of Self in Everyday Life* (London: Penguin Books, 1990), p. 114.

72. David Hesmondhalgh writes that cultural commodities have "high fixed costs and low variable costs: a record can cost a lot to make because of all the time and effort that has to go into composition, recording, mixing and editing to get the right sound for its makers and their intended audience, but, once 'the first copy' is made, all subsequent copies are relatively cheap to reproduce" (*The Cultural Industries* [London: Sage, 2007], p. 21).

73. Warner, *Publics and Counterpublics*, p. 72.

74. Robert B. Ray, *The Avant-Garde Finds Andy Hardy* (Cambridge, MA: Harvard University Press, 1995), p. 72.

75. Frederick C. Wiebel, *Backwards into the Future* (Bolsburg, PA: Bear-Manor Media, 2006), p. 254.

76. Richard Cromelin, "The Firesign Theater Reemerges," *Los Angeles Times,* February 28, 1980, p. H2. Bergman listed Shelley Berman and Nichols and May as influences (Weibel, *Backwards into the Future,* p. 48).

77. Wiebel, *Backwards into the Future,* p. 162.

78. Though inspired by the radio drama of a previous era, Firesign's success owed much to changes in FM radio during the 1960s. FM stations did not play top forty hits but more obscure album tracks, even whole albums at a sitting. Phil Austin of the Firesign Theatre stated that FM "was wide open, people would play our albums, track an entire album the way you'd read a novel . . . DJs could put our records on and be assured they could go to the bathroom for a while without anyone bothering them" (Norman Gilliland, producer, *Back from the Shadows Again: A Firesign Theatre Retrospective,* Wisconsin Public Radio, host Steve Allen, first broadcast January 9, 1994).

79. Jay David Bolter and Richard Grusin, *Remediation* (Cambridge: MIT Press, 2000), pp. 31, 53.

80. Ed Ward, "Through Tirebiter's Television," *Rolling Stone,* October 15, 1970, pp. 26–27.

81. See, for example, Dan Sullivan, "Firesign: All Things Possible," *Los Angeles Times,* April 12, 1974, p. E14; Greil Marcus, "Firesign Theatre," in *The Rolling Stone Record Guide,* ed. Dave Marsh and John Swensen (London: Random House, 1979), p. 129.

82. Greil Marcus, "The View from Highway 1," *New York Times,* October 10, 1976, p. 245.

83. Lawrence Christon, "Firesign Theater Parodies the Tube," *Los Angeles Times,* July 30, 1979, p. E14.

84. Tony Hiss and David McClelland, "The Firesign Comedians Are Hot Stuff," *New York Times,* April 20, 1975, p. X5.

85. Aniko Bodroghkozy, *Groove Tube* (Durham, NC: Duke University Press, 2001), p. 48.

86. Wiebel, *Backwards into the Future,* p. 260.

87. Philip Proctor, "Interview with the Firesign Theatre," by D. Goldberg, *Writer's Digest* 55 (September 1975): 50.

88. From Gilliland broadcast (author's collection).

89. Wiebel, *Backwards into the Future*, p. 266.

90. Derek Kompare, *Rerun Nation* (New York: Routledge, 2005), p. 46.

91. Ibid., p. 103.

92. In the stunning finale of side one of *How Can You Be in Two Places at Once,* car dealer Ralph Spoilsport reappears, now hawking pot instead of cars, until his sales spiel morphs into Molly Bloom's soliloquy from James Joyce's *Ulysses:* "and the sea, crimson, sometimes like fire, yes, yes . . . where I was a flower of the mountain, yes, yes . . . " Over the sounds of waves crashing on a beach, Ralph's voice is multitracked, the various Ralphs sometimes coming into sync, sometimes not, creating a chorus effect suggestive of the fracturing of subjectivity. In this case, Firesign's channel switching forged connections not just across different eras of screen entertainment but across high and low culture, asserting that the LP allowed the viewer to be in those two places at once as well.

93. Rick Altman, "24-Track Narrative? Robert Altman's *Nashville,*" *Cinema(s)* 1, no. 3 (Spring 1991), accessed at http://www.revue-cinemas.info/revue/revue%20no3/08-altman.htm.

94. Wiebel, *Backwards into the Future*, p. 263.

95. Mark Kernis, "The Sound of Comedy," *Washington Post,* January 10, 1979, p. A1.

96. Ken Tucker, "Records Lose Fun Second Time Around," *Hartford (CT) Courant*, September 19, 1983, p. D3.

97. Larry Kart, "Steve Martin, Richard Pryor Score Solid Hits in a Record Field," *Chicago Tribune*, February 4, 1979, p. E2.

98. Richard Cromelin, "Steve Martin Schticks to Basics on Second Album," *Los Angeles Times*, November 12, 1978, p. O77.

99. Barbara Klinger, *Beyond the Multiplex* (Berkeley: University of California Press, 2006), p. 136.

100. Ibid., p. 149.

101. Ibid., p. 157.

102. Tom Zito, "Firesign Theater," *Washington Post*, May 13, 1974, p. B4.

103. Christon, "Firesign Theater Parodies the Tube," p. E14.

104. Quoted in Wiebel, *Backwards into the Future*, p. 60.

105. Marty Chriscary, "The Firesign Theater Opens at the Ice House," *Los Angeles Times*, February 21, 1968, p. E17.

106. Ibid.

107. Steve Martin, *Born Standing Up* (London: Simon and Schuster, 2007), p. 15.

108. Cited in Coleman, *The Compass*, p. 210.

109. Peter Marks, "The Brief, Brilliant Run of Nichols and May," *New York Times*, May 19, 1996, p. H31.

110. Martin, *Born Standing Up*, p. 72.

111. Ibid., p. 12.

112. Ibid., p. 144.

113. Ibid.

114. Robert Hilburn, "Steve Martin: The Wages of Zany," *Los Angeles Times*, July 16, 1978, p. S1.

115. Lawrence Laurent, "Steve Martin: A Wild and Crazy Guy," *Washington Post*, November 19, 1978, p. A1.

116. Tom Shales, "Hey!!! It's Steve Martin!" *Washington Post*, September 15, 1977, p. 52.

117. See Robert B. Ray, *A Certain Tendency of the Hollywood Cinema, 1930–1980* (Princeton, NJ: Princeton University Press, 1985).

118. Laurel Leff, "Record Highs," *Wall Street Journal*, September 13, 1979, p. 48.

119. Philip Auslander, *Presence and Resistance* (Ann Arbor: University of Michigan Press, 1992), p. 133.

120. Richard Cromelin, "Getting Small with Comedian Steve Martin," *Los Angeles Times*, November 20, 1977, p. O92.

121. Carroll Nye, "Cantor Gives Credit Where Credit Is Due," *Los Angeles Times*, September 8, 1935, p. A6.

122. Carroll Nye, "Actor Seeks Perfect Comedy Formula," *Los Angeles Times*, June 20, 1937, p. C10.

123. Jack Gould, "They Say the Right Thing at the Wrong Time," *New York Times*, March 24, 1946, p. 100.

124. Michel Chion, *The Voice in Cinema* (New York: Columbia, 1999), p. 101.

125. Theodore Gracyk, *Rhythm and Noise: An Aesthetics of Rock* (Durham, NC: Duke University Press, 1996), p. 61.

126. Kernis, "The Sound of Comedy," p. A1.

127. Larry Kart, "Comedy," *Chicago Tribune*, October 12, 1980, p. D11.

128. Theodor W. Adorno and Max Horkheimer, *Dialectic of Enlightenment* (London: Verso, 1979), pp. 165–66.

129. Ibid., p. 167.

130. Warner, *Publics and Counterpublics*, pp. 100–103.

131. Ibid., p. 102.

132. Klinger, *Beyond the Multiplex*, pp. 181–84.

133. Leff, "Record Highs," p. 48.

134. Roland Barthes, *The Responsibility of Forms* (Berkeley: University of California Press, 1985), p. 261.

135. Jack Boettner, "Anaheim Stadium to Rock to Music Again," *Los Angeles Times*, January 10, 1975, p. 22A; see also Mike Jahn, "Grand Funk Railroad Presents Heavy Rock in Concert at Shea," *New York Times*, July 10, 1971, p. 13.

136. John Rockwell, "Pink Floyd's Great *Wall*," *New York Times*, March 2, 1980, p. D26.

137. Emily Thompson, *The Soundscape of Modernity* (Cambridge: MIT Press, 2002), p. 254.

138. Marc, *Comic Visions*, p. 15. Marc puts forth stand-up as "a surviving bastion of individual expression . . . without the protection of the formal mask of a narrative drama, without a song, dance, or any other intermediary composition that creates distance between performer and performance . . . the stand-up comedian addresses an audience as a naked self, eschewing the luxury of a clear-cut distinction between art and life . . . there is no dividing medium

from message. When performing stand-up comedy, Steve Martin is Steve Martin is Steve Martin" (pp. 12–13).

139. Martin, *Born Standing Up*, p. 169.

140. Cromelin, "Martin Schticks to Basics," p. O77.

141. Kart, "Martin, Pryor Score Solid Hits," p. E2.

142. Wm. Knoedelseder Jr., "Steve Martin: In Search of New Nerds," *Los Angeles Times*, May 27, 1979, p. M1.

143. Kart, "Comedy," p. D11.

144. Marc notes that critics have often been put off by the "totalitarian imagery suggested by the stand-up comedy spectacle," which could "conjure hallucinations of Mussolini working the crowd from a terrace" (*Comic Visions*, p. 17).

145. Kart, "Comedy," p. D11. Indeed, we might notice the shades of meaning in the term *arena*, which is often used interchangeably with *stadium*: the *Oxford English Dictionary* defines *arena* as the "central part of an amphitheatre, in which the combats or spectacular displays take place, and which was originally strewn with sand to absorb the blood of the wounded and slain . . . a scene or sphere of conflict; a battle-field."

146. Naremore, *Acting in the Cinema*, pp. 265–66.

147. Steve Martin's use of catchphrases fit in with the approach found on *Saturday Night Live*: Tony Hendra points to that show's "ever-proliferating" number of catchphrases, such as Gilda Radner's "Never mind" and John Belushi's "But noooo . . ." (*Going Too Far*, p. 441).

148. Coleman, *The Compass*, p. 281.

149. Weber, "Industrial-Strength Comedy," p. E1.

150. Naremore, *Acting in the Cinema*, p. 212.

151. See Zoglin, *Comedy at the Edge*, p. 81; Megan Mullen, *The Rise of Cable Programming in the United States* (Austin: University of Texas Press, 2003), p. 108. Of course, HBO's differentiation relied on a different regime of regulation and an economic model based on subscription fees and not advertising: "Without the financial constraints under which the networks function, HBO can target narrowly segmented niche markets, a concept essential to its branding" (Deborah L. Jaramillo, "The Family Racket: AOL Time Warner, HBO, *The Sopranos*, and the Construction of a Quality Brand," *Journal of Communication Inquiry* 26, no. 1 [January 2002]: 63). Catherine Johnson writes: "In a deliberate attempt to differentiate itself from other networks, HBO exploited its position as a subscription channel not subject to the same Federal Communications Commission (FCC) requirements as the advertiser-funded networks regarding profanity, sex and violence, and produced edgy, controversial and adult-oriented original programming" ("Tele-branding in TVIII," *New Review of Film and Television Studies* 5, no. 1 [April 2007]: 8).

152. See Zoglin, *Comedy at the Edge*, p. 34.

153. Auslander, *Presence and Resistance*, p. 129.

154. Philip Proctor, telephone interview with the author, 2008.

155. Richard Harrington, "Getting the Last Laugh," *Washington Post*, April 5, 1981, p. A1.

156. See also the denigration catchphrases in HBO's series starring Lisa Kudlow, *The Comeback* (2005).

CONCLUSION

1. William Leiss, Stephen Kline, Sut Jhally, and Jacqueline Botterill, *Social Communication in Advertising*, 3rd ed. (New York: Routledge, 2005), pp. 200, 157; Joseph Turow, *Breaking Up America* (Chicago: University of Chicago Press, 1997), pp. 30–33; Thomas Frank, *The Conquest of Cool* (Chicago: University of Chicago Press, 1997), p. 23; Richard S. Tedlow, *New and Improved* (Oxford: Heinemann, 1990), p. 372; David Hesmondhalgh, *The Cultural Industries* (London: Sage, 2007), pp. 286–88. Elana Levine, *Wallowing in Sex: The New Sexual Culture of 1970s American Television* (Durham, NC: Duke University Press, 2007), p. 26; Mark Alvey, "'Too many kids and old ladies': Quality Demographics and 1960s US Television," *Screen* 45, no. 1 (Spring 2004): 44; Roberta Pearson, "The Writer/Producer in American Television," in *The Contemporary Television Series*, ed. Michael Hammond and Lucy Mazdon (Edinburgh: Edinburgh University Press, 2005), pp. 14–15.

2. Chris Anderson, *The Long Tail* (New York: Random House, 2007), p. 40.

3. Turow, *Breaking Up America*, p. 2.

4. Ibid., pp. 3–4.

5. Richard Dyer, *Stars* (London: BFI, 1998), p. 53.

6. See Robert C. Allen, "Home Alone Together: Hollywood and the 'Family Film,'" in *Identifying Hollywood's Audiences*, ed. Melvyn Stokes and Richard Maltby (London: BFI, 1999), p. 111; Janet Wasko, *Hollywood in the Information Age* (Cambridge, UK: Polity, 1994), p. 124.

7. Rick Altman, *Silent Film Sound* (New York: Columbia University Press, 2004), pp. 22–23; Lisa Gitelman, *Scripts, Grooves, and Writing Machines* (Stanford, CA: Stanford University Press, 1999), pp. 4–5.

8. Paul Grein, "Platinum Albums Increase 84% in '77; Gold LPs, 23%," *Billboard*, January 21, 1978, p. 12.

9. Thomas L. Friedman, "Record Industry's Upheaval," *New York Times*, June 10, 1981, p. D1; Andre Millard, *America on Record* (New York: Cambridge University Press, 2005), p. 338; Jon Pareles, "Pop Record Business Shows Signs of Recovery," *New York Times*, November 28, 1983, p. C13; Barbara Isenberg, "The Record Biz Rocks 'n' Rolls to New Heights," *Los Angeles Times*, December 4, 1977, p. X1.

10. "Sounding Board," *Billboard*, March 25, 1978, p. 40.

11. Advertisement, *Billboard*, March 25, 1978, p. 37. See also "Warner Record Group Posts $528 Mil in Best Sales Year," *Billboard*, January 21, 1978, p. 8; Alexander Auerbach, "The Record Industry: How to Spin Gold," *Los Angeles Times*, August 13, 1978, p. A1.

12. Isenberg, "Record Biz Rocks," p. X1.

13. Paul Grein, "*Fever* Sells at White Hot Pace Setting New Record," *Billboard*, April 22, 1978, p. 77.

14. Ed Harrison, "*Pepper* Sets Production Record," *Billboard,* July 29, 1978, p. 1.

15. Alexander Auerbach, "Record Sales: The Music Is Turning Sour," *Los Angeles Times,* July 6, 1979, p. B1; Patrick Goldstein, "Get Tough Policy From CBS Records," *Los Angeles Times,* October 14, 1979, p. P81.

16. "Nu-Disk: A CBS Stratagem," *New York Times,* July 9, 1980, p. D1; "Music to Beat Inflation By," *New York Times,* July 27, 1980, p. F17; see also Sam Sutherland, "Record Business: The End of an Era," *High Fidelity,* May 1980, p. 96.

17. "Nu-Disk," p. D1; Friedman, "Record Industry's Upheaval," p. D1; Robert Palmer, "The Pop Record Industry Is under Electronic Siege," *New York Times,* November 28, 1982, p. H1; Auerbach, "Record Sales," p. B1.

18. See Millard, *America on Record,* p. 355.

Further Reading

POSTWAR CULTURE

Allyn, David. *Make Love, Not War: The Sexual Revolution, an Unfettered History.* Boston: Little, Brown, 2000.

Anderegg, Michael. *Orson Welles, Shakespeare, and Popular Culture.* New York: Columbia University Press, 1999.

Belgrad, Daniel. *The Culture of Spontaneity: Improvisation and the Arts in Postwar America.* Chicago: University of Chicago Press, 1998.

Bodroghkozy, Aniko. *Groove Tube: Sixities Television and the Youth Rebellion.* Durham, NC: Duke University Press, 2001.

Bogle, Donald. *Primetime Blues: African Americans on Network Television.* New York: Farrar, Straus and Giroux, 2001.

Cassidy, Marsha F. *What Women Watched: Daytime Television in the 1950s.* Austin: University of Texas Press, 2005.

Cohan, Steven. *Masked Men: Masculinity and the Movies in the Fifties.* Bloomington: Indiana University Press, 1997.

Cohen, Lizabeth. *A Consumers' Republic: The Politics of Mass Consumption in Postwar America.* New York: Knopf, 2003.

Ehrenreich, Barbara, Elizabeth Hess, and Gloria Jacobs. *Re-making Love: The Feminization of Sex.* New York: Anchor Books, 1986.

Erenberg, Lewis A. *Steppin' Out: New York Nightlife and the Transformation of American Culture, 1890–1930.* Chicago: University of Chicago Press, 1981.

Escoffier, Jeffery, ed. *Sexual Revolution.* New York: Thunder's Mouth Press, 2003.

Levine, Elana. *Wallowing in Sex: The New Sexual Culture of 1970s American Television*. Durham, NC: Duke University Press, 2007.

Lhamon, W.T., Jr. *Deliberate Speed: The Origins of a Cultural Style in the American 1950s*. Cambridge, MA: Harvard University Press, 1990.

Lynn, Susan. *Progressive Women in Conservative Times: Radical Justice, Peace, and Feminism, 1945 to the 1960s*. New Brunswick, NJ: Rutgers University Press,

May, Elaine Tyler. *Homeward Bound: American Families in the Cold War*. New York: Basic Books, 1988.

Meyerowitz, Joanne, ed. *Not June Cleaver: Women and Gender in Postwar America, 1945–1960*. Philadelphia: Temple University Press, 1994.

Osgerby, Bill. *Playboys in Paradise: Masculinity, Youth and Leisure-Style in Modern America*. Oxford: Berg, 2001.

Radway, Janice A. *A Feeling for Books: Book-of-the-Month Club, Literary Taste and Middle-Class Desire*. Chapel Hill: University of North Carolina Press, 1997.

Rubin, Joan Shelley. *The Making of Middlebrow Culture*. Chapel Hill: University of North Carolina Press, 1992.

Spigel, Lynn. *Make Room for TV: Television and the Family Ideal in Postwar America*. Chicago: University of Chicago Press, 1992.

———. *Welcome to the Dreamhouse: Popular Media and Postwar Suburbs*. Durham, NC: Duke University Press, 2001.

Wilinsky, Barbara. *Sure Seaters: The Emergence of Art House Cinema*. Minneapolis: University of Minnesota Press, 2001.

CHILDREN AND CONSUMER CULTURE

Cook, Daniel Thomas. *The Commodification of Childhood: The Children's Clothing Industry and the Rise of the Child Consumer*. Durham, NC: Duke University Press, 2004.

Cross, Gary. *Kids' Stuff: Toys and the Changing World of American Childhood*. Cambridge, MA: Harvard University Press, 1997.

DeCordova, Richard. "The Child Audience, the Hays Office and Saturday Matinees." In *Looking Past the Screen*, ed. Jon Lewis and Eric Smoodin. Durham, NC: Duke University Press, 2007.

———. "The Mickey in Macy's Window." In *Disney Discourse*, ed. Eric Smoodin. New York: Routledge, 1994.

Formanek-Brunell, M. *Made to Play House: Dolls and the Commercialization of American Girlhood, 1830–1930*. Baltimore: Johns Hopkins University Press, 1993.

Garvey, E. Gruber. *The Adman in the Parlor: Magazines and the Gendering of Consumer Culture, 1880s to 1910s*. New York: Oxford University Press, 1996.

Jacobson, Lisa, ed. *Children and Consumer Culture in American Society*. Westport, CT: Praeger, 2008.

———. *Raising Consumers: Children and the American Mass Market in the Early Twentieth Century*. New York: Columbia University Press, 2004.

Jenkins, Henry, ed. *The Children's Culture Reader*. New York: New York University Press, 1998.

Leach, William. *Land of Desire: Merchants, Power, and the Rise of a New American Culture*. New York: Vintage Books, 1993.

Sammond, Nicholas. *Babes in Tomorrowland: Walt Disney and the Making of the American Child, 1930–1960*. Durham, NC: Duke University Press, 2005.

Schor, Juliet B. *Born to Buy: The Commercialized Child and the New Consumer Culture*. New York: Scribner, 2005.

Seiter, Ellen. *Sold Separately: Children and Parents in Consumer Culture*. New Brunswick, NJ: Rutgers University Press, 1995.

Small, Christopher. *Music, Society, Education*. Hanover, NH: Wesleyan University Press, 1977.

MARKETING AND NICHE AUDIENCES

Alvey, Mark. "'Too many kids and old ladies': Quality Demographics and 1960s US Television." *Screen* 45, no. 1 (Spring 2004): 40–62.

Anderson, Chris. *The Long Tail*. New York: Random House, 2007.

Davila, Arlene. *Latinos Inc.: The Marketing and Making of a People*. Berkeley: University of California Press, 2001.

Frank, Thomas. *The Conquest of Cool: Business Culture, Counterculture and the Rise of Hip Consumerism*. Chicago: University of Chicago Press, 1997.

Leiss, William, Stephen Kline, Sut Jhally, and Jacqueline Botterill. *Social Communication in Advertising*. 3rd ed. New York: Routledge, 2005.

Marchand, Roland. *Advertising the American Dream*. Berkeley: University of California Press, 1985.

Mittell, Jason. *Genre and Television*. New York and London: Routledge, 2004.

Pearson, Roberta. "The Writer/Producer in American Television." In *The Contemporary Television Series*, ed. Michael Hammond and Lucy Mazdon. Edinburgh: Edinburgh University Press, 2005.

Turow, Joseph. *Breaking Up America: Advertisers and the New Media World*. Chicago: University of Chicago Press, 1997.

Wasko, Janet. *Hollywood in the Information Age*. Cambridge, UK: Polity, 1994.

MEDIA TECHNOLOGIES AND PHONOGRAPH CULTURE

Altman, Rick. *Silent Film Sound*. New York: Columbia University Press, 2004.

Anderson, Tim J. *Making Easy Listening: Material Culture and Postwar American Recording*. Minneapolis: University of Minnesota Press, 2006.

Barlow, William. *Voice Over: The Making of Black Radio*. Philadelphia: Temple University Press, 1999.

Bolter, Jay David, and Richard Grusin. *Remediation: Understanding New Media*. Cambridge: MIT Press, 2000.

Eisenberg, Evan. *The Recording Angel: Explorations in Phonography*. New York: Penguin, 1987.

Gitelman, Lisa. *Scripts, Grooves, and Writing Machines: Representing Technology in the Edison Era*. Stanford, CA: Stanford University Press, 1999.

Gracyk, Theodore. *Rhythm and Noise: An Aesthetics of Rock*. Durham, NC: Duke University Press, 1996.

Gray, Ann. *Video Playtime: The Gendering of a Leisure Technology*. London: Routledge, 1992.

Jarrett, Michael. *Sound Tracks*. Philadelphia: Temple University Press, 1998.

Katz, Mark. *Capturing Sound: How Technology Has Changed Music*. Berkeley: University of California Press, 2004.

Keightley, Keir. "Long Play: Adult-Oriented Popular Music and the Temporal Logics of the Post-war Sound Recording Industry in the USA." *Media, Culture & Society* 26, no. 3 (2004): 375–91.

———. "'Turn It Down!' She Shrieked: Gender, Domestic Space, and High Fidelity, 1948–1959." *Popular Music* 15, no. 2 (1996): 149–77.

Kenney, William Howland. *Recorded Music in American Life*. New York: Oxford University Press, 1999.

Klinger, Barbara. *Beyond the Multiplex: Cinema, New Technologies, and the Home* . Berkeley: University of California Press, 2006.

Kompare, Derek. *Rerun Nation: How Repeats Invented American Television*. New York: Routledge, 2005.

Millard, Andre. *America on Record*. New York: Cambridge University Press, 2005.

Robertson Wojcik, Pamela, and Arthur Knight, eds. *Soundtrack Available*. Durham, NC: Duke University Press, 2001.

Wasser, Frederick. *Veni, Vidi, Video: The Hollywood Empire and the VCR*. Austin: University of Texas Press, 2001.

PERFORMANCE

Auslander, Philip. *Liveness: Performance in a Mediated Culture*. London: Routledge, 1999.

———. *Presence and Resistance: Postmodernism and Cultural Politics in Contemporary American Performance*. Ann Arbor: University of Michigan Press, 1992.

Barber, Karin. "Preliminary Notes on Audiences in Africa." *Africa* 67, no. 3 (1997): 347–62.

Bauman, Richard. *Verbal Art as Performance*. Prospect Heights, IL: Waveland Press, 1977.

Chion, Michel. *The Voice in Cinema*. New York: Columbia, 1999.

Coleman, Janet. *The Compass*. New York: Alfred A. Knopf, 1990.

Glenn, Susan A. "'Give an Imitation of Me': Vaudeville Mimics and the Play of the Self." *American Quarterly* 50, no. 1 (1998): 47–76.

Goffman, Erving. *Frame Analysis*. Boston: Northeastern University Press, 1986.

Hendra, Tony. *Going Too Far*. New York: Doubleday, 1987.

Keller, Florian. *Andy Kaufman*. Minneapolis: University of Minnesota Press, 2005.

Kercher, Stephen E. *Revel with a Cause: Liberal Satire in Postwar America*. Chicago: University of Chicago Press, 2006.

Marc, David. *Comic Visions: Television Comedy and American Culture*. Boston: Unwin Hyman, 1989.

Martin, Steve. *Born Standing Up*. London: Simon and Schuster, 2007.

Murray, Susan. *Hitch Your Antenna to the Stars: Early Television and Broadcast Stardom*. New York: Routledge, 2005.

Nachman, Gerald. *Seriously Funny: The Rebel Comedians of the 1950s and 1960s*. New York: Backstage Books, 2004.

Naremore, James. *Acting in the Cinema*. Berkeley: University of California Press, 1988.

Schechner, Richard. *Performance Theory*. London: Routledge, 2005.

Warner, Michael. *Publics and Counterpublics*. New York: Zone Books, 2002.

Watkins, Mel. *On the Real Side: A History of African American Comedy*. Chicago: Lawrence Hill, 1999.

Wexman, Virginia Wright. *Creating the Couple: Love, Marriage, and Hollywood Performance*. Princeton, NJ: Princeton University Press, 1993.

Zoglin, Richard. *Comedy at the Edge: How Stand-up in the 1970s Changed America*. New York: Bloomsbury, 2008.

Index

TEXT
10/13 Sabon Open Type

DISPLAY
Sabon Open Type

COMPOSITOR
BookComp, Inc.

PRINTER AND BINDER:
IBT Global